PRESENCE AND THOUGHT

HANS URS VON BALTHASAR

Presence and Thought

*Essay on the Religious Philosophy
of Gregory of Nyssa*

Translated by Mark Sebanc

A COMMUNIO BOOK
IGNATIUS PRESS   SAN FRANCISCO

Title of the French original:
Présence et pensée
Essai sur la philosophie religieuse de Grégoire de Nysse
© 1988 Beauchesne Editeur, Paris

Cover by Roxanne Mei Lum

© 1995 Ignatius Press, San Francisco
All rights reserved
ISBN 978–0–89870–521–8
Library of Congress catalogue number 94–79302
Printed in the United States of America

CONTENTS

Foreword 9
Introduction 15

PART ONE
The Philosophy of Becoming and Desire

1. The Concept of Spacing 27
2. Becoming and the Immanent Infinite 37
3. Spirit and Matter 47
4. Real Becoming 57
5. Ideal Becoming 65
6. The Solution to the Anthropological Problem 71
7. Desire and Knowledge 89
8. The Twofold Mystical Paradox 97

PART TWO
The Philosophy of Image

1. The Definition of Nature 111
2. Monad, Mirror, and Window 121

PART THREE
The Philosophy of Love

1. Human Nature and Incarnation 133
2. Transposition of Becoming 153
3. Transposition of the Image 163

Conclusion 171
Final Note 181
Bibliography 183
Bibliographical Note 189

Εἰ γὰρ πάντα ἡμῖν ἦν καταληπτά
οὐκ ἂν χρείττων ἦν ἡμῶν ὁ κρείττων.

If all things were within our grasp,
the higher power would not be beyond us.

— Gregory of Nyssa

FOREWORD

The situation of the theologian in today's world is strangely paradoxical. In terms of vocation, he is devoted to a study of the past,
where God has manifested himself. Even beyond this study of the
past, though, he is a man devoted to a contemplation of the Eternal. But by the very fact of his existence, he is immersed in a world
that is teetering on its foundations and seems ready to collapse. Very
much absorbed as he may be by prayer and his professional research,
if he has taken any trouble at all to look around him and to rise high
enough above the fray to seek to understand what is happening, he
cannot but think that he belongs to an "epoch", as Péguy said, not
to a "period". He belongs to an epoch where the established order,
to all outward appearances still solid, is in reality sapped from within,
deserted already by a life that can at any given moment reject it and,
transformed, leave it like an empty shell destined to turn to dust at
the slightest breeze. Undoubtedly there remains for him the contemplation of "the eternal verities". He knows well enough that they, at
least, do "resist" the tumultuous storms of our time. Does he not,
however, know quite as vividly that these eternal verities, in order
to be living and active—real and true in both an earthly sense and
a heavenly sense at the same time—must be incarnated in temporal
forms?

But where are these temporal forms to be found? The historical period that was inaugurated by Descartes is ended. How will the theologian be able to work at the task of bringing to birth and nurturing a
theology that will be reclaimed by a new humanity? As for this new
humanity, we can catch glimpses here and there of its lineaments.
But its contours remain so blurred, its internal structure so embryonic, that one would risk making enormous and fruitless mistakes in
conceiving a wish to describe it prophetically, rather than waiting for
its slow maturation and perhaps, as well, the profoundly disruptive
disorders and sudden catastrophes that will liberate it from an overly
oppressive and haunting past.

In a present that is so ambiguous, between a death that is being
consummated and a life that is being born, what can the theologian
do? What ought he to do? His first move will be to return once more

to the past. This return will be beneficial, but only on one condition: that he understand well that history, far from dispensing us from creative effort, imposes it on us. Our artists, and in particular our architects, all acknowledge this. A Greek temple, a Romanesque church, a Gothic cathedral all merit our admiration, because they are witnesses to a beauty and truth that are incarnate in time. But to reproduce them now in our present day would constitute an anachronism, all the more appalling to the extent the copies were more minutely exact. The intent to revive them, to adapt them to the needs of the time, would be even worse. Such an effort could only beget horrors. All attempts at "adaptation" to current tastes are doomed to the same fate. No more than architecture does theology escape this universal law. In neo-Greek style, the column of antiquity loses its original qualities of simplicity and becomes an intolerable imitation. And the same may be said of Saint Thomas: "A great and estimable doctor, renowned, authoritative, canonized, and very much dead and buried" (Péguy). We should not imagine that there are other estimable figures who in our eyes are better capable of withstanding such treatment! We have turned our gaze on a more distant past, but we have not done so in the belief that, in order to give life to a languishing system of thought, it would suffice to exhume the "Greek Fathers" and adapt them for better or worse to the needs of the modern soul. We are not ingenuous enough to prefer a "neopatristic" theology to a "neoscholastic" theology! There is never a historical situation that is absolutely similar to any of the ones that preceded it in time. Thus there is no historical situation that can furnish us with its own solutions as a kind of master key capable of resolving all the problems that plague us today. When it comes to shaping one's personal behavior, all the rules of morality, as precise as they may be, remain abstract in the face of the infinite complexity of the concrete. Even when these rules of morality are applied to "cases of conscience" where they are limited in scope and complement one another reciprocally, the fact that they are combined with one another means that they cannot provide an exact coincidence with a human "situation", which is always susceptible to an infinite analysis. If one goes right to the limits of the thing, from rules of conduct to a conduct that is regulated, there always subsists a gap that can only be surmounted by the decision of a love that is free. The same is true of theology. As precise as one may suppose it to be, the history of dogma will never yield more than fragmentary formulas that will never provide a decisive, "ready-made" solution to the difficulties of our contemporary situation, a situation that is entirely unique!

Without a doubt, the theologian may appeal for help to tradition, which the Catholic Church makes use of in her struggle against all forms of theological individualism and Protestantism. But it is important to understand exactly what this tradition is, so that we may know what we can expect from it and what it absolutely cannot give us. One would be quite mistaken to imagine it as a relay of runners, each of whom, at the end of his segment of the race, hands off the "witness", the "message", a piece of wood, or a written work that, through space and time, is preserved of itself in its immovable materiality. If there were indeed a witness and a message to preserve, a more correct image would be that of the torch, as in the Olympic races of antiquity. For even while it remains identical to itself, a living flame can lay claim to being protected, at every moment, against a constant succession of dangers and being sustained by a substance that is ever new. In very truth, this living Flame is that of the Spirit of love, who, having come down from heaven to the Holy Land, is jealously preserved by the Church and transmitted by her through all human generations in order to inflame the world. Tradition, therefore, is the very consciousness of the Church and, in a more particular way, her memory, in which are accumulated the experiences of her sons and daughters, who succeed in keeping the "sacred deposit" alive and intact in an incredibly diverse panoply of situations. The treasure-house of these memories is at the disposal of the theologian in the same way that the storehouse of his lived experiences is available to the individual. But it is evident that recalling the problems and solutions of the past does not admit, for either the theologian or the individual, of a literal resumption of previous solutions and their mechanical application to the difficulties of the present. For a new problem there must be a new solution. Without a doubt, between these two variable conditions of past and present there always subsists an identity of relationship. But precisely because the second of these terms is always different from what it was up to the present moment, the formal identity of relationship cannot be preserved by the purely material repetition of the first term. To unravel each one of the problems that life poses for him, man must also act each time according to an immanent rule in such a way as to maintain, in the midst of the most diverse situations,

the coherence of his own personality. He will succeed in this only on
the condition that he discover a new attitude each time. "Only those
who change remain akin to me", said Nietzsche. Without giving way
to any kind of superficial relativism, one may even apply these words
to the life of the Church herself. In order to remain faithful to herself and her mission, the Church must continually make an effort at
creative invention. Paul had to be inventive in order to cope with the
problem of the Gentiles who were obliged to enter into a Church that
was heir to the Synagogue. The same applies to the Greek Fathers in
the face of Hellenistic culture, and also to Saint Thomas in the face
of Arabic philosophy and knowledge. We, indeed, for our part, must
do the same in the face of the problems of our day.

Being faithful to tradition most definitely does not consist, therefore, of a literal repetition and transmission of the philosophical and
theological theses that one imagines lie hidden in time and in the con-
tingencies of history. Rather, being faithful to tradition consists much
more of imitating our Fathers in the faith with respect to their attitude
of intimate reflection and their effort of audacious creation, which are
the necessary preludes to true spiritual fidelity. If we study the past,
it is not in the hope drawing from it formulas doomed in advance
to sterility or with the intention of readapting out-of-date solutions.
We are asking history to teach us the acts and deeds of the Church,
who presents her treasure of divine revelation, ever new and ever
unexpected, to every generation, and who knows how, in the face of
every new problem, to turn the fecundity of the problem to good
account with a rigor that never grows weary and a spiritual agility
that is never dulled. To understand ever better the intimate reality of
our Mother, behold what draws the eyes of the theologian toward the
Church's past and the development of her dogma. All the rest is the
job of the historian. All this rest interests us only to the extent that
it is necessary in order to be in communion with the Church and
to learn from her, in our turn, the unique actions that are required
by the situation of our time—actions that no one, absolutely no one,
will discover in our stead.

It is in this spirit that we should like to undertake a series of studies in the theology of the Greek Fathers. The first such study, on
Gregory of Nyssa, will be followed by two others, on Origen and
on Maximus the Confessor. In each case, the central point of view
governing the choice and grouping of the ideas is not, therefore, the

desire to present what would seem in their case to have more potential to interest and influence modern theology. We are not attempting
any kind of material transposition. We should like rather to penetrate
right to those vital wellsprings of their spirit, right to that fundamental and hidden intuition that directs every expression of their thought
and that reveals to us one of the great possibilities of attitude and approach that theology has adopted in a concrete and unique situation.
We shall explain at length, in our study of the theology of Origen,
why the thought of the Greek Fathers, taken in its materiality, often offers but little support to the task of the theologian today, why
there might even be a danger in wishing to rejuvenate it without a
total critique. And yet this system of thought was great and strong,
harmonious and serene. We remember it, as a man remembers the
profound intuitions he had as an adolescent. If he cannot relive them
just as they were, because his situation, his life, indeed, the whole
world have changed for him, he can at least fortify himself with the
thought that that purity of inspiration, that burning and impatient res-
onance of his whole being is his very self! We should like to reread
a few pages of that intimate journal written by the Church when she
was seventeen years old. This we do from the same distance of age
but also with the same respectful admiration for the person we once
were. It would be a want of taste to desire, when we are forty, to
bring laboriously to a conclusion one of those blazing fragments we
had carelessly left undone when we were twenty. Youthful fire is not
meant to warm up those who are old. We shall not collect the living
and sacred documents of our life (and the history of the Church is
our life) as a person would collect stamps or butterflies. That would
be to demonstrate that we are already dead. Let us read history, our
history, as a living account of what we once were, with the double-
edged consciousness that all of this has gone forever and that, in spite
of everything, that period of youth and every moment of our lives
remain mysteriously present at the wellsprings of our soul in a kind
of delectable eternity.

INTRODUCTION

Only a very small number of initiates have read and are aware of Gregory of Nyssa, and they have jealously guarded their secret. Scarcely a handful of studies, and quite austere ones at that,[1] have appeared on him, mostly in German. Here and there, too, there are a few scattered references to him,[2] together with a translation of his *Great Catechesis*[3] into French. From the critical point of view, the text of his works is the most neglected of the whole patristic era.[4] Who would suspect that under this unprepossessing exterior we are to find the most profound Greek philosopher of the Christian era, a mystic and incomparable poet besides? Yet Saint Maximus even designated him the Universal Doctor,[5] and the Second Council of Nicaea confirmed him in his title as Father of Fathers.[6] Scotus Erigena, subtle expert on Greek thought that he was, cites him as frequently as he does Saint Augustine. Less brilliant and prolific than his great master Origen, less cultivated than his friend Gregory Nazianzen, less practical than his brother Basil, he nonetheless outstrips them all in the profundity of his thought, for he knew better than anyone how to transpose ideas inwardly from the spiritual heritage of ancient Greece into a Christian mode. And he accomplishes this in that fundamentally Hellenistic spirit that allows him to translate religious experience seamlessly into

---

[1] See the Bibliography.

[2] What we have in mind here above all are the articles of the much-lamented Father Gabriel Horn, the articles of Father Malevez, and the critical studies of Father Jean Daniélou, which we await with impatience.

[3] Under the French title of *Grande catéchèse*, edited by Louis Méridier (see the Bibliography).

[4] The critical edition of Werner Jaeger (*Contra Eunomium*, 2 vol. [Berlin, 1921]) and of G. Pasquali (*Epistulæ* [Berlin, 1925]), which was abandoned for a length of time, has been taken up again by M. F. Müller, at the Institute for the Study of Antiquity at Münster, in Westphalia. The remainder of his theological works will appear shortly. For the sake of convenience we shall make our citations according to Migne (PG 44, 45, 46 = I, II, III). For earlier editions, see O. Bardenhewer, *Geschichte der altkirchlichen Literatur* 3:188–220, and Berthold Altaner, *Patrologie* (Herder, 1938), 191.

[5] ὁ τῆς οἰκουμένης διδάσκαλος (*Opusc. theol.*, PG 91, 161 A.)

[6] Mansi, 13, 293.

its conceptual expression, that spirit for which the crystalline clarity of thought is lit from within and becomes a mystical life. If the Bishop of Hippo enraptures us with a more human inspiration, it is often his lyric flights rather than the clarity of his thought that sweep us to such heights. Gregory's attractiveness lies in the perfect harmony that reigns between the "system" and its religious realization, between the idea and the drama.

There is in his Christian detachment a certain indefinable, naïvely fervent attachment to all the beauties of the earth, to all human and cosmic values. This quality gives his thought the earmark of youth and a kind of morning freshness. The bitter experience of the vanity of things that he relived in making his commentary on Ecclesiastes seems in no way inconsistent with his manifold curiosities about the composition of the human body, the evolution of nature, and the thousand little details of daily life. And if sometimes his education as a rhetorician causes him to decorate his phrases with an excessive flourish of images, which the more refined taste of Gregory Nazianzen was discreet enough to avoid, he redeems this defect by a deeper and more substantial poetry, the poetry of the ideas themselves. All mystics, it is true, speak through images. But in the case of Gregory, the mystical bent that animates all his writings produces an authentic metaphysics as well, a metaphysics marked by an irreproachable logic and the adequate translation of his interior drama.

It is only, we believe, in emphasizing this twofold character that is at once dramatic and conceptual, "existential" and "essential", that we shall succeed in reviving and rethinking the work of Gregory. The studies that have appeared on him so far have brought out only the second of these two characteristics.[7] It is for this reason, perhaps, that several of these studies have thought it incumbent to consider Gregory a second-class thinker. Especially attentive as they are to the influences that acted on him, it is small wonder his philosophy seemed to them like a syncretistic concoction of preexisting givens. Which is to say that, in their eyes, Platonism and Stoicism accounted for his anthropology, Origenism and Irenaeism for his idea of original sin, and finally Plotinianism and Christianity for his conception of

---

[7] Note especially the quite serious work of Franz Diekamp, which lacks, however, adequate understanding of the spirit that is peculiar to the thought of Gregory.

the mystical vision. But what great thinker is not at the confluence of diverse tendencies? Is Saint Thomas not the fruit of the meeting between Augustinianism and Aristotelianism? Did Kant not take his rise from the conflict between Leibniz and Hume? Never will looking backward toward the sources and the basic elements replace a looking forward that endeavors to grasp the synthesis that has been effected, the irreducible novelty that has been attained. The fruit of these labors, even though it is contained in the roots, is always something new and unexpected. We should like to try to see this fruit ripen. Perhaps, if our experiment succeeds, we shall, in plucking this fruit, be convinced that Gregory of Nyssa is something other than a mere compiler.[8]

But the objections that can be raised on this issue have not yet admitted to defeat. Ought one not to admit, the argument goes, that, in spite of everything, the thought of Gregory, as profound as it may be, remains anemic to a certain extent? Does he not too often give contradictory responses precisely with regard to the fundamental themes of his philosophy? And shall we not be authorized because of this to seek out the sources and opposing influences that underlie the contradictions? Is there or is there not an immediate vision of God? Is there or is there not a means of escaping the realm of undefined becoming and losing oneself in God?[9] Is the primitive state of man situated in this realm of historical becoming, or is it not? Or must we seek

---

[8] We believe we can dispense with entering into obscure questions concerning the relationship of Posidonius, Gregory of Nyssa, and Cicero. Even if in places Gregory depends, for the substance of his ideas, on Posidonius, his *De hominis opificio* possesses a spirit so new and so original that it definitely conveys the personal thought of Gregory. Finally one would have to agree with J. Bayer, when he writes: "Here, too, it becomes obvious that, with regard to the depth of his query and his incessant struggle with the problems, Gregory offers his own thoughts in spite of his affinity to earlier and contemporary ideas" (*Gregors von Nyssa Gottesbegriff* [Diss., Giessen, 1935], 38).

[9] This was the subject of a controversy between Diekamp and Koch, recently taken up again by Endre von Ivánka. Ivánka's work marks a considerable progress in the question. He does not, however, seem to us to be free of prejudice about "sources". In his subtle analysis of knowledge in Plato, Aristotle, Augustine, and Gregory, he concludes that there is a deep-seated Aristotelianism in Gregory with respect to natural knowledge and a certain Plotinianism with respect to mystical knowledge. But although his results seem accurate to us, they still leave us somewhat indifferent, since his elaborate outlines seem too abstract to be capable of grasping the living sinew of Gregory's thought. As for Diekamp, he applies scholastic conceptions to this Father of the Church, while Koch strives to reduce him to the level of Philo.

out a higher world? And is human "nature" a Platonic idea, or is it not?[10] There are so many questions, as scholars will acknowledge, that touch on the very heart of Gregory's philosophy and that remain sharply disputed. Let it suffice at the moment for us to counter these questions with the response already suggested. Would these "contra-dictions", if indeed there are any, not be the simple and necessary expression of a unique, but dramatic, vision? The outlines of a sys-tem of thought that is in progress? And once this progress has been accomplished, could these contradistinctions not be harmonized and diminished in a "synthetic" outlook that embraces all the winding, sinuous turns of thought that have been traversed? But let us leave this an open question. Only the completion of his thought as a whole can provide a satisfactory answer to it.

However, before we undertake this, let us linger a moment still to ask ourselves what the governing principle should be as we embark on this odyssey across the landscape of Gregory's thought, the principle that would serve us as a guide and compass on this journey. It is my firm belief that this is none other than Gregory's very Christianity. Although it is possible that there may be influences drawn from the mysticism of Philo[11] or Plotinus,[12] especially with regard to the idea of infinite desire and eternal progress in the knowledge of God, above all else there is Christ, the living way. And there is the Father, our personal and supremely free Creator. There is the Spirit, the myste-rious heart of the Trinity, revealed last in the order of time, after the Father and the Son, after the Law and the Gospel, "so that our nature may receive its perfect nourishment, the Holy Spirit, in whom there is life".[13]

What distinguishes Gregory at once from Philo and Plotinus is the radical opposition between the triune God and the creature, an oppo-sition that is not mitigated by any kind of intermediary zone. In Ori-gen's Trinity, the Son and the Spirit, even though they were formally affirmed as being God, served as ontological mediators between the Father and the world. After Arius, something like this is no longer

---

[10] See especially the articles of Father Malevez.
[11] H. Koch, "Das mystische Schauen beim hl. Gregor von Nyssa", *Theol. Quartalschrift* 80 (1898): 357–420.
[12] Gabriel Horn, "Le Miroir et la nuée", *R.A.M.*, 1927, 113.
[13] *Sermo de Spiritu Sancto*, PG 46, 697 B.

conceivable.[14] The divine essence is absolutely one[15] and equal[16] in three Persons. From then on it was no longer possible to infer Divine Persons on the basis of different regions of the world.[17] Rather there is a "common operation" *ad extra*.[18] The Son can no longer be envisaged as the instrument of the Father in creation[19] or, consequently—and this is even more serious—as the world of ideas, a virtually multiple entity: τῷ ὑποκειμένῳ ἓν πολὺ ταῖς ἐννοίαις, as Origen put it.[20] The mystical aspiration that sought, as in the case of Origen at times and even more often in the case of Eunomius, to go beyond the sphere of the Son in order to reach the kingdom of the Father had been exposed by Basil as an act of impious pride.[21] Gregory follows him in this line of thought.[22] At the same time Plotinus' realm of "*nous*" finds itself excluded from the domain of reality. Personalized by Origen, who identified it with the Logos, *nous* had retained an intermediary place between the Father (βύθος) and the soul in Christian metaphysics. But once the absolute transcendence of the divine essence was recognized, this place became untenable. Augustine will try to maintain it, but not without skirting the edges of contradiction.[23] Gregory, who

---

[14] Letter XXIV (III, 1089 D): "Since, then, we conceive of no distinction with respect to that which is incomprehensible in the three Persons. (For it cannot be that one Person is more incomprehensible and the other less so. But there is only one basis for incomprehensibility in the Trinity.) For this reason we, who are guided by the ungraspable and inconceivable itself, say that there is no difference of being in the Holy Trinity."

[15] *De communibus notionibus* II, 176–77.

[16] The victory brought off by Basil and Gregory in their treatises *Contra Eunomium* on the idea of a possible gradation in the divine essence ("The more and less of being": *C. Eunom.* 1; II, 305 B) is in truth the most conspicuous victory of Christian thought over Greek thought. It is the replacement of a profoundly rooted habit of thought (Tertullian, Hippolytus, Origen!) by another kind of thinking, a thinking demanded by the concrete givens of revelation.

[17] As was advocated by Origen (*Peri Archon* 1, 3. 5–7) and Eunomius, II, 297 BC, 326 C, 354 AB.

[18] Ibid. II, 374 B; 382 D.

[19] *C. Eunom.* 4; II, 662 D. Cf. 2; II, 554 B.

[20] *In Jer.* 3, 3 (Lat.) Baehrens 8, 313; 8, 2 (Greek) M. 13, 338.

[21] *Adv. Eunom.* 2, 13; PG 29, 596 C, 600: "to go beyond the beginning".

[22] *C. Eunom.* 10; II, 831 D; 834 AB. Cf. *C. Eunom.* 9; II, 821 AB.

[23] "We are not saying that Augustine did not strive to distinguish conceptually between an intellectual knowledge of ideas, a mystical view of God, and the beatific vision, only that he did not succeed in his critique of knowledge. And this was necessarily the case, for, with the acceptance of Plato's fundamental theory, the identification of the knowledge of Ideas and the beatific vision is inescapable, unless one does as Plotinus did and hypostatizes Ideas within

is more categorical, abandons it. This fundamental dogma of Platonism is completely absent from his philosophy. But what happens in such a case to universal and necessary being, to the spiritual realm? Christian metaphysics divides the elements of it into three regions of being. Its formally divine aspect is linked to its true proprietor, God himself, whose absolute transcendence will henceforth preclude any distinction, no matter how tentative, between divine being and "the things that are possible."[24] Its psychological aspect returns to the soul, whose proper operation remains irreducible to the operation of the senses,[25] whose very being, insofar as it is spiritual, keeps a mysterious character of concrete universality. Finally its existential aspect is absorbed into the realm of the angels, which Gregory readily calls the spiritual world (κόσμος νοητός). But in his eyes they are sheer creatures like souls, inasmuch as they are not an object of essential knowledge for the latter[26] and do not themselves have a knowledge of God that is more perfect than that which souls have.[27] Thus the impersonal domain of Ideas finds itself completely absorbed by three categories of personal beings, of which the last, that of angels, plays only a secondary role in the religious philosophy of Gregory. The drama is played out between the soul and God. And whereas, in the case of Plotinus, *nous*, inasmuch as it is the sum total of things that are intelligible, remains the first object of knowledge, behind which there emanates the unfathomable depths of the ἕν, depths that are adequately distinguished from the intelligible world and thus absolutely transcendent, superintelligible, superbeing, these two domains

---

an independent realm of being that is between God and the soul. But this was repugnant to Augustine for metaphysical reasons." Ivánka, "Vom Platonismus zur Theorie der Mystik. Zur Erkenntnislehre Gregors von Nyssa", *Scholastik*, 1936, 175.

[24] The reader is referred farther on in this book to my Conclusion. God is "action and wholly active". *C. Eunom.* 12; 988 B.

[25] In this way Gregory escapes Stoicism and its materialistic tendencies.

[26] For this reason there is in Gregory a disappearance of that Plotinian and gnostic parallelism, favored yet by Origen, between the stages of mystical ascent, the metaphysical degrees of being, and the realms of cosmology. There remains only the soul and God. Certainly he does not escape that paradox entertained by all ancient cosmologies, namely, situating the "place perceptible by the mind" (τόπος νοητός), in this case the realm of angels, beyond the celestial sphere, whose fire, by virtue of its subtle character, provides for the transition between the "sense-perceptible" (αἰσθητόν) and that which is "perceptible by the mind" (νοητόν) (*C. Eunom.* 12; II, 1004 A; *In hexaëm.* 80 D–81 ACD, 116 B, 121 A). But this having been said, is it that much easier to escape the cosmological antinomies of Kant?

[27] *In Cant.* 8; I, 949 B; 6; I, 893 B.

constitute only one entity for Gregory. Herein we grasp the profound difference between the theology of Plotinus and Christian theology.[28] For Plotinus, Ideas are objects, "things", above which, by a supreme "separation" or χωρισμός, there rises the One, the ἕν. For Gregory, ideal knowledge has no other object than the Supreme Being himself. The multiplicity of ideas in the knowing soul corresponds with her incapacity to grasp this unique object,[29] while in the divine object this multiplicity corresponds with its richness of infinite life.[30] Here also, as in Plotinus, the decisive moment will thus be "negative". In renouncing the possibility of its being grasped by the idea, the object itself will appear. But the positive aspect of the *via eminentiæ* [the way of standing out from] can, thanks to an absolute identity of "Ideas" and of "God", be stressed even more. Gregory accepts from Origen the notion of objective knowledge by "particular aspects" (ἐπίνοιαι).[31] For the same reason he is able to give God the fundamental attribute of Being,[32] instead of exalting him, like Plotinus, above the Idea of Being.[33] For being is for Gregory precisely not an idea. It is first and foremost the negative residue of all of God's qualitative attributes.[34] In the impossibility of knowing "what" God is (πῶς ἐστίν), it becomes clear "that" he is (ὅτι ἐστίν).[35] "The fact of not being this or that is not, for all that, a circumscription of being."[36] But this negative residue is revealed as being eminently positive. From the incapacity to attribute "this" and "that", which is to say, the nonbeing of things,

[28] "A comparison between Gregory . . . and Plotinus immediately reveals the *proximity* of the personal God in Gregory, no matter how much he may insist on the categories of being in the remainder of his work" (Bayer, 36).

[29] *C. Eunom.* 12; II 1068 C–1069 B.

[30] Ibid., 913 D–916 A, etc.

[31] Ibid., 969 C; 972 CD; 1013 A.

[32] "The peculiar mark of divinity, namely, true being ['Ίδιον θεότητος γνώρισμα τὸ ἀληθῶς εἶναι]" (Ibid. 10; II, 840 D). "Really existing ["Οντως ὄν]" (*Vit. Moys.* I, 333 A). "He underlies that which is [Τῷ ὄντι ὑφέστηκε]" ibid., B. "Truly he is one and only [Μόνος ὡς ἀληθῶς ἔστι]" (*C. Eunom.* 8; II, 768 C), etc. Being is "some such character of true divinity [οἱόν τινα χαρακτῆρα τῆς ἀληθινῆς θεότητος]" (*C. Eunom.* 8; II, 772 A).

[33] Plotinus, *Enn.* VI, 8, 11; V, 5, 6.

[34] *Vit. Moys.* I, 317 B. God is called "He who Is" because he does not have a name that could designate his essence (*C. Eunom.* 11; II, 873 A).

[35] *In Cant.* 11; I, 1009 C. Cf. *C. Eunom.* 12; II, 916 A: "He comes to a knowledge of being, . . . although he is not freely given a knowledge of essence [εἰς γνῶσιν ἔρχεται τοῦ εἶναι, . . . οὐ τὴν γνῶσιν τοῦ τί ἐστι χαριζόμενος]."

[36] *De anima et resurrectione* III, 41 B.

to God, there arises Being itself.[37] On the one hand, this Being manifests itself in a "feeling of Presence" (αἴσθησις παρουσίας τινός).[38]
On the other hand, this feeling finds itself ceaselessly augmented by
the failure of all attempts to grasp it conceptually. Thus the concept
indirectly reveals *being*: "It indicates being, but not by confiding what
indeed it is, since being is not graspable. It reveals it only indirectly
[παραδηλοῦν]."[39] What we are witnessing here is nothing less than a
reflex, philosophical realization of the "idea" of Existence. In the face
of "ontological mystery", pagan philosophy saw that only a twofold
affirmation was possible. On the one hand, there was the affirmation
of "ousia", which expresses the "essence" (τὸ τί εἶναι), of a thing, and,
on the other hand, the affirmation of something mysteriously beyond
"ousia", which enjoys a transcendent relationship to being. The Christian consciousness[40] can no longer escape by taking one of these two
ways. The being that is present in essence must be found, without,
however, confusing it with essence or expressing it by way of essence.
All knowing that is "essential" already presupposes an "existential"
faith. "First, we must believe that a thing is, and only then can we de-
fine what this object that is believed in is."[41] The structure of human
judgment is completely adapted to this indirect knowledge, "so that it
is necessary to think of one thing when we are positing being and of
something else when we are positing that which is added to being for
the purpose of knowledge." In every judgment about God, "being is
understood", and it is toward this mysterious "being" that thought
ought to direct (προαπαρτίζει) its concepts, under pain of falling into
the void (κατὰ κενοῦ τὴν προσηγορίαν πίπτειν). In this way we learn
that there is in all being a duality between existence and its manifestations, between *actus* and *actio*.[42] Only the assigning of attributes remains "around being" (περὶ τὸ ὄν). Existence itself stays in obscurity
(ἐν ἀδήλῳ).[43] Therefore we understand why Gregory does not need

---

[37] " 'Ousia' is seen by means of movement toward that which is irresistible" (*C. Eunom.*
12; II, 1040 C).

[38] *In Cant.* 11; I, 1001 B. We shall be examining the notion of *parousia* much more closely
in our study of Origen.

[39] *De comm. not.* II, 177 B.

[40] *Quod non sint tres dii* II, 133 C.

[41] *C. Eunom.* 7; II, 761 B–D.

[42] Ibid., 764 AB.

[43] *De beat.* 6; I, 1268 C.

to go beyond being in order to affirm God. God is ὑπὲρ πᾶσαν φύσιν
καλοῦ παντὸς ἐπέκεινα.[44] He is ὑπὲρ τὸ ἀγαθόν. Since, for Gregory,
"God" denotes the attribute of universal Providence (θεὸς, from the
verb θεᾶσθαι),[45] God is even "above God".[46] But to say that God is
above Being would make no sense, since Being *is* that Great Beyond.
It is he we touch by all that we posit and all our negations.[47] He is
the "underlying agent" (ὑποκείμενον) who cannot be designated in
any other way than by εἶναι.[48] We shall see farther on how this εἶναι
has been forgotten, not only as it concerns the knowledge of God,
but almost as much insofar as it concerns the knowledge of creatures.
For the moment, it suffices for us to have noted this point. There
are in Gregory's thought ideas that are more apparently opposed to
Neoplatonism. But none of them marks a more radical divergence.
Our whole study will be merely a proof of this affirmation, which it
has been our intention to set forth right at the outset as a thesis to
be proven.

The three parts that follow are successive approaches toward this
central mystery of existence. On this path of approach we shall encounter all the problems described above, not as questions that would
occupy our attention for their own sakes or that could find a satisfactory solution outside of the principal question, but as stages of
the problem itself as it progressively unfolds. The three parts do not
therefore correspond to three different problems, or to three diverse
solutions to the same problem, but rather to a successive resumption
of the same problem, each time on a higher plane. This higher plane,
by its very manner of posing the question, transcends the lower plane
even while it safeguards the essential solution.

---

[44] *C. Eunom.* 2; II, 469 D.
[45] *Quod non sint tres dii* II, 121 D.
[46] *C. Eunom.* 5; II, 684 B.
[47] "From a denial of the qualities that are not present and from an assent to the qualities
that are sacredly perceived about him, what is apprehended is that he is . . . [ὅτι ἔστι κατα-
λαμβάνεται]" (*C. Eunom.* 12; II, 957). (And not, as is proposed by Franzelin, who is followed
in this by Diekamp: "what he is [ὅ τι ἔστι]" [Diekamp, 187, note].)
[48] *C. Eunom.* 1; II, 320 CD.

PART ONE

The Philosophy of
Becoming and Desire

I

THE CONCEPT OF SPACING

Every time he undertakes a development of the fundamentals of his metaphysics, Gregory begins from the irreducible opposition between God and creature.[1] God is he who possesses Being as his Nature: ὃ τῇ αὐτοῦ φύσει τὸ εἶναι ἔχει.[2] As a result, it is impossible to find action or passion in him.[3] Nor do we find any category of limited being in him, inasmuch as: "That which is without quality cannot be measured, the invisible cannot be examined, the incorporeal cannot be weighed, the limitless cannot be compared, the incomprehensible does not admit of more or less."[4] Everything that exists outside of God is like nothing before his eyes. "Not absolutely nothing, but like nothing",[5] like a spider's web.[6] "He who looks at it sees nothing."[7] All of this is suspended in God, and, in order to be able to subsist, it participates in the inexhaustible source of being.[8] But if it turns away from this source with a desire to belong to itself, it no longer merits the name of being.[9] This profoundly ontological privation of being is sin,[10] which is veritably an annihilation (ἐξουδένωσις).[11]

The first essential characteristic of the creature is therefore negative. It consists of the very fact that the creature is not God. In taking its referential bearings entirely from him, the creature distinguishes it-

---

[1] For example: *In Cant.* 6; I, 885 C; *C. Eunom.* 1; II, 333 CD; *C. Eunom.* 8; II, 793 CD–796 A.
[2] *Vit. Moys.* I, 333 B.
[3] *C. Eunom.* 12; II, 1036 C–1037 A.
[4] *In suam ordin.* III, 552 B.
[5] *C. Eunom.* 12; II, 952 C; cf. 989 B.
[6] *In Ps.* 1, 7; I, 462 D.
[7] *In Eccles.* 1; I, 624 C.
[8] *Vit. Moys.* I, 333 AB.
[9] Ibid. I, 381 B; *In Ps.* 2, 14; I, 586 B; *In Ps.* 2, 15; I, 595 C.
[10] *In Eccles.* 5; I, 681 C; 7; I, 725 B.
[11] *In Ps.* 1, 8; I, 479 AB.

self from him by this self-same referential relationship: "It is precisely through its comparison and union with the Creator that it is other than him."[12] This abyss that separates the two forms of being is the fact of creation, which in and of itself surrounds that which is created with a magic circle, which it will never escape. There is no stratagem by which the creature will ever understand its own origins.[13] "The question of knowing how each thing came to be remains completely excluded from the domain of research." Even the prophets and those blessed with special inspiration are incapable of receiving a revelation on this question.[14] Our being reveals to us the fact of creation and how it is "in every way ineffable and incomprehensible".[15]

There is, in effect, in a created being a fundamental character that at one and the same time reveals to it and hides from it its origins. This is the διάστημα, or the διάστασις, which is to say, spacing.[16] Gregory, moreover, calls it αἰών. What does he mean by this? To summarize things somewhat imprecisely, to be sure, we may say that he is talking about the categories of time and space, considered, not as qualities added in some way to finite being, but as the intimate substance of its being. In God all diastasis is excluded, be it in the distinction between his Persons[17] or in his nature as such.[18] It is necessary, therefore, that this diastasis be linked to the idea of creation itself. In effect: "When it speaks of aeons, it is the intention [of Scripture] to designate all visible and invisible creation by that which contains it [ἐκ τοῦ περιέχοντος]."[19] And to be more precise: τὸ διάστημα οὐδὲν ἄλλο ἢ κτίσις ἐστίν (spacing is nothing other than creation).[20] We may

[12] C. Eunom. 1; II, 368 C.
[13] In Cant. 10; I, 980 B.
[14] De an. et res. III, 121 AB.
[15] Or. cat. 11; II, 44 B.
[16] Balthasar, in his nomenclature for this concept, oscillates back and forth between the French word "espacement", which I regularly translate as "spacing", and the Greek terms diastēma and diastasis. He does, though, seem to favor the Greek diastēma in terms of frequency of use, recurring to the actual word in Greek script or a transliteration of it or even the French equivalent, "diastème". To save at least some awkward, emphasized transliteration and intrusive quotation marks, I have Englished diastasis, diastēma, and their cognates into plain, unadorned form as follows: diastasis, diastema, diastematic, etc.—TRANS.
[17] Quod non sint tres dii II, 129 AB; De comm. not. II, 180 C; C. Eunom. 1; II, 360 AB-361 D, 364 A-D; C. Eunom. 1; II, 304 D; 445 B.
[18] De mortuis III, 517 B.
[19] C. Maced. II, 1321 B.
[20] In Eccles. 7; I, 729 C.

picture to ourselves this nonidentity of the creature, for it is in this
way that we find the meaning of this concept of spacing, conceiving
of it as a kind of exterior limit, which would envelop finite being
with nonbeing from both the front and the rear, as two periods of
night envelop a day on either side[21] or, better still, as a circle, which
would enclose the creature on every side: ἐν ἑαυτῇ ἀεὶ μένει.[22] And
the same circle surrounds the spiritual activity of the creature: "The
limit of man's movement and spiritual activity is the aeon."[23] But, as
it stands, this description remains completely exterior and characterized by images. It is important, if we are to go farther, to consider
that the limits of a finite being are at the same time its contours, its
form, indeed, its beauty. It is in fact Divine Wisdom that "has cir-
cumscribed each being within its own proper dimensions, by giving
it a suitable rhythm as a limit, so to speak, so that it may be included
in the rightful harmony of the universe".[24] This limitation is part
and parcel of the being itself to such a degree that, in reaching its
boundaries, it "loses its being".[25] The limitation is not exterior to
it. It traverses it through and through, for it is its internal finitude.
Spacing is a transverse (διαμετροῦν) measure that actively traverses the
whole being (διαλαμβάνον).[26]

But at this point, we hasten to add that, in the work of Gregory,
the term "spacing" denotes two things we must carefully distinguish.
Without this distinction we risk getting ourselves all tangled up in
inextricable contradictions. The term "spacing" is applicable, on the
one hand, as we have seen, to the whole creature, and this in virtue
of the fact that it is a creature. It corresponds in a way to the *Ævum*
of the scholastics. On the other hand, it denotes a particular form
of nonidentity, that of the material world. In this sense, the spiritual
nature is excluded from the "characteristics of place and spacing".[27]
And the diastema is confounded here with the notion of time and
space.

In this latter sense, spacing is that "receptacle" of all material being

---

[21] *C. Eunom.* 9; II, 820 C.
[22] *In Eccles.* 7; I, 729 B.
[23] *C. Eunom.* 1; II, 365 C.
[24] Ibid., 365 B.
[25] *De an. et res.* III, 141 A.
[26] *C. Eunom.* 1; II, 365 B.
[27] *In hexaëm.* I, 84 D; cf. 81 D.

which God created in the beginning: χώρημα δεκτικὸν τῶν γινομένων προκαταβαλλόμενος,[28] and which is "time and place".[29] It is evident that what is at stake here is only a logical preexistence, since time could not exist either before itself or before any being.[30] Gregory, moreover, explains himself clearly. If God created "in the beginning" (ἐν ἀρχῇ), this means that he created everything at once, in a moment that precedes the possibility of spacing.[31] But since the limit of our being and our intelligence is in very truth spacing, this indivisible (ἀκαρές) moment is for us incomprehensible. Therefore Moses expresses it by way of the darkness that reigns over the abyss.[32] For our limited intelligence, the simultaneity of creation is construed in two ways. First, when we position ourselves in God, we say that all times are present to his eternity, which is an endless presence,[33] and that his Providence encompasses all times in one solitary gaze.[34] And, second, when we position ourselves from the point of view of the world, we say that God created everything in the very first moment, without adding anything to his handiwork later on.[35] The time that is unfolded is limited, or, better still, it is the very limit of material being. There is no such thing as undefined time, because there is no such thing as undefined material being.[36] The notion of time is construed identically by the notions of beginning and end, which are both joined together by a *path* (ὁδός).[37] It is an ordered unfolding (τάξις καὶ ἀκολουθία).[38] On the one hand, it is a kind of manifestation of the parts of a being, a distension of its members (παρά-στασις).[39]

---

[28] C. Eunom. 1; II, 365 D; cf. Ibid. 9; II, 801 D.

[29] Ibid., 368 A.

[30] Cf. Philo, De opificio mundi I §26 (Mang. p. 6).

[31] "For the beginning of the whole concept of diastema is a marvel. Just as the point that is the beginning of a line or of a material substance is indivisible, so also is a moment of the temporal diastema" (In hexaëm. I, 72 A).

[32] Ibid., 72 C.

[33] C. Eunom. 8; II, 793 D;–1; II, 565 B;–12; II, 1064 C.

[34] De hom. op. 16; I, 185 D; In Ps. 2, 13; I, 569 B.

[35] In Ps. 6; I, 610 BC.

[36] "And time did not come to be something other after the time that had been proclaimed as having effect when the cosmos was undergoing its preparation. But the nature of time was marked out with boundaries by means of a week of days" (ibid.).

[37] De mortuis III, 520 C.

[38] C. Eunom. 1; II, 364 C.

[39] "Diastematic manifestation [παράστασις διαστηματική]" (C. Eunom. 1; II, 364 C). "Diastematic manifestation [παράστασις διαστηματική]" (C. Eunom. 12; II, 1104 D).

On the other hand, this spacing is also a movement (διαστηματικῶς ἔκ τινος εἴς τι τῇ ζωῇ διοδεύουσα),[40] an emanation (ἡ ῥοώδης κίνησις),[41] and thereby a tension. This apparent contradiction is translated into the order of knowledge by a rending of consciousness with respect to a memory of the past and a prevision of the future (τῆς ζωῆς σχι-ζομένης κατὰ τὴν τοῦ χρόνου διαίρεσιν), even though this consciousness remains that of a unique subject possessing the πάθη πρὸς ἐλπίδα καὶ μνήμην (passions of hope and memory).[42] The measure of this tension is time in the strict sense.[43] This movement "is not a displacement of locale, for nature does not go outside its limits. It is a progression by alteration." As the flame of a lamp seems always to be identical and is not, though, at any given moment the same (οὐδέποτε ἐπὶ τοῦ αὐτοῦ μένουσα), but is ceaselessly renewing itself (ἀεὶ καινὴ) and perpetually reborn (πάντοτε γινομένη), in the same way all material nature is in continuous change.[44] It is therefore a perpetual death, a "living death",[45] which moves toward its foregone end, not as it would toward an end set arbitrarily, but because its spacing is identical to its limitation. The tension of hope is necessarily directed toward an end, toward its proper bounding limits: πρὸς τὸ πέρας ταῖς ἐλπίσι συμπαρατείνεσθαι.[46]

---

[40] C. Eunom. 12; II, 933 B.

[41] In Ps. 6; I, 609 C.

[42] C. Eunom. 1; II, 367 AB.

[43] "For time is coextensive . . . with all movement" (C. Fatum II, 160 B). "Positively everything that moves moves in time" (In hexaëm. I, 120 A). "For beginnings and endings are definitely observed in any manifestation. But all manifestations are measured out by means of time" (C. Eunom. 9; II, 812 C). "Time is coextensive with everything that happens" (In Eccles. 6; I, 697 C).

[44] De an. et res. III, 141 BC.

[45] In Cant. 12; I, 1022 D.

[46] C. Eunom. 8; II, 793 D. Compare the proof given in C. Eunom. 1; II, 359–63, to the effect that there cannot be any diastema between the Father and the Son. This proof rests in its essence on the finitude of all spacing. Cf. C. Eunom. 12; II, 1104 D: "It takes its rise from nonbeing and ends at nonbeing."

What are the sources of this philosophy of time that is apparently so original? It is certain that we shall not have cause to look for these sources in Aristotle's totally cosmological concept: "A measure of movement and an enumeration of what happens before and after" (Phys. IV, 11; De cælo I, 9). Gregory conceives of time as a profound, ontological reality, as an intrinsic mode of created substance rather than as one of its accidents. Plutarch was the first to have interpreted time thus: he saw in it the principle of harmony and order in the universe and even considered it the living nature of the cosmos. Time and the cosmos are, in the same order of things, images of divinity and all life. All cosmic movement unfolds in the

While this notion of time is abundantly developed, we find only a few rare indications concerning diastema as "space". There are enough of them, however, for us to suppose that place is merely another as-

---

great reality of time (*Quæst. platonicæ* 1007 B–D). In this case, Plutarch merely develops the celebrated passage from the *Timaeus*, according to which time is the living image of eternity, an image that encompasses all cosmic space and that will be destroyed together with the celestial sphere (*Tim.* 37 C–38 B).

But it was only the Stoics who accepted the notion of diastema in their definition of time. "For of the Stoics, Zeno spoke of time as a diastema of absolutely all motion, while Chrysippus called it a diastema of the motion of the cosmos" (*Simplicius in categ.*, ed. Kalbfleisch [1907], 350). "A diastema of motion, but nothing else, as some of the Stoics [say]" (Plutarch, *Quæst. platonicæ* 1007). A definition that was taken up by Philo (*De opif. mundi* I): "Inasmuch as time is a diastema of the motion of the cosmos" (cf. *De ætern. mundi*, ed. Cumont, 16). But this concept merely expresses a mechanical law and refers us therefore with much more force to the cosmological milieu of Aristotle than to that of Plato. It is only by combining the Stoic concept with the Neoplatonic idea of time that we approach the conception of Gregory of Nyssa. According to Plotinus, God is beyond movement and rest. *Nous*, which moves round about God, is at once movement and rest, in a life that is supratemporal and eternal (*Enn.* III, 9, 3). But whereas *nous* possesses God in this tranquil movement, the cosmic Soul tends toward him with a certain restlessness (*Enn.* IV, 4, 16). This restlessness is not itself in time. It is rather the very source of temporality. The Cosmic Soul itself is time, and all that it contains is completely penetrated by time (*Enn.* III, 7, 11). Whereas eternity can be defined as "the life of the existent in being, in its full, uninterrupted, absolutely permanent totality" (*Enn.* III, 7, 3), time is defined as "the life of the soul, which passes from one vital manifestation to another in its movement" (*Enn.* III, 7, 11). One cannot therefore say, according to Plotinus, that time is a diastema of motion, since the diastema of motion is itself in time, as is motion (*Enn.* III, 7, 7–8). But since all particular souls together form the total Soul, the definition of time as life is applied to each one of them: time is in us, it is our life (*Enn.* III, 7, 13).

The later Neoplatonists, however, favor more and more those elements that, in the definition of Plotinus, were opposed to a Christian conception. Time, Proclus tells us, imitates eternity so well that it ought itself to be designated as something eternal (*In Platonis Timæum commentaria*, ed. E. Diehl [1904–1906]; 244 D, 246 B). Temporal motion is circular motion and, as such, eternal, perfect, infinite movement. But Proclus goes farther, claiming that time is by its motion the perpetuation of temporal things. It is very much a δύναμις (power), but a purely active power, which draws things within its center of energy in order to take their measure in accordance with Ideas and to assimilate them to Ideas. Time, in its essence, is motionless. It only moves in that which it moves. Thus Proclus is merely being consistent with this when he makes time a kind of divinity ("Time itself is a god . . ." ibid., 248 D). The closed circle of temporality that is also described by Iamblichus (cf. *Simplicius in categ.*, 345) is thus in no wise the motion that is proper to created being as such. It is rather an expression of intrinsic independence on the part of the "hypostasis" or the "idea" of time. It is an infinite, periodic movement that tends to identify itself with eternity itself. Already Plotinus conceived of the latter as a life that is at once in movement and at rest. Iamblichus explicitly distinguishes an intelligible, immaterial time and a physical, material time (*Simplicius in phys.*, 787). Even while they multiply intermediary emanations between pect of the fundamental spacing of material being: "For there exists no being in this created world which does not have its being in either space or time."[47] Just as the idea of the initial "receptacle" (χώρημα δεκτικόν) is conveyed by its temporal nonidentity, it can also be conceived of as a "spatial receptacle" (χώρημα τοπικόν),[48] in which all being is comprehended (ἐν ᾧ τὰ καθ' ἕκαστον εἶναι καταλαμβάνεται).

Spacing is therefore the character of the creature that establishes quantity and number. The whole method of the treatise κατὰ εἱμαρμένης (*Contra fatum* [Against destiny]) consists of reducing all appearance of qualitative difference in the movement of the stars to pure quantity, which, in itself, is incapable of being the cause of several qualitatively different effects.[49] As for number, it is defined as a "synthesis of unities" (σύνθεσις μονάδων).[50] But "that alone can be calculated through synthesis which is conceived of in its limits."[51]

God and the world, the Neoplatonists tend to elevate time right to the level of God. It enters into the supracosmic realm of ideal beings.

Gregory of Nyssa, therefore, brings an absolutely new element to the problem by interpreting time as the very sign of the creature and thus of the fundamental passivity of created being. In this way the three elements of the Greek philosophy of time find themselves profoundly modified. The Stoic diastema becomes an ontological concept that designates a being that is not identical to itself, a being that is in some way torn apart, divided from itself. Plotinus' ontological time aptly maintains its character of restlessness and of tense vitality but is more pronounced in its orientation toward the indigence, the poverty, the insufficiency of the creature. Circular time is finally stripped of its infinite, eternal radiance. To the contrary, the circle becomes the symbol of finitude. The circuit is followed only one time. Once it has arrived at its end term, the created being reaches at the same time the goal of its existence. It dies, it does away with itself. (See Dr. Hans Leisegang, *Die Begriffe der Zeit und Ewigkeit im späteren Platonismus*, Bäumkers Beiträge 13, no. 4, [Münster, 1913].)

[47] *C. Eunom.* 1; II, 368 A.

[48] Ibid. 12, II, 1104 D.

[49] "For there is one measure of motion in everything that moves from one place to another: namely, there is a change either from the place in which it is or into the place in which it is not. But if neither the rushing of streams nor the movement of ships nor the walking of men when it is measured out makes fateful destinies of the diastemas of time, how can you fashion the temporal signs of the motion of the stars into the cause of destined fate?" (II, 160 C). For the mutual dependence of time and number, compare this with Philo, *De opif. mundi* I, 55–61 (Mang. 12–13).

[50] *In hexaëm.* I, 85 C.

[51] *Quod non sint tres dii* II, 132 A. Thus human persons, by virtue of what they have particularly, can be considered "quantitative in their composition" (κατὰ σύνθεσιν ἐν ἀριθμῷ): ibid., 120 B. Gregory does not apply this possibility to the Divine Persons. For in God one cannot distinguish "that which underlies him" (ὑποκείμενον) and "that which is shared in common" (μετεχόμενον), and thereby nothing of "that which is composed of dissimilar

What we have described up to now is the diastema of the material world. But since all diastema is, as we have seen, inseparably linked to the idea of creation, the categories of time and space cannot be completely foreign to spiritual beings. Indeed, many of the passages cited are applicable to "the entire creation",[52] and it is not always easy to see whether spiritual creation is included in this or not. It is necessary, however, to maintain two affirmations. On the one hand, spiritual being finds itself, by the very fact of being created, in a παράστασις, which gives it a certain movement, a progress.[53] On the other hand, this progress does not proceed, as does that of material being, toward an end term (πέρας). This last affirmation, however, includes two aspects that are apparently contradictory but equally true. On the one hand, the fact of its not extending itself to its own proper limits renders the spirit limitless[54] and infinite in a certain way: "The nature of souls and of angels does not know limits, and nothing stops their respective natures from progressing to the infinite."[55] On the other hand, this same fact can be conveyed by the very negation of "spacing" (which is the limitation of a "scattered" being) and, consequently, by the identity of the origin and the end.[56] Angels are thereby removed from time, insofar as time is "passivity"[57] and entails the notion of being in spite of itself (ὁδεύουσα φέρεται).[58] Their nature is "perfect" in that their nature possesses its proper end: "Without spacing, their end was created in such a way as to correspond with their origins . . . , at the same moment as their beginning, their final perfection was manifested in being [ὁμοῦ τῇ ἀρχῇ]."[59] These

---

things" (σύνθετον ἐξ ἀνομοίων): C. Eunom. 1; II, 321 C. Number is "the sign of quantity" (C. Eunom. 1; II, 312 B), but in God there is no quantity.

[52] "Creation" (Ἡ κτίσις): C. Eunom. 1; II, 365–68. "The order of nature in creation" (Ἡ ἐν τῇ κτίσει φύσις): ibid. 8; II, 793 C. "For all the things that come to be" (πᾶσι τοῖς γινομένοις): ibid. 9; II, 812 D.

[53] De mortuis III, 520 C.

[54] In Cant. 6; I, 885 C.

[55] C. Eunom. 8; II, 792 D.

[56] "But for moving things, their boundary is the limit of diastematic nature. In accordance with this limit, the order of nature that is perceptible by the mind and unvarying is found to be free of characteristics that are peculiar to the notions of place and diastema" (C. Eunom. 9; II, 812 C).

[57] This is "fateful" (εἱμαρμένη) time (C. Fatum II, 160 BC), time as characterized by necessitas, in its Augustinian sense: cf. De an. et res. III, 104 B.

[58] C. Eunom. 1; II, 365 B.

[59] In Cant. 15, I, 1109. It is true that this passage is applied to the first creation of man. But

two aspects, namely, possession of its own proper end and infinity, are so far from being mutually exclusive that, on the contrary, they convey exactly the distinctive character of the spirit: total reflection. It is for this reason that, from the first moment of their creation, the Spirit of God, which is light, hovered over the waters that were below the firmament, which is to say, it hovered over the angels.[60] Created spirit, therefore, has "finitude" and "infinity" at the same time. It lives "for aeons without end, and its finitude (πέρας) is not having an end (ἀπειρία)".[61]

What is not yet apparent in this description is how this possession of self does not exclude a radical diastasis. In order to see this, a deeper analysis of the becoming of the creature will be necessary.

---

we shall see farther on why it can be applied to spiritual nature as such. Compare as well the idea of the ubiquity of the soul after death: according to Gregory, it remains in union with dispersed matter: "Therefore the realm of unvarying nature, united as it is to things that are spatially dispersed and divided, is in travail" (*De an. et res.* III, 48 A).

[60] *In hexaëm.* I, 85 A.

[61] *De an. et res.* III, 81 C.

2

BECOMING AND THE IMMANENT INFINITE

If time constitutes the foundation of material being, this physical movement is itself founded on a primordial movement, a metaphysical movement, so to speak, which is common to all creatures: namely, the passage from nothingness to existence. "Already the transition from nonbeing to being is a movement and a change."[1] "Only uncreated Nature is incapable of movement. All the rest is subject to change, because, without exception, it began by way of an alteration, when it was drawn by divine power from nonbeing to existence."[2] But we know already that this "beginning" of being should not be understood in a temporal way, time being a category of created being. The being that comes to be does not cease to become, or, rather, it is quite entirely becoming. The idea of change that comes into play here is therefore subjacent to all its being: "Since it possesses the beginning (ἀρχή) of its being by way of change, it is impossible that it should not be entirely variable (τρεπτός)."[3] For the material creature, this perseverance in change is precisely time. For the spiritual being, on the other hand, it is participation in the cause of being not only insofar as it is source but also insofar as it is end. Since its existence is, so to speak, a continuous effort to maintain itself in being, its perfection consists of a perpetual effort toward God. This effort is the spiritual participation in God: "Creation stands within the realm of the beautiful only through a participation in that which is the best. It has not begun merely at one point or another to exist, but at every moment it is perceived to be in its beginning stages on account of its perpetual growth toward that which is the

---

[1] *De hom. op.* 16; I, 184 C.

[2] *Catech.* 6; II, 28 D.

[3] *Catech.* 21; II, 57 D; cf. 8; II, 40 AB: "Having begun to exist directly as a result of change, it always goes forward by means of alteration."

best.''[4] It follows from this that, just as the finitude of material being engenders a certain eternity of emanation, albeit in the horizontal scheme of the quantitative and of number, similarly the finitude of spiritual being, which by its participation in God as source and as end constitutes itself in a nature that is opposed to God, engenders an aspiration that is even more appropriately infinite, a vertical ascent that is limitless: "Never will the soul reach its final perfection, for it will never encounter a limit, . . . it will always be transformed into a better thing.''[5] The reason for this infinite becoming is the very infinity of the source, which the creature seeks to be reunited with: "Since the First Good is infinite in its nature, communion with it on the part of the one whose thirst is quenched by it will have to be infinite as well, capable of being enlarged forever.''[6] Thus, there are two forms of becoming, the two of them together yielding the total formula for the analogy of being. One of these two is the horizontal movement of created being, which is to say, its foundation of nothingness, which separates it eternally from God, inasmuch as pure potentiality (time) is in itself κένωμα καὶ οὐδέν [emptiness and nothingness].[7] The other expresses the ascending movement of becoming,[8] which is the innate idea and desire for God in the creature.[9] We shall be obliged to show farther on in this essay in what way these two aspects are linked and inseparable in all of created being. Let it suffice at this point merely to have adverted to this fact.

At this point we must examine more closely the specific character of these two forms of becoming, and particularly that of material becoming, whose immanent infinity has not yet been clearly revealed to us. We had even, in a contrary sense, identified time and limit. But if it is true in a general and abstract fashion that material being is the movement between a beginning and an end, both of which transcend

---

[4] C. Eunom. 8; II, 797 A.
[5] C. Eunom. 1; II, 340 D.
[6] Ibid.
[7] In hexaëm. I, 80 C.
[8] Cf. Erich Przywara, Analogia entis (Munich, 1932), 73ff.
[9] "The notion of the divine lies in all men naturally" (De beat. 5; I, 1249 D). Obviously we are not dealing here with innate ideas in the sense of modern philosophy (cf. J. Bayer, Gregors von Nyssa Gottesbegriff [Diss., Giessen, 1935], 8), but rather in the sense of the Stoics (Cicero: De nat. deor. II, 12). Cf. Heinemann, Poseidonius metaphysische Schriften II, 125ff., 172.

it, we also noticed that this limitation was bound to be conceived as an utterly intrinsic characteristic, which is applied to each of its moments and each of its elements. It has existence only as a perpetual transition between two extremes that are not it.

> This material and fleeting [ῥοώδης] life of bodies, which advances in a perpetual movement, possesses force of being in virtue of the very fact that it never ceases to move. But the situation may be likened to a river. A river that follows its course is able to show that the bed in which it flows is always full but that it is never the same water staying in the same place, inasmuch as one part of the stream withdraws from any given place while another part draws near. Similarly the matter of this life changes within the context of a certain movement and a certain flux, even while it admits opposite impressions within a state of perpetual transition. Thus it is impossible for it to cease from this process of alteration, but [in place][10] of the possibility of remaining at rest it possesses an untiring movement through a change of similar [qualities]. And if ever it ceased to move, it would at the same moment cease to exist.

Thus must fullness empty itself and emptiness fill itself. Sleep must succeed waking. "None of this can have indefinitely long duration. Rather each state must yield place to another, for by such substitutions nature restores itself."

> If the forces of the living being are in a perpetual tension, members that are excessively stretched will end up being broken and torn of necessity. Contrariwise, a prolonged loosening of the body will produce a fall and a dissolution of the organism. For nature, the power of continuance, therefore, consists of the art of touching the two extremes at the right moment [κατὰ καιρόν] and in the right measure [μετρίως]. And, by a perpetual transition toward the opposite, it takes its rest in a series of pairs.[11]

And not only that which is alive but rather the whole world also is conceived according to this law. "Divine artistry was capable, by way of rest and movement, of giving becoming to nonexistent things and continuity to beings."[12] "Stability" is given to the earth, and "movement" is given to the heavens, so that creation may find itself moving between the extremes (μεταξὺ τῶν ἐναντίων κτίσις). On all sides

---

[10] The Greek text needs to be corrected.
[11] *De hom. op.* 13; I, 165 AC.
[12] Ibid. 1; I, 128 C.

creation is threatened by an excess (ὑπερβολή) of movement or of rest, but it is also in itself the fruit of these extremes ("for that which appears in this world is none other than the result of movement and stability"). In dissociating them, creation unites them (μιγνὺς ἅμα καὶ διαιρῶν) and thus produces the great kinship of all beings.[13] But the extremes themselves are not exempt from contradiction. The heavens, which appear to be pure movement, possess at the same time the immobility of nature. The earth, on the other hand, which is apparently pure stability, undergoes alterations of substance. Divine Wisdom had two equally profound reasons for this. One of them was so that no part of the world might remain without contact with the others but rather that "each part might incline toward the other" "and that all of creation might be united with a view to the same harmonious aspiration [συμπνέοι πρὸς ἑαυτὴν ἡ κτίσις]". The second reason, which proceeds immediately from the first, is so that no part of the universe may be taken for divine, neither the heavens on account of their immutability nor the earth on account of its stability. But with a mixture of contrasts in the one and the other, all appearances of divinity were bound to disappear.[14] Everything in this world is essentially relative. Everything holds together only by being counterbalanced by an opposite "excess". All the beauty of the world, all its worth, all that harmony that arises from the rhythm of becoming, is founded on those elements in it that are, properly speaking, opposed to the divine.[15] Polytheism arose when men marveled at the world, no longer in its entirety, but rather in its parts,[16] whereas the words of Genesis "and God saw that it was very good" can be applied only to the whole.[17] For the good is never one of the oppositions, since the latter are only "good" in relation to one another.[18] It is the continuity of the whole (συνεχές ἐστι τὸ πᾶν ἑαυτῷ) that leads without any slackening from one extreme to the other (οὐκ ἔχει τινὰ λύσιν ἡ ἁρμονία) and that ties opposites together indissolubly (οὐκ

---

[13] Ibid., 128 C–129 B.

[14] Ibid., 129 C–132 A.

[15] It will be recognized without difficulty how fundamentally opposed this vision of the world is to that of Pseudo-Dionysius, where all the beauty and worth of the cosmos issue from the immanence of the ἕν (One), from Participation in the supreme Unity.

[16] C. Eunom. 5; II, 682 B.

[17] De mortuis III, 500 BC. Cf. In hexaëm. I, 92 CD.

[18] De mortuis III, 500 CD.

ἀπέσχισται τὸ πᾶν τῆς πρὸς ἑαυτὸν συναφείας).[19] It is this world full of "vicissitudes, of transmutations of all kinds",[20] that caused God to utter the phrase λίαν καλόν (very good). For the perfection of this universe is a symphonic perfection that requires a diversity of sounds and instruments in order to form a rhythm and a harmony that are at once multiple and unique.[21] In this immense mixture (τοῦ παντὸς κρᾶσις), the mutual touching of the elements (αὐτὴ ἑαυτῆς ἁπτομένη) produces that unique stability that is ordered and invariable rhythm (διά τινος τεταγμένου τε καὶ ἀπαραβάτου ῥυθμοῦ), "a veritable song of praise for the unapproachable and unspeakable glory of God".[22] In this system of harmonious agreement, each quality emphasizes, by its very opposition, the other quality, "in such a way that there arises in movement that which is stable and in tranquillity that which is perpetually in movement". Incarnated in this universal fellowship of feeling (συμπάθεια πάντων) is the pure idea of music (ἡ πρώτη τε καὶ ἀρχέτυπος καὶ ἀληθής ἐστι μουσική), which the Wisdom of God has itself composed.[23]

Man is by the constitution of his body a microcosm. His harmonious proportions are an image of the music of the world. And since "all that is in accordance with nature is dear to nature", man recognizes himself in music as in a mirror (ἀναθεωρεῖ ἑαυτὴν ἡ φύσις).[24] In the polyphonic melody of becoming, the soul perceives, as it were, an echo of the divine infinity to which she aspires, and she risks letting herself be seduced by its very beauty. This time, it is a seduction, no longer by a part of the world that has been erected into an absolute, but by the song of becoming in its wholeness.

However, when the infinite soul would like to take her fill of the infinite becoming of the world, she realizes that she is like a man "who pursues the shadow of his head. She ends up running after something that is ungraspable."[25] For all sensual delight that is material is ex-

---

[19] *In Eccles.* 7; I, 724 D.

[20] *In Christi resurr.* 3; III, 672 D.

[21] "The ordered regulation of the whole universe is a kind of musical harmony that is richly and multifariously tuned internally according to a certain order and rhythm. It is a harmony that is never separated from this symphonic order, even if many differences are visible in its individually existing parts" (*In Ps.* 3; I, 440 C).

[22] Ibid., 440 D–441 A.

[23] Ibid., 441 B–C.

[24] Ibid., 444 A.

[25] *De beat.* 4; I, 1245 A.

tinguished with the achievement of the pleasure. The sensual delight must be interrupted "in order that the desire for enjoyment might return".[26] Thus it is that desire is perpetually recovered by means of disgust.[27] Material infinity resembles "the building of sand castles by a child. The pleasure the child takes in constructing them dies out coextensively with his joy in doing such work . . . , and the sand collapses, leaving no trace of the things that were made with such painstaking care."[28] "Even as those who write in the medium of water might work hard to sketch things with their hand . . . but nothing remains on the surface of the water, . . . the same applies to all quests and all activities that pursue sensual pleasure."[29] The soul would like to give the illusion of orderly progress toward an end. "But, like beasts that toil at a millstone, we turn round and round, our eyes blinkered, tethered as we are to the millstone of this life. . . . I shall enumerate to you the following round of things: hunger, satiety, sleep, waking, evacuation, repletion. Always one follows the other, and the other follows the one, and then again the other, and never does this round of activities have an end, until such a time as we escape from this millstone."[30] The soul would still like to give herself the illusion that her infinite desire alone causes her to rise up in some way. But she is "like those who scale a sandy slope. Even if they look like they are traversing great tracts of ground on foot, they tire themselves to no avail. Each time the sand slides to the bottom, in such a way that there is a great effort of movement but no progress."[31] We cannot stop the flowing current of becoming and appropriate to ourselves the thing that is happening: "None of these passing things belongs to us. How do we hold that which is dissolving and flowing away from us? If it is true that what is spiritual and immaterial remains, but that matter passes away in a perpetual alteration and flux, he who lets go of what is stable must himself end up swept away by the current of what is unstable, and he who loses the stable and the unstable finds himself betrayed by both of them."[32] But in that case how should

---

[26] Ibid., 1244 D.
[27] *In Eccles.* 2; I, 648 D.
[28] Ibid. 1; I, 628 CD.
[29] Ibid. 4; I, 677 D–680 A.
[30] *Or. de Placilla.* III, 888 D.
[31] *Vit. Moys.* 405 CD.
[32] *In Cant.* 2; I, 804 BC.

one behave in the face of this symphonic arrangement of the world? A sense of the relativity of each of its elements must be reacquired so that their transparency might then be seen. Only those who are foolish wish to erect sensible things around themselves like a wall that blocks their view of the spiritual things beyond it.[33] In this case only, true spiritual thirst is transformed into a kind of sickly thirst, like that suffered by those who have been bitten by a snake,[34] and desire becomes cursed like the water vessel of the Danaides,[35] so that, at long last, there is nothing left in the soul but shame.[36] Thus the mold in which the bricks are baked is found each time to be empty and burning hot.[37] The miser—and whoever would like to put a stop to becoming in order to seize it is a miser—resembles the sea in the immensity of his desire, since rivers flow down to the sea without surcease, and yet the sea never becomes more full on this account.[38] Everything in this world that appears to have absolute perfection is in fact defective in that it possesses something more perfect: "*Terra stat in æternum!* [the earth stands eternally!] But what is more tedious than this fixity without movement? The sea is stirred up with boundless movement—yet what is more meaningless?"[39]

But in contemplating this world, is man not contemplating himself? "O men, when you consider the universe, you are comprehending your own nature!"[40] The same limitation by way of extremes is to be found in the life of the spirit. In this realm, too, there reigns "a certain harmony that results from opposites",[41] a vital eurhythmy (ἡ τῆς ζωῆς εὐρυθμία) that is the fruit of a just measure that falls between too strong a tension of the strings and their excessive looseness.[42] For "all the tendencies of our soul are mutually opposed without possible union. They terminate one in the other and are limited one by the

---

[33] *De an. et res.* III, 21 D–24 A.

[34] *In Eccles.* 8; I, 737 A.

[35] *De beat.* 4; I, 1244 B.

[36] The phenomenon of modesty and shame occupied Gregory's attention many a time: *In Eccles.* 3; I, 650 D; *In Ps.* 4; I, 447 A; *De an. et res.* III, 92 B.

[37] *Vit. Moys.* I, 344 A.

[38] *In Eccles.* 1; I, 628 C.

[39] Ibid., 625 A–628 A.

[40] Ibid., 625 B.

[41] *Catech.* 6; II, 25 C.

[42] *In Ps.* 3; I, 444 ABC.

other."[43] Thus there is no particular virtue that can be perfect in itself:
"It is impossible for an aspect of virtue, separated from the others,
to be capable of being designated as a perfect virtue on its own."[44]
Only a true synthesis is no longer a kind of immanent harmony of
the parts between each other, as in the material world. Unity can
come only from a more fundamental aspiration, from a more ardent
spiritual becoming, which snatches the soul from the horizontal plane
of matter in order to elevate her to God, the infinite good, who is
alone capable of freeing her from an unachievable concern for what
is immanently infinite. "For this is the supreme success of mutability,
namely, progress in the good, where, in a happy state of alteration, we
find ourselves ceaselessly transformed in the direction of that which is
the most divine. In this case, what appeared formidable—I mean the
mutability of our nature—is thus revealed to us as the eagle's wing
that will carry us toward greater things."[45] This wing is love, which
alone establishes "equilibrium between the too much and the too little",[46] for it goes beyond the whole region of relative oppositions and
surges up toward the infinite good, in which "one cannot hope for
satiation or experience distaste, but where aspiration does not slacken
in communion and where desire retains all its ardor in the fullness
of joyful possession."[47] "He who receives in himself what he desires
is full of the desired thing. For in this instance it is not as it is in
the filling up of a body that empties itself after having been filled.
The drink does not remain inactive in it. But the divine source, if it
penetrates someone, transforms by its agency the one who touches
it and transmits to him its own power."[48] This power is the power
to be always more desirous, "for God has no end. And thus there is
no other possible outcome. The desire of the one who participates
can have no rest [στάσις], because such a one has soared up into the
indeterminate and the infinite."[49] Whence we have the definition of
created spirit: "To wish ever to possess more fully the beautiful is

[43] *In Cant.* 5; I, 873 D.
[44] *De beat.* 4; I, 1241 CD.
[45] *De perf. Christ. forma* III, 285 BC.
[46] *De beat.* 5; I, 1252 B.
[47] *In Eccles.* 2; I, 648 D–649 A.
[48] *In Ps.* 5; I, 452 BC.
[49] *Vit. Moys.* I, 301 AB.

perhaps the perfection [τελειότης] of human nature."[50] This is a quite dynamic definition, the complete meaning of which will be revealed in the second part of this study. It suffices for us at this point to understand that the infinity of created spirit is ineluctably opposed to the infinity of matter, just as it is opposed to the infinity of God. It is ineluctably opposed to quantitative infinity, which is the infinity of number, of emptiness (κένωμα καὶ οὐδέν), of time, and thereby of the finite itself, just as it is opposed to the uncreated infinite, "which is eternally that which it is, always equal to itself, above all growth and all decline, incapable of receiving a new goodness".[51] Between desire without satiation and possession without desire, created spirit realizes that paradoxical synthesis of a desire that can only grow in joy, because the infinity of the object loved increases and rejuvenates (ἀνανεάζουσα) in it for all eternity (εἰς τὸ ἀΐδιον)[52] an impetus that tends (τόνος) toward an end that cannot be attained.[53] Thus the mystical works of Gregory of Nyssa are all built on the idea of a perpetual surpassing of self: "Always higher, always greater than oneself." The life of Moses, the commentary on the Song of Songs, and the sermons on the beatitudes are mystical ascents without any possible end (in this they differ essentially from the ascents of a Saint Teresa). Since the object is infinite, the journey toward it is also infinite. All limited computations henceforth disappear. Once the soul has arrived at a new summit, it is as if she had not yet taken her first step.[54]

But with this analysis of twofold, infinite becoming, the one horizontal, the other vertical, we are still far from having a concrete philosophy of man. For what we are essentially lacking is a doctrine concerning the relationship between matter and spirit in general, and more particularly the unity of the two in the human composite. We are not trying to hide the fact that this doctrine is only partially elaborated by Gregory and that the general picture has many difficulties. Even so, it forms an indispensable presupposition for his entire religious anthropology.

---

[50] Ibid., 301 C.

[51] *In Cant.* 6; I, 885 D.

[52] *C. Eunom.* 8; II, 792 D.

[53] *Vit. Moys.* I, 401 AB.

[54] *In Cant.* 6; I, 892: "It learns that it is as far from having reached its end as those who have not yet undertaken their first faltering steps."

3

SPIRIT AND MATTER

"Since our nature is twofold, a mixture of the spiritual and the sensible, our life also is twofold as a consequence."[1] "Man is twofold, comprised of both body and soul. His life is also twofold."[2] But already we have seen that these two realities are not without analogy. Material becoming released, as the fruit of its undefined movement, something indefinably spiritual, which was law, order, rhythm, music. Spiritual becoming, on its part, had its deep roots in temporality (αἰών), which was often confounded with materiality itself. It is difficult to say in exact terms what this materiality that Gregory attributes to the created spirit as such actually is. There is no doubt that the spirit maintains a certain relationship with time and place.[3] Indeed Gregory seems to envisage as possible a certain materialization of souls as a result of an excessive love of earthly things.[4] This would explain the appearance of ghosts in cemeteries.

Whatever degree of materiality there may be in the created spirit, the inverse assertion, that of the spirituality of matter, finds ample development in Gregory's work. Indeed, matter is comprised entirely of qualities (ποιότης), such as color, surface, thickness, weight, which by their coming together constitute the body. Now these qualities are in themselves spiritual (νοητόν). They are universal predicates that we attribute to a subject (ὑποκείμενον). Their convergence alone constitutes the sensible object.[5] It is possible to resolve a body into definite concepts, of which not one is identical with the particular subject.[6]

---

[1] *In Eccles.* 8; I, 736 B.

[2] Ibid. 6; I, 709 D.

[3] See the texts collected by F. Diekamp, *Literargeschichtliches zu der Eunomianischen Kontroverse*, Byzant. Zeitschrift 18 (Leipzig, 1909), 230⁻31.

[4] *De an. et res.* III, 88 BC.

[5] *De hom. op.* 24; I, 212 D⁻214 B.

[6] "Each kind of quality can be distinguished by the concept of the universal predicate. But

47

Outside of these concepts (λόγος), nothing more remains.[7] "In re-solving the phenomenon into that which constitutes it . . . , I do not see what could remain as an object of knowledge."[8] The qualities of matter "thus constitute, for the one who studies it, a limit beyond which he can imagine nothing [ἐν φαντασίᾳ λαβεῖν]".[9] Gregory says expressly that these qualities are "perceived by the spirit and not by the senses",[10] since it is only the result of their synthesis that pro-duces the sensible object. They are, "taken in themselves, thoughts [ἔννοιαι] and pure concepts [ψιλὰ νοήματα]".[11] It should no longer be necessary to say that when they are attributed to a preexistent subject they become material. This subject could not be other than spacing itself, but Gregory enumerates it in like manner among "thoughts". It is only by a synthesis of all these points of view (νοήματα) that matter becomes real (ὕλη γίνεται).[12] But what is the subject of these thoughts? It goes without saying that Gregory has absolutely no in-tention of excluding man, since the latter is capable of resolving the phenomenon into its constituent parts. But the primary subject re-mains God. For God alone can give a proper life to his ideas. He alone can create interiorized concepts. These "spiritual principles" of bodies (νοερὰς ἀφορμὰς πρὸς τὴν τῶν σωμάτων γένεσιν) Gregory also calls "spiritual forces" (νοητὰς δυνάμεις).[13] In his explication of the Hexaëmeron, he insists above all on the fact that the word (λόγος) of God, which called forth the successive appearance of beings, was an in-terior word that was spoken to these very same beings, a living voice,

---

this concept is something spiritual and not something that can be seen corporeally" (ibid., 212 D).

[7] De an. et res. III, 41 A. Therein lies the difference between Gregory's theory and that of the Neoplatonists, who were themselves also bent on dissolving matter into spiritual qualities. Plotinus and Origen (C. Cels. IV, 56) discern a final material suppositum. Gregory dissolves "all of matter" (πᾶσαν τὴν ὕλην) (De hom. op. 24). In Gregory's thought, there is, however, the "receiving receptacle" (χώρημα δεκτικόν), the "aeon" (αἰών), which in a certain way replaces "matter" (ὕη). He did not express an opinion on the relationship between the "aeon" and spiritual qualities. (Cf. Hans Meyer, Geschichte der Lehre von den Keimkräften von der Stoa bis zum Ausgang der Patristik, nach den Quellen dargestellt [Bonn, 1914], 109ff.)

[8] C. Eunom. 12; II, 949 A.
[9] In Cant. 6; I, 885 C.
[10] De an. et res. III, 124 D.
[11] In hexaëm. I, 69 CD.
[12] Ibid.
[13] De hom. op. I, 213 B.

which was the work itself.[14] "The word is the work." "He placed his words in them. ['Έθετο ἐν αὐτοῖς τοὺς λόγους]."[15] "The word is immanent in Creation."[16] This word of God is thus a force that is at once living and constructive: "a skillful power" (τεχνικὴ δύναμις),[17] a voice that bursts forth from within: δι' αὐτῶν ἐκφωνούμενος.[18] Its spiritual splendor "surpasses all human thought [πᾶσαν ἔννοιαν παριὼν ἀνθρωπίνην]" and for this reason appears to us through the hazy mist of the senses.[19]

Let us draw two conclusions from this theory. The one is epistemological, the other ontological. With regard to knowledge, the spiritual will thus appear as something that is at once superior and interior to the given datum of the senses. The senses, which only apprehend what is concrete (that is to say, comprised of spiritual elements), can only draw near to the simplicity of the spiritual by way of abstraction, dissection, and elimination without reaching it in itself. "Wherever we explore things with our reason, feeling our way like blind men along the walls of a room toward the door . . . , we discover (corporeal) qualities . . . , and thus we are overcome by discouragement and tempted to believe that (the spiritual) does not exist at all."[20] But if the resolution of our body into its spiritual elements suppresses it, at the same time it delivers up to us the spiritual being, which is sought in vain by the senses. And thus "we are guided by the very activity of the senses toward a thing that is beyond the senses, toward an idea."[21] The senses "are signposts for penetrating deeper into the invisible from the visible".[22]

Is Gregory therefore an idealist or a Platonist? An idealist, yes. A Platonist, no, or, at least, only in certain limited respects. His philosophy is situated boldly between Plato and Aristotle. From Plato he borrows the concrete universal. But in so doing he rejects "separation" (χωρισμός). No other ideas exist except these concrete beings

---

[14] *In hexaëm.* I, 73 A.
[15] Ibid., C.
[16] Ibid., B.
[17] Ibid., 113 C.
[18] Ibid., 88 C.
[19] Ibid., 76 A.
[20] *De an. et res.* III, 41 B.
[21] Ibid., III, 28 C.
[22] Ibid., III, 33 BC.

that are at the same time forces, entelechies. From Aristotle he holds that immanentism that is determined by the incorporeal idea, the εἶδος ἔνυλον, but without letting go, for all that, of universality and the spirituality that is not merely abstractive but conceptually existent. Only his consistent idealism permits Gregory to maintain this intermediary position. The concept can be at once universal as thought and concrete as power.[23]

These explanations were necessary in order to come to an understanding of Gregory's anthropology. In abandoning the ontological structure of pure, created spirit, a structure that is poorly illuminated by Gregory, we are well able nonetheless to conceive of a being such as man, who is at once spiritual and material, at once a concrete unity of nature and a multiplicity of individuals. He is spiritual, not only in the way that matter is spiritual (which is to say, thought by another subject), but by the superior power of reflection. By this same power, he escapes the multiplicity of the sensible so as to be a perfect unity, universal and concrete at the same time. On the other hand, insofar as it is material (whatever way this contact with matter has been caused), human nature is communicated to innumerable individuals, isolated in time and space, but participating in the same, identical, universal, and concrete nature. Number in no way affects this unity. Here we can apply Gregory's words regarding "spiritual riches": "They are like the sun, which allows all those who look at it to partake in it and passes entirely into the possession of each one of them."[24] Thus every man participates in this nature in an absolutely identical manner. The first man was no more a man than the last,[25] even though nature is transmitted by procreative generation. The following fact, then, must be realized at all costs: human nature, inasmuch as it is spiritual, is a concrete universal that is perfectly one, while, inasmuch as it is material, it is this same concrete universal participated in by innumerable individuals. *The one is unthinkable without the other*, the idea taken as a whole being an entelechy. Human nature does not exist outside of the totality of concrete individuals. But this totality

---

[23] In Philo already "power" (δύναμις) and "thought" (λόγος) are confounded (Brehier, *Philon* [1925], 156–57). But Philo does not yet possess the metaphysical boldness of Gregory.

[24] *De beat.* 1; I, 1196 D.

[25] *C. Eunom.* 1; II, 304 BC. This is asserted as much against Philo (*De ep. m.* 141) as against Eunomius.

supports a universal unity that is at once *ante rem* (before the fact) and *in re* (in the fact). We have already seen that the created spirit as spirit was defined by the identity of first principle and end, without intermediary spacing (on a material or temporal level). If, by way of contrast, this same spirit is at the same time material—and this is the case with humanity—this possession of its own end without mediation (ἀδιαστάτως) will have to be coupled with a temporal diastasis, which will be the history of humanity. In this order, human nature enters into material becoming, it is "transfused" by procreative generation.[26] We see that obviously *neither "creationism" nor "traducianism"* can be applied to this conception, for transmitted nature (body and soul) is not in the dimension of time, inasmuch as it is *the* human nature. But it is precisely human nature that is directly and immediately created by God. "One should not be obliged to say, strictly speaking, that Adam engendered a being other than himself [οὐσίαν παρ' αὐτὸν ἄλλην] but rather that from himself he engendered another himself."[27] Just as each individual man "is a veritable nation of men, wherein no member is lacking, be it fetus, infant, boy, adolescent, man, father, or old man",[28] and just as each one is in spite of this an "individual", it is the same with humanity. Gregory loves to recognize humanity in that sheep that Christ took on his shoulders.[29] Thus it signifies many concrete men, but only insofar as their unity is itself concrete. Gregory calls this unity by the most diverse names: "nature's pleroma",[30] "universal nature",[31] "our nature",[32] "humanity",[33] and so forth. The reasoning of a series of short treatises on the Trinity, which seems strange to us at first glance, ends in convincing us that this unity is

---

[26] *In Cant.* 13; I, 1052 D; *In illud* I, 1312 AB; *In Ps.* 8; I, 479 AB; *C. Eunom.* 3; II, 592 CD.

[27] *C. Eunom.* 3; II, 592 D. Stephanou (*Echos d'Orient* [1932], 304ff.) would like to conceive of Gregory as a pure traducianist. It is true that the image of the offshoot planted in the earth, which acquires an independent life for itself (*De an. et res.* III, 125 C), would lend itself to this, if one isolated it from the whole body of his doctrine. But it is precisely this whole body of doctrine that is opposed to so univocal a label.

[28] *De an. et res.* III, 141 CD.

[29] *In Eccles.* 2; I, 642; *C. Apollin.* II, 1153 C; *C. Eunom.* 2; II, 546 C; *C. Eunom.* 4; II, 635 B; *C. Eunom.* 12; II, 890 AB; *In Cant.* 2; I, 801 A.

[30] *De hom. op.* 17; I, 185 C.

[31] Ibid., B.

[32] *C. Eunom.* 12; II, 989 D.

[33] τὸ ἀνθρώπινον (humanity): *De hom. op.* 17; I, 180 C.

in no way "generic" from the point of view of logic. Why, it was objected, is it not possible to speak of several Gods, on the pretext that the nature of the three Persons is identical, since, in the same circumstances, one would speak of several men? The response does not admit of any hesitation. We speak of several men only by an error of usage (καταχρηστικῶς). We do it only for practical reasons, even as, in a similar way, only practical reasons forbid us to speak of three Gods. In fact, the difference remains between the atemporal simultaneity of the Divine Persons and the temporal and material succession of men, the latter giving rise to number and thereby to a somewhat different distinction.[34] It is nonetheless true that, far from understanding divine essence as an abstract essence, Gregory prefers to compare the concrete essence of humanity to it.

Henceforth we understand the subtle, reciprocal priority given by the *De hominis opificio* to the creation of man. "There is a certain duality in the foundation of our nature."[35] This double constitution corresponds to the two accounts of Genesis: creation in the image of God and the forming of earthly clay into man and woman. The image resides in man's whole nature, for the image can belong only to the spirit. And our common nature is precisely (by the immediacy of the first principle and of the end) that which is spiritual in man. "The image is not found in a part [μέρος] of our nature, and beauty [χάρις, grace] is not found in a particular property. But this virtue [δύναμις] extends in an equal manner over the whole race. The proof of this is that spirit [νοῦς] resides in all men in an identical fashion [ὡσαύτως]."[36] But here is what is most characteristic: the "spiritual" creation of humanity is first,[37] not only in the account of Moses, but because, of necessity, that which is more spiritual precedes that which is more material.[38] But this anteriority of spiritual creation can be ef-

---

[34] While human hypostases are distinguished numerically (κατὰ σύνθεσιν ἐν ἀριθμῷ [quantitative in their composition]: *Quod non sint tres dii* II, 120 B), God is absolutely simple (παντελῶς ἁπλοῦν: *C. Eunom.* 1; II, 324 D) and without composition (ἀσύνθετον: *C. Eunom.* 10; II, 848 A). It is only limited beings that are able to be counted: *Quod non sint tres dii* II, 132 A.

[35] *De hom. op.* 16; I, 181 B.

[36] Ibid., 185 C.

[37] Ibid., 181 CD.

[38] Cf. ibid. 24; I, 213 B: "The same intellectual starting points that arise from incorporeal nature underlie the generation of bodies." It is evident that all *temporal* priority of a unique nature with respect to individuals is to be excluded, as A. Krampf justly remarks (*Der Urzu-*

fected only by the knowledge of God, embracing "beforehand" in a
single gaze all *individual* men who were to participate in this nature:

> When it is said "God created man", the imprecision of these words
> shows that they refer to human nature in its entirety. For the creature
> is not immediately named Adam, as he is later in the story. Rather the
> name of man is applied to the created being, not as a proper name, but as
> a common name. By this common designation of its nature, we are thus
> led to believe that by divine foreknowledge and power all of humanity
> was encompassed in this first formation. For it is impossible to admit of
> something indeterminate in the works of God. But what must rather be
> believed is that every existing being has its limit [πέρας] and its measure.
> In the same way that a particular man is defined by the dimensions of his
> body . . . , thus, it seems to me, the fullness of humanity was embraced
> by the power of God's Providence [προγνωστικῇ δυνάμει] as if it were a
> single body.[39]

---

stand des Menschen nach des Lehre des hl. Gregor von Nyssa [Würzburg, 1889], 13, n. 1) in opposition to Hayd (preface to the translation of Gregory of Nyssa, Bibliothek der Kirchenväter
187, [Munich, 1880] 1:51ff.) Only Krampf interprets the first creation as a purely "ideal"
creation (as do Moeller and Hilt: "the πλήρωμα . . . is merely a universal concept", 17–18;
J. B. Aufhauser, *Die Heilslehre des hl. Gregor von Nyssa* [Munich, 1910], 46) and likens it, as
do most interpreters, to a Platonic "idea" (cf. Aufhauser, 62, and Slomkowski: *L'État primitif
de l'homme dans la tradition de l'Église avant saint Augustin* [1938], 106–8).

[39] *De hom. op.* 16; I, 185 BC. The idea that underlies this conception of universal being
is the Stoic idea of the "whole" (καθόλον) constituted by its concrete parts. That which
is universal is the world itself and is not a reality distinct from the world. Let us advert to
Marcus Aurelius: "All particular beings are in their substance like a fig from a fig tree" (X,
17), "just as the nature of the leaf is a part of the nature of the plant" (VIII, 7). "This body
that is so great is perfected by means of all bodies" (V, 8). The whole thing is thus very much
a *result*: "The world, which is made up of all things, is indeed one" (εἷς ἐξ ἁπάντων: VII,
9). But all this is not, for all that, a mere accumulation of juxtaposed parts. The concrete
totality is a true totality that is organic and vital, which by the immanence in its parts renders
these parts similar and connected among themselves (οἰκείως ἔχει: IX, 1). "No part, it may
be said, is a stranger to the others, for all of them have been ordered together and contribute
together to the good order of the whole world" (VII, 9). "All of them are linked one with
the other, and all of them, for this reason, are on friendly terms with one another" (VI, 38).
Each being, in relation to the other, is ὁμόφυλος, συγγενής, κοινός (of the same stock, kin to
each other, of common origin) (III, 11). They meet each other in an identity that springs,
not from ideas, but from the earth, from the light, from the air (IX, 8).
There is thus nothing more false than to conceive of Stoic "cosmopolitanism" as arising
from a liberal individualism, from a social atomism. The λόγος κοινός, a reason that is common (IV, 4) to all rational beings, is a truly identical thing like the identical character of "the
air we all breathe", with the difference that in this case the common atmosphere is conscious
in multiple individuals: "Indeed, the more a being is superior to others, the more it is ready
to mix and intermingle with that which is similar to it" (IX, 9). There follows a description

What is excluded with all possible force in this text is the idea of a purely ideal unity, a unity whose particular applications are yet to be determined. No, in order to be constituted *beforehand*, this nature must have precise, existential limits. It is, in a very exact sense, the concrete sum of the beings that constitute it. The circle of the mutual constitution of the "real" and the "ideal", of the "spiritual" and the "material" is thus absolutely closed. Here we find ourselves quite far from Plato, and even from Plotinus.

A last point should be addressed. Even if one excludes the anthropomorphic idea of a creation of "humanity" that is temporally ante-

---

of the social instinct in all the degrees of being, which forms a prelude to the celebrated pages of the Areopagite and which provides evidence as to how, for Marcus Aurelius, this instinct is founded on a natural unity, one that is "physical": "However much they flee from one another, they are now together, for nature is the strongest force." And this unity does not come (as one might think in simplifying the opposition between Platonism and Stoicism) from below: "The nature of the sinner himself is to be my parent, who participates, not in the same blood and the same seed, but in intelligence [νοῦς] and in a portion of divinity" (II, 1).

If one remembers how much Origen is imbued with Stoicism, one will keep oneself from affirming too hastily the individual and atomistic character of his "city of spirits". The celestial city is presented by him as a mother who carries all her children in her bosom (*frag. in Cant.* Migne, 17; 270, *frag. in Prov.* 17, 201). It is the true Adam who carries all of us in him (*In Rom.* 5, I; M. 14, 1010, which is to be compared to 6, 4; M. 14, 1029). All the spirits are united in an ontological participation in the unique Logos. In Christ and in God, every creature constitutes only one single sun (*frag. in Eph.*; ed. Gregg, *Journal of Theol. Studies*, 1902, 413). For Gregory of Nyssa, the character of nature's concrete and spiritual unity is even more accentuated.

We must not, therefore, think here of opposing an impersonal conception of nature (which, like the "racist" state, would have its point of departure from below), where individuals would be only imperfectly individualized (*ratione materiæ*) to a "personal" conception (of a liberal state, an abstract unity of independent individuals). Marcus Aurelius saw things in a true light when he affirmed that only the mode of distinction between nature and individuals changes to the extent that a person ascends the scale of the degrees of being: The independence of the parts increases without detriment to their unity ("as they grow yet greater and more independent . . . , their unity remains": IX, 9. French trans. by Trannoy, coll. des Univ. de France, 1925). The unity becomes "moral" even while it remains "physical". It remains an a priori principle even while it becomes an a posteriori result.

Saint Thomas will explain the independence of the individual by way of "essential" categories (an angel constituting a "species"). Suarez will perhaps be happier explaining it by way of "existence". It is important to note that individuation is accomplished only de facto by Gregory of Nyssa *ratione materiæ* (by reason of matter). If men did not have sin, they would multiply themselves spiritually like pure spirits. What is certain is that he does not "Platonize": "Plato and the Greek circle remain abandoned. They are gone forever, even though the same words may still be echoed" (Willms, ΕΙΚΩΝ I [1935] 116).

rior to the creation of Adam, does there not remain a hesitation about the "real" or "ideal" character of this creation? Is not the question all the more difficult since the spirit possesses its τέλος ἀδιαστάτως, since it does not seem, therefore, that one could, strictly speaking, admit them both, by placing the "ideal" state at the beginning of history and the "real" state at its end (διάστημα)? There is only one solution that allows an escape from this dilemma: the categories cannot be applied *disjunctive* (disjunctively) to the spirit. The character of this creation encompasses both categories at once. It is "ideal" insofar as it logically precedes real history. It is "real" in being, as we have seen, the result of this history. But one could equally say that it is "real" as a point of departure of the evolutionary process (the λόγος-δύναμις which is νοερὰ ἀφορμή) and "ideal" at its arrival, where it realizes totally its reflexive consciousness.

Nevertheless, our lucid philosophical construction has forgotten one thing, which risks obscuring everything: the role of sin and freedom, the exact place of the original fall. Was sin committed by "humanity" or by the "first man"? And where, from that time on, is paradise situated in concrete terms? It is here, at a first glance, at any rate, that Gregory seems to fall into open contradictions. Whether one situates oneself within a "spiritual", "Origenist" point of view on the preexistence of "ideal" humanity, or whether one adopts a "realist", "Irenaean" perspective, which envisages man as the product of a natural evolution of the earth, in both cases one can draw a beautiful and coherent doctrine from Gregory, but a doctrine that is incapable of incorporating the givens posited by the opposite aspect. Could this dualism be his final word on the matter? We, for our part, do not believe so. But, in order to prove it, we must strive to penetrate the meaning of each of these opposing aspects.

4

REAL BECOMING

What we must show, then, in a first, cursory study is the coming to be of spirit from matter, or, if you will, the "temporal" priority of the "real". Not without regret, we shall refrain from giving an extended analysis of those inspired works that are represented by the *Hexaëmeron* and *The Constitution of Man*, in order merely to recapitulate some few brief ideas from them. Gregory's evolutionism claims to be an interpretation of Genesis. But Moses speaks in "stories", in "images".[1] He describes in an exterior manner that which was interior, the λόγοι of God. He shows us in the guise of a mythical account "none other than a philosophy of soul, which contemplates the perfect thing [τέλειον], according to a certain necessity of order and succession, as the final result. For in the rational being all the rest is recapitulated [περιείληπται]." In describing this "order and this logical connection [τάξις καὶ ἀκολουθία]"—it is here that we find the very foundations of his *Hexaëmeron*—Gregory is energetically opposed to a tropological interpretation, such as "several men before us"[2] have attempted. He wishes "through the meaning, in its full sense", to disengage the *interior* meaning (τῶν ῥητῶν ἐξετάσαι διάνοιαν).[3] This ties in, then, to a comprehension of the text that is neither only literal nor uniquely allegorical: "Thus at one and the same time we safeguard the meaning of the letter and we disengage the philosophical meaning [φυσικὴ θεωρία]."[4]

It is interesting to note that this exegetical method corresponds exactly to the antiplatonist theory of real becoming. Origen, who held to the preexistence of souls and a quite intimate link between the

---

[1] ἱστορικῶς (historically): *C. Eunom.* 12; II, 996 D; 1064 D.
[2] *In hexaëm.* I, 81 D.
[3] Ibid., 68 D.
[4] Ibid., 124 B.

material world and sin, preferred to separate the literal and material meaning from the spiritual meaning. Gregory rejects this dualism. "Those who claim that the city of souls is more ancient than life in the body do not seem to me to be untainted by the pagan doctrines of the Greeks concerning the migration of souls."[5] No, in the seeds of all things (ἀφορμαὶ καὶ αἰτίαι καὶ δυνάμεις),[6] matter and life, body and soul, were already perfectly one.[7] For this σπερματικὴ δύναμις (seminal power)[8] was, as we know, at once λόγος and δύναμις. It is thus this active power that God created "at the beginning" and that he allowed to be developed "little by little" (διὰ βαθμῶν), "as it rose from the least perfect to the most perfect".[9] For the heavens were not created afterward, nor was any other part of the world added. But "creation is self-contained, without experiencing the need for a new intervention and without diminution, as it continues in its arrangements."[10] The "life force",[11] pure potentiality at the starting point,[12] made its first appearance in the ordered disposition of matter, and then it demonstrated its "plastic vitality"[13] in the blossoming of successive degrees of life. Must it be said, therefore, that plant, animal, and man are not irreducibly distinct? This would be precisely to fall into the gross error of those who confound all natures in order to justify universal transmigration.[14] It must rather be said that there is continuity and discontinuity at one and the same time. Let us take an example from the realm of ontogeny. Nobody doubts (οὐκ ἄν τις ἀμφιβάλοι) that the seed deposited in the womb of the mother develops "without any new power coming to be added", but that the soul in its entirety is to be found therein, governing the stages of "unfolding", even though it is still "potential [τῇ δυνάμει] and not apparent [μὴ φαινομένη]".[15] But, on the other hand, nobody would want to call (οὐκ ἄν τις προσείποι)

---

[5] De hom. op. 28.

[6] In hexaëm. I, 72 AB.

[7] De an. et res. III, 125 C.

[8] In hexaëm. I, 77 D.

[9] De hom. op. 8; I, 148 B.

[10] In Ps. 6; I, 610 BC.

[11] De an. et res. III, 60 A.

[12] "But energy was not yet individualized . . . which is the same as saying that it was and it was not" (In hexaëm. I, 77 D–80 A).

[13] ὕλη ζωοπλασθεῖσα (matter in its plastic vitality): C. Apollin. II, 1256 A.

[14] De hom. op. 28; I, 229–33; De an. et res. III, 109 B.

[15] De hom. op. 29; I, 236 C.

"an embryo which has not come to term a man, but merely a life power [δύναμις] that would result, if it were brought to term, in the production [γένεσις] of a man. But inasmuch as it is incomplete, it is something else and not a man."[16] The two assertions are equally true, for in this duality there reappears the mystery of the priority (ἀρχή) and the posteriority (τέλος) of the spiritual.

But let us remain within the compass of real becoming. In studying the ascending stages of nature, we shall discover therein not only a law of necessary progression (ἀναγκαία τις τῆς τάξεως ἀκολουθία)[17] but also a law of necessary foundation (ὑπόβαθρα). Each stage is the necessary condition for the possibility of a higher stage. Animal life could not exist without vegetable life, human life could not have been united to matter or even to vegetable life without the foundations of sensory life: "The intelligent being cannot be incorporated in any other way than by intermingling itself with a sensoriness."[18] This law has such a rigorous application that spiritual activity itself requires this sensory foundation in order to exist: "Sensation does not exist without matter, nor does spiritual action [δύναμις νοερά] exist without sensory activity [αἰσθήσεως ἐνέργεια]."[19] For that which is properly spiritual in the soul is its "ability to discern and to contemplate".[20] But this discernment presupposes a matter to synthesize or to analyze.[21] We are not therefore astonished to see that time itself enters into spiritual activity through the mediation of sensation,[22] for we know that every spiritual being is, despite its possibility of reflection, torn by the diastema.[23] Human thought is a νόημα διαστηματικόν (diastematic thought).[24] This attachment of the spirit to nature is shown practically in this fact of experience: "If nature goes at a good and healthy pace [εὐοδουμένης] within the terms of its own constitution,

---

[16] C. Apollin. II, 1320 A; cf. 1256 A: "But that basic matter, with a plastic vitality endowed to it by divine power, becomes a man."

[17] De hom. op. 8; I, 148 B (we substitute τῆς for the τῇ in the edition of Migne).

[18] Ibid. I, 145 B.

[19] Ibid. 14; I, 176 B; cf. De an. et res. III, 60 CD.

[20] De an. et res., III, 57 B.

[21] See the texts in F. Hilt, Des hl. Gregor von Nyssa Lehre vom Menschen systematisch dargestellt (Cologne, 1890), 62ff.

[22] "Through an analysis of time, always examining closely matters that are greater than those that are currently being discovered" (In Eccles. 7; I, 729 C).

[23] "Life is split apart in accordance with the sundering of time" (C. Eunom. 1; II, 368 A).

[24] De infantibus III, 172 C.

the spirit also, for its part, is able to act. But if nature falls prey to any accident, the movement of thought finds itself fettered."[25] The same goes for sensory life, properly speaking, for the πάθη (passions). The latter are far from being useless to the spiritual life. They "carry the soul on their back in a way and raise her toward the heights".[26] This is true of anger as well as concupiscence. "Reason, in dominating them, transforms each of them into a special virtue . . . , and thus one finds that all these motions, raised as they are for their part, as well, by the transcendence of the spirit, are conformed [συσχηματίζεται] to the beauty of the image of God."[27]

Thus the admirable role of man with regard to the world begins to be revealed. He who is the supreme fruit[28] of this ascent of nature has it as his duty to unify the ascent in his spirit and to present it thus in its entirety to God. We ought first of all to cite the beautiful passage where Gregory describes how earth becomes man, matter being diversified into living organs. And he does all this in order to prove the indissoluble unity of the spirit and the body and their common history.[29] For man, the whole universe is a vast instrument, as it were, which permits him to communicate himself and to blossom forth:

> Since the spirit is in itself something thinking and immaterial, it would have a savage [ἄμικτον] and incommunicable beauty if its interior movement had not been capable of being revealed by an ingenious [ἐπίνοια] invention. It is to this end that this organic constitution was necessary, so that the interior movement might succeed in being interpreted [ἑρμηνεύσῃ] through the varied formation of articulations by touching, like a plectrum, the organs destined for the voice.[30]

Gregory describes at his leisure how this admirable instrument slackens (λύσις) its strings, so to speak, during sleep and how the soul in this case extracts only fantastic, confused harmonies, namely, dreams.[31] But in spite of these dependencies, the world is only the multiple instrument that serves unity of spirit. After Origen[32] and before Au-

---

[25] De hom. op. 15; I, 177 C.
[26] In Ps. 8; I, 478 C; cf. De beat. 6; I, 1276 A.
[27] De hom. op. 18; I, 193 BC.
[28] "Like a fruit" (De an. et res. III, 128 A).
[29] De hom. op. 30; I, 252 B–253 A.
[30] Ibid. 9; I, 149 BC.
[31] Ibid. 13; I, 165 B–172 A.
[32] Origen, Hom. 21 in Luc. (Rauer 9, 141–42).

gustine, Gregory admires the vast "interior city of the spirit [τὴν τοῦ νοῦ πόλιν]", the inexhaustible receptacle of the memory, which accumulates all that the different senses furnish it without mixing anything up and which unifies from within these multiple givens, just as wayfarers, who, having entered by different gates, meet together in the center of the city.[33] For it is not eyes that see nor ears that hear. But it is the one spirit that looks about and hears things through the medium of the senses.[34] Far from subjugating the spirit to themselves, the senses liberate it. So that man should no longer have to seek out his nourishment with his mouth, his hands are formed in such a way as to serve him as an instrument. Thus his mouth finds itself freed for the service of the spiritual word.[35] In this way man is, by his twofold nature, prepared for his cosmic task. He is the place where there is brought about, "in accordance with Divine Wisdom, the fusion and the intermingling of the sensory and the intelligible, so that all things may partake likewise in beauty". He is "the point of junction between the divine and the earthly". From him "one sole grace of equal value is diffused over all of creation."[36] The body, matter in its entirety, receives the spiritual reflection of the soul. It becomes the image of the Image.[37] Gregory loves to describe this lofty royalty of man in the universe: "Living image of the universal King", "independent and free" in his actions,[38] man finds himself in that unique and privileged situation of being "capable of two joys: his rejoicing in God, because there is something of the divine in his nature, and his rejoicing in earthly goods through the sensation that is kin to them."[39] He is "partly witness to, partly ruler over the wonders of this world in order to receive, on the one hand, through his joy, knowledge about the one who bestows these wonders and, on the other hand, through the beauty and grandeur of visible things, a certain impression of the unutterable and uncommunicable Power of the Creator."[40] By man and for man, matter receives a supreme sanctification sacramentally:

---

[33] *De hom. op.* 10; I, 152 B–153 C.
[34] Ibid. 6; I, 137 D–140 A; cf. *De an. et res.* III, 29 B–33 C.
[35] *De hom. op.* 8; I, 141 BC.
[36] *Catech.* 6; II, 25 C–28 A.
[37] *De hom. op.* 12; I, 164 A.
[38] Ibid. 4; I, 136 B–D.
[39] Ibid. 2; I, 133 B.
[40] Ibid., 133 AB.

Man is composite and not simple, and for this reason . . . similar and connatural means of salvation were appropriate to him. For his body, which appears visibly, palpable water was appropriate, while for his invisible soul it was the invisible Spirit that was appropriate. . . . Do not therefore scorn the divine bath! . . . This sacred altar as well . . . is according to its nature an ordinary rock . . . , but once it is blessed, it becomes a holy table, an immaculate altar. . . . The bread, too, is first of all ordinary bread, but, sanctified by the sacrament, it is called and indeed is the Body of Christ. The same applies to the mystical oil, the same to the wine. . . . The wood of the Cross brings salvation to all men . . . , the bush revealed to Moses the presence of God, and the dead bones of Elisha raised a dead man, a little bit of earth gave back sight to the man born blind. And all this, which was made up of dead and insensible matter, conveyed great miracles and received in itself the force of God.[41]

And finally, in a last supernatural "evolution", the earth bore that unique fruit which was the human body of Christ[42] and which would turn out to be the beginning of the eternal deification of the earth. For man is too much one, the body has participated too intimately in the adventure of the soul not to have the same destiny. "The soul, indeed, is not separate from the body, not when it comes to committing a theft or an act of plunder, nor again when it is a matter of giving bread to those who are hungry or quenching the thirst of those who are thirsty. In every action, the two of them are united. How is it therefore that you could want to lead her alone, without the body, before the judgment seat of God?"[43] If this unity, which is so intimate, as we have seen, from the first moment of being, obliges the soul to love her body and not to be perfectly happy without it, is this situation not something just and praiseworthy?[44] Gregory's theory of the resurrection is, whatever Diekamp may say of it,[45] quite

---

[41] *In baptismum Christi* III, 581 B-584 B.

[42] *In Christi resurr.* 5; III, 688 B.

[43] Ibid. 3; III, 677 BC.

[44] *De an. et res.* III, 105 D-108 A.

[45] He would like to see in Gregory's thought an eclectic position somewhere between that of Origen and Methodius (*Literargeschichtliches zu der Eunomianischen Kontroverse*, Byzant. Zeitschrift 18 [Leipzig, 1909], 44, n. 2). He does not seem to be taking into account Origen's *De resurrectione* or his commentary on Psalm 1, where he develops the theory of the surviving *eidos*, which at the resurrection will once again become the same body that it had been, but glorified.

materially identical to that of Origen. Only a nuance separates them. For Origen, human equilibrium takes place by the adhesion of the body to the soul, which spiritualizes it. For Gregory also, there exists a legitimate adhesion of the soul to the body. The body is a thing which is the soul's own, something "connatural and fitted to her [τὸ συγγενές τε καὶ τὸ ἴδιον]", for which she has a "certain innate tenderness [στοργὴ]" and toward which "she is attracted by a natural attraction."[46] The eschatological ideal toward which such a conception tends is not at all Origen's city of souls but a unity of the spiritual and material world that is at the extreme opposite of the vision of Plotinus:

> We are not permitted to believe that the Word wants the life of the just to be torn asunder by a dualism [ἐν δυάδι νοεῖσθαι] [a dualism, that is to say, of spirit and flesh]. But after "the separating wall of evil" will have been lifted in our abode, the two ought to become one, founded on a superior harmony [εἷς οἱ δύο τῇ πρὸς τὸ κρεῖττον ἀνακρίσει συμφυέντες γίνονται]. For if the Divine, as we believe, is simple, seamless, and formless, man also ought, by this process of "pacification", succeed in ridding himself of this dualism [κατὰ τὴν διπλῆν σύνθεσις] . . . in order to become truly one, so that the hidden interior may completely recover the apparent exterior, and the apparent exterior the hidden interior. . . . Thus he will be able to be called in all truth a child of God.[47]

Such, in Gregory's doctrine, is the ascending evolution, both material and spiritual, from a life force to the most divine blossoming of this same unity. Let us now look at the complementary aspect of this question.

---

[46] *De hom. op.* 27; I, 225 BC.
[47] *De beat.* 7; I, 1289 D–1292 A.

5

IDEAL BECOMING

Porphyry's tree recognizes two series of ideas. On the one hand, there is the category of realized ideas, which includes matter, plants, animals, and man. On the other hand, there is the category of reflex or logical universals, including genus, species, and the individual. The first of these two series has evolved within the ambit of "real" becoming. The second series poses the problem of "ideal" becoming. Let us not, however, forget in what sense we are taking the concept of the universal. We have considered it from the outset as a concrete universal. Within these limits, the problem of ideal becoming returns quite simply to the question of the preeminence of "genus" over and against the individual. We have seen Gregory affirm this logical and metaphysical priority thus: "The image of God, therefore, which declares itself in the totality of human nature, was perfected [τὸ τέλος ἔσχεν]. But Adam did not yet exist."[1] It is clear that this priority and this discrepancy have no place in "real" becoming. What is at stake is another dimension of being. It is true that, after having considered the beauty of the earth before the appearance of man,[2] as if to mark a caesura in creation, Gregory shows us how, according to the account of Moses, God "improvised" the world, so to speak, up to that point (ἀποσχεδιάζεταί πως ἡ κτίσις), but then he seems to retire within himself in order to deliberate over the living image he is going to create.[3] It is no longer Prâkriti (ἡ πάντα τεχνιτεύουσα φύσις),[4] it is rather God himself who undertakes the work. This is expressed in the distinction between "gift" and "participation": God has "by his magnanimity given the rest of what is good to human nature. As for spirit and thought, he has not, properly speaking, given [δέδωκεν]

---

[1] *De hom. op.* 22; I, 204.
[2] Ibid. 1; I, 132 AB.
[3] Ibid. 3; I, 133 CD.
[4] Ibid. 30; I, 253 D.

them, but he has caused them to be participated in [μετέδωκεν] by imparting to his image the particular beauty of his own nature."[5] For the unity of the spirit cannot be explained on the basis of matter. In this unity the image properly resides.[6] For this creation, the forms presented by Prâkriti are like a material that has been prepared beforehand (ὡς καὶ ὕλην αὐτῷ τῆς συστάσεως προετοιμάσαι), a material to which God, on his part, would add the form of his likeness (καὶ ἀρχετύπῳ τινὶ κάλλει τὴν μορφὴν ὁμοιῶσαι).[7] We should notice that there is no question here of "a body drawn from the soil of the earth" and of a "soul" breathed into this body. It is a question, on the one hand, of the preceding creation in its entirety and, on the other, of that properly divine character that is "the image", which is not capable of being reduced to a natural formation. It is quite evidently not a matter any longer of certain "supernatural" gifts in the modern sense, gifts that would come to graft themselves on a ready-made nature. The image, to the contrary, is νοῦς καὶ φρόνησις,[8] accompanied, to be sure, by the whole panoply of virtues.[9] No transition could have produced this image by evolution. Man is the *analogatum princeps* (chief of analogies) of life: "If there exists outside of him something that participates in life, we call it living only through a current misuse of terms."[10] "For nothing that exists receives its name in the strongest sense of this word except on the basis of its perfection."[11] We must therefore call only the soul of man a soul, the others being merely life forces (ἐνέργεια ζωτική).[12]

The question that is posed at this point is one of knowing how to visualize this "first creation" and, to be more precise, of knowing in what place and in what time paradise should be located. In this regard two series of remarks complement one another. Gregory gives a spiritual interpretation to the principal facts in the account from Genesis. "Eden" signifies joy.[13] The tree of life and the tree of good

---

[5] Ibid. 9; I, 149 B.
[6] Ibid. 6; I, 137 D-140 B.
[7] Ibid. 3; I, 136 A.
[8] Ibid. 9; I, 149 B.
[9] Ibid. 4; I, 136 CD.
[10] Ibid. 30; I, 256 B.
[11] Ibid. 15; I, 176 C.
[12] Ibid., 177 A.
[13] *In Cant. proœm.* I, 761.

and evil, both of which are "in the middle" of paradise (Genesis 2:9; 3:3), must be one single reality, even though they are distinguished in the account. "Nobody will make us believe that this tree . . . was one fruit tree among many others. . . . To the person who does not train his gaze on the truth with due regard for its spiritual content, the account will always seem incoherent and fantastic. These are people who do not look at things closely enough."[14] "The tree of life is God himself, eternal life. The tree of the knowledge of good and evil is this same life, but a life that is partaken of in a deficient or perverse manner, evil being nothing other than a deficiency of good."[15] "Every tree of the garden [τὸ πᾶν]" does not denote something else. Rather the expression shows that God is all good in himself:[16] "It is not permitted to think of a passing and provisional nourishment during a sojourn in paradise." Then comes the fall, caused by the jealousy of Satan, who could not tolerate the greatness of humanity, "arisen from a nature that was inferior to him"[17]. And then they cover themselves with "tunics of skin", which is to say, mortal flesh.[18] After this spiritual exegesis, what remains of the "earthly paradise"? Nothing, no allusion even to an exteriorly privileged state of the first man, except for that beautiful description of the earthly garden before the appearance of man. But this Eden is the whole earth and such as it occurs at all times. Nevertheless Gregory rejects the allegorical interpretation, as he had done in the case of the *Hexaëmeron*. The account is not a myth: ἔστι δὲ ὁ λόγος οὐ μυθώδης διήγησις. It receives its full justification through an existential analysis of our nature: ἀλλ' ἐξ αὐτῆς τῆς φύσεως ἡμῶν τὸ πιστὸν ἐπαγόμενος.

This process bears a strong resemblance to the Platonic method of anamnesis: "The reason we have so little pity on ourselves is that we do not have an adequate grasp of our wretchedness. We almost resemble those who have lost their reason, those for whom a surfeit of unhappiness has caused them to lose a sense of their suffering besides. But he who recognizes himself, who recognizes what he once was and what he is at present, . . . will always have pity on himself."[19] This is

---

[14] *In Cant.* 12; I, 1021 C–1024 A.
[15] *De hom. op.* 19; I, 196 D–197 A.
[16] *Catech.* 6; II, 28 B.
[17] *De mortuis* III, 524 D; *Vit. Moys.* I, 333 C; *Catech.* 8; II, 36 C; *De an. et res.* III, 148 C.
[18] *Catech.* 6; II, 25 B.
[19] *De beat.* 5; I, 1260 B.

a reflection that each person can and should undertake: "Anyone who would not spend his whole life in tears and lamentation, if he has arrived at a knowledge of himself, of what he is, if he realizes personally what he has possessed and what he has lost [καὶ γνοίη καθ' ἑαυτὸν ἅ τε εἶχεν, ἅ τε ἀπώλεσεν], in what conditions nature found itself in the beginning and in what conditions it is in at the moment".[20] At that time there was no such thing as the phrase "mine and yours, those hateful words". Everything was commonly held, grace and the vision of God. We had the integrity of angels, an unspeakable beauty.[21] It is our ancient "homeland, from which we have been expelled", the household that we have left behind, like the prodigal son.[22] "We men once had a share in God."[23] It is "mankind that has been thrust aside from its familiarity with God".[24] There can be no doubt about Gregory's thought on this issue: each man had his part in the celestial paradise, not individually, as Origen had imagined, but socially. The transcosmic priority of spiritual nature (φύσις ὑπερκόσμιος)[25] corresponds exactly to paradise. Gregory always presents it as a celestial place: it is the third heaven, to which Paul was carried off,[26] the place to which Jesus sent the good thief and which is none other than the "hand of the Father".[27] It is the entrance to heaven,[28] an unchangeable place,[29] "without corruption, a blessed place, where nothing is lacking, an independent place, without sorrow".[30] It was a life without any passions (πάθος)—and what an impassioned existence we have received in exchange for it![31] But this earthly life is only an enforced sojourn,[32] an existence (ἐν ἀτόποις). Our return to heaven will be a "reentry into our natural condition".[33]

---

[20] *In Eccles.* 6; I, 708 C.
[21] Ibid.
[22] *Or. dom.* 2; I, 1144 C.
[23] *De beat.* 3; I, 1225 D.
[24] *De an. et res.* III, 133 BC.
[25] *Catech.* 6; I, 28 A.
[26] *In hexaëm.* I, 121 D.
[27] *C. Apollin.* II, 1156 AB.
[28] *De beat.* 8; I, 1292 A–D.
[29] Ibid.
[30] Ibid. 3; I, 1225 D.
[31] Ibid., 1228 B; cf. 5; I, 1257.
[32] *De mortuis* III, 512 B.
[33] *De beat.* 8; I, 1292 B.

From all this it clearly emerges that: (1) There is no paradise other than the celestial paradise (the account from Genesis not being a myth but rather an account that denotes an ideal becoming (τὴν περὶ ψυχῆς φιλοσοφίαν) under an image of a real becoming (ἱστορικῶς);[34] and (2) "God, by his foreknowledge, honored the totality of human nature with a unique action, so that it shares in an elevated, angelic lot."[35] But if this is perfectly coherent, the reconciliation of this aspect with that of real becoming is only more difficult. The whole problem revolves around the problem of sin. We catch a glimpse already of a certain mysterious relationship between existence in its earthly passions (βίος παθητικός) and the original fall. But to what point exactly does sin extend its influence?

---

[34] *De hom. op.* 8; I, 144 D.
[35] Ibid. 17; I, 189 C.

6

THE SOLUTION TO THE
ANTHROPOLOGICAL PROBLEM

The solution proposed by Gregory as an "hypothesis"[1] can be summed up in a few words: God foresaw that created nature, "which cannot exist without change because the transition from nothingness to existence is already a certain movement",[2] and which "has a kinship to this mutability",[3] was going to move freely toward evil. Even before the sin was committed, that is to say, from the beginning and in view of the sin, God added sexual difference to nature. This difference is a material πάθος (pathos), and by this expedient an animal and irrational (ἄλογον) nature was intermingled with the image of God.[4]

This ingenious solution permits Gregory to situate himself at an equal distance from Origenism, which claimed to construe the material world in its entirety as a consequence of sin, and from a naïve naturalism, which denied all connection between πάθος and sin. Two assertions are, for Gregory, indisputable: on the one hand, "we became flesh and blood through sin",[5] and, on the other hand, it is a "blasphemy" to say "that any man or any earthly thing does not begin to exist except through sin, the source of any entry into existence".[6] But in spite of everything, the breadth of this paradox surpasses any explicitly proposed attempt at a solution. This explanation is the centerpiece, as it were, of a broader conception. It demands, on its part, if not an explanation, at least clarification through the whole body of Gregory's thought and work. In attempting to supply it, we are conscious of the fact that Gregory did not furnish it "systematically".

---

[1] *De hom. op.* 16; I, 180 C.
[2] Ibid. 16; I, 184 C.
[3] Ibid., 184 D.
[4] Ibid. 22; I, 205 A.
[5] *C. Eunom.* 12; II, 889 CD.
[6] *De an. et res.* III, 116 C.

But even so we do not believe we are going beyond the limits of a more thoughtful refinement of what he himself expressed essentially. Indeed, the whole of his thought extends in two ways beyond the "hypothesis" broached in *De hominis opificio*. On the one hand, Gregory does not hide his tendency to ground free human action in its entirety within the realm of "pathos" and thereby in the realm of matter. On the other hand, he seems to put free action and sin at the basis not only of the sexual "pathos" but of all "pathos" and of materiality itself. Before we enter into an examination of these two tendencies, let us, however, exclude a solution that is still apparently possible, namely, that of "preternatural" gifts that could have been bestowed on Adam in order to dominate the other passions that were necessarily given along with sexual passion. We do not find any hint of this solution in Gregory, for the simple reason that we find no hint of any earthly paradise. The question that asks, "Would Adam have been immortal, if . . .", does not make any sense as it stands, because, with sexuality, death was foreseen.[7] For Gregory, the sole disputable question is the following one: What would Adam's earthly nature have been if he had not received the imprint of sexuality? And he imagines a form of wholly spiritual procreation, similar, he supposes, to that of the angels.[8]

Let us therefore imagine this first man. Since he received a share in animal nature, through his sexuality "he also shared the rest of what can be observed in this animal nature."[9] This was quite simply the heritage that fell to him by way of the real becoming: "For irrational life had appeared beforehand in the world."[10] We see, therefore, that all of man's evolution, starting with the embryonic stage, is tied for Gregory to his anticipated sin. The soul "would have been perfect from her very beginning if nature had not been maimed by sin [ἐκολοβώθη ἡ φύσις]. But, because of sin, participation in sensual, animal generation does not allow the immediate appearance of the divine likeness in the formed being but leads man to perfection through a series of successive states, caused by the fact that the soul possesses material and animal dispositions."[11] We must at this point recall our

---

[7] *De hom. op.* 22; I, 205 BC.
[8] Ibid. 18; I, 192 B.
[9] Ibid.
[10] Ibid. 30; I, 253 D–256 A.
[11] *De an. et res.* III, 60 CD.

whole development of the subject of real becoming, which showed us how much the spirit is rooted in matter, indeed, presupposes it and is based on it: "Just as . . . the faculty of thought cannot reside in a body except through the mediation of sensation, just as, moreover, sensation exists already in the anterior degree of the animal realm, our soul, in uniting herself to sensory life, necessarily makes contact with all the rest of the nature of animals."[12] (Let us note in passing that in this text the point of contact is not sex but quite simply the distinctive characteristic of animal nature in general, namely, sensation.)

It must, therefore, be affirmed, on the one hand, that if sex is intermingled in a mysterious way with sin—for Gregory it is the anticipated punishment for it, chosen for a profoundly symbolic reason: namely, that it expresses the fluid inconsistency (πρὸς τὸ ὑλῶδες ῥοπή) of sin[13]—all that it is afterward participates in this same contagion. To be sure, the passions are not bad in themselves,[14] nor is procreation in the womb of the mother.[15] But it is also true that "*everything* partaking of irrational life that has been intermingled with human nature was not in us before we had fallen into 'pathos' by way of sin",[16] and that in order once more to become that "divine thing" (θεῖόν τι χρῆμα)[17] that we were before the fall, we shall have to leave behind all "that we have received with the garment of skin: that is to say, sexuality, conception, birth, defilement, suckling, nourishment, excretion, growth from childhood to maturity, manhood, old age, sickness, death".[18] Therefore we understand how Gregory can say that sin will depart from man only "at the hour of his death". He will say in an analogous way that, "wheresoever a man is born, sin, so to speak, is born with him", because "evil is, so to speak, a constituent element of our nature."[19] For this reason Gregory considers original sin as having been transmitted by way of procreation.[20] Not that procreation is bad in

---

[12] *De hom. op.* 17; I, 192 A.

[13] *De an. et res.* III, 61 A.

[14] *Catech.* 28; II, 73 A.

[15] *De an. et res.* III, 148 B.

[16] Ibid., 148 A.

[17] Ibid.

[18] Ibid., 148 C–149 A.

[19] *De beat.* 6; I, 1273 A.

[20] "It was transmitted to a great multitude by the successive generations of posterity" (*In illud* I, 1312 AB). "It was spread out" (*In Ps.* 8; I, 480 B). "Produced at the same time"

itself, but it is, as it were, the sacrament of sin: an efficacious sign, insofar as it is a symbol (exemplary effect), on the one hand, and, on the other hand, insofar as it is a cause of the transmission of a sinful nature.[21]

The problem becomes more serious in the psychological order. If God has given us passions in expectation of our sinning, are they not then, in the order of time, causes or, at least, inevitable occasions of sin? "Matter is heavy and it drags things down . . . , all passions carry in themselves a burning and irresistible desire for their satisfaction, . . . it is impossible to rise completely above the passions and sensuality in a sensory life."[22] The fact that Christ was conceived without "passion" and that he died without the "pathos" of corruption assumes henceforth a very pronounced importance.[23] "For there is in truth no πάθος which does not lead to sin."[24] But in that case, what are we to say of the "passions" that were so visible in Christ? Was he not subject, like us, to "procreation, nutrition, to growth, to sleep, and to tiredness"? Here Gregory makes distinctions. It is something of an abuse to name all these states of nature (ἔργον τῆς φύσεως) "passions". Only that which is opposite to "the impassiveness that accords with virtue", to the ἀπάθεια κατὰ τὴν ἀρετήν, can be named a "pathos" in the strong sense of the term.[25] But further explanation demonstrates quite vividly that the whole domain of the "passions" is in some way afflicted by a "sickness". The divinity of Christ touches them without being affected by them, as it touches everything in this world. It was precisely this substantial contact that was bound to heal nature.[26] Let us concede that real becoming and all that it includes of "passions" in the broad sense is not the cause

---

(*In Ps. 6 sermo*; I, 610 D). *In Cant.* 12; I, 1024 D: "By successive generations of the young"; *In Cant.* 13; I, 1052 D.

[21] "To take up again the memory of the common penalties of human nature, anyone who has a common share in this nature also shares altogether in these penalties" *Or. dom.* 5; I, 1184 AB.

[22] *De beat.* 2; I, 1216 A.

[23] *Catech.* 13; II, 45 A–D.

[24] *C. Eunom.* 6; II, 721 B.

[25] Ibid., 721 CD. This explanation recurs every time it needs to be explained why the Incarnation was not contrary to divine dignity: *Catech.* 16; II, 49 BC.

[26] "It was fitting for him who had thus healed to heal the passions by his touch. It is not indeed because he cures sickness that he himself is therefore deemed to have become swayed by the passions" (*C. Eunom.* 6; II, 724 B).

of sin: "For the Creator would himself be the author of sins if the compulsion to transgress emanated from the passions. It is the use that our free will makes of them" that determines the fault.[27] The "passions" belong to that indifferent (μέσον) region that the spirit can elevate to the realm of the good or that it can render bad by abusing it.[28] But this is not the question. It is a matter of ascertaining whether, through real becoming, the temporal priority of sensory life does not create for man in the concrete an obstacle so great that it is equivalent to a constraint to sin. Indeed the judgment of the senses is false,[29] and whoever follows it is sure to be lost.[30] However, as Origen had already remarked,[31] every man must pass through this delusive stage in order to go beyond it. Thus the habit of falsehood is born and grows with us (συντρεφόμεθα τῇ κατ' ἀρχὰς ἐγγινομένῃ περὶ τῶν ὄντων κρίσει).[32] This is so true that even God's pedagogy raises us only by degrees above the domain of the senses,[33] and, in the end, our whole "spirituality" rests on a sensory foundation. We saw above that our intelligence presupposed the senses and thereby time. The same goes for our morality. The material world is its object (καλῶν ἢ κακῶν ὕλη),[34] and the moral act is in its very roots a choice and a discernment (κρίσις).[35] And since all material objects are subject to time, the latter enters into play as the supreme criterion in moral matters. The measure (μέτρον) of becoming is time. Morality is founded on measure (ἡ ἀρετὴ μέτρον ἐστὶ τῇ μεσότητι τῶν παραθεωρουμένων μετρούμενον).[36] So therefore time is the criterion of a morality of becoming.[37] Here the idea of the *kairos* assumes a quite capital importance. Moral symmetry (συμμετρία) is none other than *situation*, εὐκαιρία.[38] At this point we reach the most profound point

---

[27] *De an. et res.* III, 61 A.

[28] Ibid. III, 57 BC.

[29] *In Eccles.* 8; I, 736 A.

[30] *In Cant.* 2; I, 804 D–805 A.

[31] *In Ierem.* 5, 15; PG 13, 318 C.

[32] *In Eccles.* 8; I, 736 C.

[33] *In Ps.* 2; I, 438 A. This is to be compared with the following chapter of our study.

[34] *In Eccles.* 8; I, 752 D–753 A.

[35] Ibid. 6; I, 697 B.

[36] Ibid. 697 C.

[37] "Time therefore has been considered by us as equal to measure. Wherefore time is a measure of all individual measures" (ibid., 700 B).

[38] Ibid., 700 B.

of Gregory's anthropological paradox. This paradox, the contrasts of which we have managed to develop only on the basis of the theory in *De hominis opificio*, can therefore be summed up in this way: the free and sinful act is at once the first cause of the whole series of real, material becoming and its last effect, presupposing this whole series. We believe that we have shown that the theory of *De hominis opificio*, as ingenious as it is, provides the total solution only in an implicit way and in an abridged form, so to speak. Was Gregory conscious of a more comprehensive and more audacious synthesis, all of whose elements are included in his work? This, indeed, is what we believe. The theory that sex was added "last of all", which, when all is said and done, is somewhat anthropomorphic, this somewhat incoherent theory, inasmuch as sex can be added only to a nature that is already material and inasmuch as, on the other hand, sex itself entails materialization—such a theory, we maintain, would in this case merely be an inoffensive exponent of a more radical pattern of thought, a pattern of thought that would be engaged in answering the anguishing question: "How could Being have been subjugated by nonbeing, how can nothingness govern what is real?"[39]

In undertaking to explain the constitution of man, Gregory has a conscious feeling that he is undertaking an apparently impossible synthesis: "Even what appears in man to be a contradictory state . . . ought to be synthesized into a necessary, ordered sequence, as much in terms of scriptural doctrine as in terms of rational conclusions, . . . so that the apparent contradictions may be resolved in one, unique end-point, divine power being capable of finding a hope where there is no more hope and a pathway in the midst of the impossible."[40] What constitutes the "impossible", to be sure, is that inextricable dialectic between the normal, celestial state of humanity and its real, fallen state (ἐν ἀτόποις). It is a dialectic that operates through the reciprocity of causal priority. The philosophers, says Gregory somewhere, divide the soul into a rational part, a concupiscible part, and an irascible part: "The spirit, it is said, is attached to the chariot of these two, and it guides them, restraining [συνέχειν] the chariot, and in this way it is led [ἀνέχεσθαι] by them."[41] Now all the mystery

[39] Ibid. 2; I, 637 C.
[40] *De hom. op. procem.*; I, 128 B.
[41] *Vit. Moys.* I, 353 C.

resides herein: namely, in the reciprocity between συνέχειν (leading) and ἀνέχεσθαι (being led). Let us now advert to the following text, where Gregory elevates this reciprocity to the high level of a cosmic law:

> Since the Divine is the supreme beauty and the highest of goods, toward which anything that desires the beautiful is inclined, for this reason we say that spirit [νοῦς], formed in the image of the highest beauty, remains, itself, within the beautiful for as long as it participates, insofar as it is capable of this participation, in a likeness to the archetype, but that it finds itself deprived of beauty the moment it leaves the domain of beauty in any way. Spirit, according to us, is adorned with beauty through its likeness to the prototype, like a mirror that bears on it the form of the reflected object. Likewise it seems to us that nature, organized and administered as it is by the spirit, is suspended from the spirit and is itself also adorned by this beauty that is near neighbor to it. And it seems to us that in this way it becomes the mirror of a mirror. Finally the material base from which nature breaks free is, in its turn, dominated and held together by it. As long, therefore, as the one remains suspended from the other, participation in true beauty is communicated analogically across all the degrees, since the superior degree renders beautiful the degree that is suspended from it. But if, in this fine system of cohesion, a rupture is produced, or if, counter to right order, the superior degree begins to follow the inferior one, then the deformity of a matter abandoned by nature is revealed (matter in itself is in fact shapeless and artless), and this formlessness destroys at the same time the beauty of nature, which received its beauty from the spirit. And thus the ugliness of matter, by its communication with nature, penetrates right into the spirit itself, in such a way as to cause the disappearance in its structure of the image of God.[42]

But this, it will be said, is from Plotinus! What does it matter, we shall answer, provided that it is true and it clarifies our problem! And this passage seems happily to give us the key to it. Evil, and here Gregory breaks away profoundly from Plotinus, evil is not matter. Evil is spiritual disorder, turning away from God (ἐπιστροφή).[43] But this disorder entails a revolution in the lower spheres, a revolution communicated stage by stage, starting with the lowest. By an entirely spiritual sin, "creatures have been wounded, because they have not

---

[42] *De hom. op.* 12; I, 161 C–164 A.
[43] Ibid., 164 B.

been used in a way that accords with their meaning."[44] "The Meaning of the world is that in all of creation the Power that surpasses
all might be glorified thanks to intelligent nature. Celestial things and
earthly things have been harmonized together toward this unique goal
through this very activity, through gazing, I mean to say, on God.
The act of gazing on God is none other than a life that is proportional
to the spirit."[45] Thus the death of the soul is first. The death of the
body is merely a consequence of the death of the soul.[46] But, since
time for Gregory is a fundamental quality of being and therefore analogical in all the degrees of being, the man who participates in two
different planes of being also lives in two times that have nothing in
common. This explains how that which is a cause on a superior plane
can be an effect on an inferior plane. Man, as Gregory says, is Janus.

At this point a profound mystery finds its solution, which is itself
paradoxical. Sex and the "passions", Gregory tells us, are a *punishment*
inflicted by God for the sin arising from our freedom. On the other
hand, it is undeniable that, in the perspective of "real" becoming,
these passions, sexuality itself, are an undeniable *favor* bestowed on
the spirit. But the one does not exclude the other. To illustrate our
thought, let us consider kingship in Israel. It is well enough known
that, in its origins, it was a concession of Yahweh to his people and
at the same time a punishment inflicted by him for Israel's refusal to
let itself be guided by God alone. And God announced to his people all the evils that, according to his foresight, would arise from
this institution. In spite of this, David was king in accordance with
the will of God, and it is from his family line that the Messiah was
destined to be born. The same reciprocal causality of good and evil
holds sway when we approach Gregory's problem. If sex is the anticipated punishment for sin, it is at the same time a favor from God,
who did not wish to deliver men to death.[47] Through things that
are γεννητικά (begotten or born), nature finds itself kept integral and
immortal (ἀθανασία συντηρεῖται τῇ ἀνθρωπότητι). There is more. If,
through sex, man finds himself weighed down earthward, inclined
toward his animality, through marriage he finds an alleviation of his
hard and mortal life on this sad and wretched earth (ἐν ᾧ ὁ γάμος

[44] *In Eccles.* 8; I, 753 A.
[45] *De infantibus*, III, 173 BC.
[46] *C. Eunom.* 2; II, 546 BC; cf. 8; II, 797 CD–800 A.
[47] *De hom. op.* 28; II, 73.

παραμυθία τοῦ ἀποθνήσκειν ἐπενοήθη).⁴⁸ The same goes for death it-self. Although it is the supreme punishment for man's original fault, it is death, nonetheless, that detaches us from the world and purifies us of all concupiscence (οὐδὲν γὰρ ἄλλο τί ἐστιν ἐπ' ἀνθρώπον ὁ θάνατος, εἰ μὴ κακίας καθάρσιον).⁴⁹ Death is the entry into man's original life —a life that has never existed in its integrity—and therefore death is a good thing: ἀγαθὸν ἂν εἴη ὁ θάνατος.⁵⁰

This twofold interpretation is also at the basis of the treatise *De anima et resurrectione*. Only in this treatise, Gregory seems, for anyone who does not look into it closely enough, to waver uncertainly be-tween two incompatible conceptions. The first definition of the soul, given by Macrina, is entirely "ideal" and spiritualist (νοερὰ οὐσία). It does not seem to admit of the "passions" or even the empirical body, except as a strange burden imposed on it from without. Mac-rina goes so far as to call them warts (μυρμηκίαι) on the intelligent portion (τοῦ διανοητικοῦ μέρους τῆς ψυχῆς).⁵¹ Gregory, however, can-not be content with this definition. He stresses the indispensable role of the passions (ὧν ἄνευ οὐκ ἔστιν ἀνθρωπίνην θεωρηθῆναι φύσιν), the harmonious union of the entire vital cosmos within man (ὡς πᾶσαν ἐκπεριειληφότος τὴν ζωτικὴν ἰδέαν),⁵² the necessity (ἀναγκαίως) of the soul's contact with her broad animal base. He also stresses briefly that whole "Posidonian" side, that Stoic immanence that lays claim to the rights of the corporeal world against the Neoplatonic flight into the spirit. Gregory knows what he is doing. He knows that within the realm of concrete nature he is protecting the tares along with the wheat. Did not God himself protect them against his overzealous ser-vants?⁵³ Here again Gregory is not the eclectic compiler, which some would like to make him out to be. He is the conscientious philoso-pher who is wary of one-sided systems where an excess of clarity holds sway, who prefers the apparent contradiction to the simplistic solution. It is not the body that begets the seeds of evil (οὐ τὸ σῶμα

---

⁴⁸ *De virg.* III, 376 A.
⁴⁹ *Or. de Pulcheria* III, 876 D; cf. *Or. cat.* 8; II, 33 Bff. 35; II, 88 Dff.: "According to the economy of things, death was affixed to human nature on account of divine Provi-dence."
⁵⁰ Ibid. III, 877 A.
⁵¹ *De an. et res.* III, 56 C.
⁵² Ibid., 60 B.
⁵³ Ibid., 65 AB.

τάς τῶν κακῶν ἀφορμάς ἐμποιεῖ) but free will (ἀλλ᾽ ἡ προαίρεσις).[54]
In the order of reality, however, it is very much the effects of sin that
push the will toward sin.

From now on, it must be affirmed that death is at once natural (in
the real order) and against nature (in the ideal order). Indeed, mortality resides in the very constitution of corporeal matter, for "everything that is composed naturally decomposes [πᾶν τὸ σύνθετον καὶ
διαλυτὸν ἐξ ἀνάγκης]".[55] Death is thus a "necessary consequence of
nature".[56] It is a "natural process" (φυσικῶς).[57] But it is nonetheless
true that death is, in the ideal order, the consequence of sin.[58] The
two assertions need to be adhered to simultaneously.[59]

---

[54] De mortuis III, 529 A.

[55] De an. et res. III, 20 C.

[56] De mortuis III, 528 B; 497ff.; Or. cat. 32; II, 80; 32 C; 52 A; 45 A; De an. et res. III, 128
Bff.

[57] De mortuis III, 512 C.

[58] De hom. op. 20; I, 200 D; Or. cat. 8; II, 33 B; In Cant. I, 1021 D, etc.

[59] It is only in this way that we shall avoid the inextricable difficulties in which the learned
commentators on Gregory have mired themselves. After we have gone through all the preceding arguments, we must distinguish four stages in his thought: (1) The state of man who
would not have sinned, a purely ideal state (in the sense of "purely possible"), in which
man would have multiplied himself in a spiritual and angelic fashion. (2) The creation of
"humanity", a true creation, but ideal (in the sense of Platonic "realism" and even more so
in the sense of Stoic "realism"). This creation is that of the concrete idea of actual humanity
in its entirety and has thus nothing to do with a state of earthly paradise. (3) The state of
the first real man, situated in the "earthly paradise" (which is the whole earth), endowed
with sexual organs and consequently ("Of necessity through the one [man] . . .": III, 61 A)
"passions", albeit sinless. (4) The state of sinful man.
  The main point of the first error, therefore, is that it confounds the idealness of the first
and second states. (Thus, for example, Huber: Philosophie der Kirchenväter [1859], 199ff., and
Hilt: Des hl. Gregor von Nyssa Lehre vom Menschen [1890], 98, who confounds the πλήρωμα
of humanity with the hypothetical state of man without sin.) The consequence of this is that
Hilt gives the historical Adam a wholly spiritual corporeality (no corporeal nourishment,
no digestive processes), marked only by sexual difference. This difference would not even
constitute a restriction on man's original wholeness (Hilt, 97–98)! But this theory is too
openly in opposition to Gregory's intentions not to appear false. We must therefore concede
that Huber is right (189ff.), as are Rupp (Gregors, des Bischofs von Nyssa, Leben und Meinungen
[1834], 175 n.), Stigler (Die Psychologie des hl. Gregor von Nyssa [1857], 13), and Aufhauser
(Die Heilslehre des hl. Gregor von Nyssa [1910], 46ff.), who see in sexuality an injury to original wholeness. Consequently Krampf attempts to establish a subtle structure that situates
the condition of the first man at an equal distance, roughly, from Hilt's hypothesis and ours:
Adam would have had a sexualized body and thus a nonspiritualized one, except that the
exercise of the sexual act as well as the necessity for corporeal nourishment would have been
excluded from it. What is more, the πάθη (passions), conditioned as they are by normal

The mystery of reciprocal priority appears under yet another image: "We know by the account of creation in Scripture that the earth first

---

corporeality, would have been suspended by preternatural gifts: σοφία, ἀπάθεια, ἀφθαρσία (wisdom, passionlessness, incorruption) (Krampf, *Der Urzustand des Menschen nach der Lehre des hl. Gregor von Nyssa* [1889], 15ff.). But who is so blind as not to see that this Adam, endowed with a body like our own, but deprived of nourishment, is an idle fancy? The idea, moreover, that the passions (πάθη) were present in a potential state, but bound by preternatural gifts, is a gratuitous invention, about which Gregory does not say a word. We must therefore allow that Huber, Rupp, and Hayd are right in dismissing an ideal earthly state to the domain of pure possibility. The same criticism must be made with regard to Aufhauser (47).

Hayd (and before him Bergardes: ἡ περὶ τοῦ σύμπαντος καὶ τῆς ψυχῆς τοῦ ἀνθρώπου διδασκαλία Γρηγορίου τοῦ Νύσσης [Thessalonica, 1876]) perfectly understood that the idealness of human nature in its totality was something completely other than a pure possibility or even a Platonic idea in the divine intellect. For Hayd, this whole idea is real, but of a reality that is pre- or suprahistorical, and it is toward this plane which is incommensurable with history that the economy of salvation is proceeding. Man, according to him, "first existed in another life, a happy one, exempt from earthly mortality". This state "was not historical and real in the commonly understood sense, . . . it was no more so than the state that must follow the resurrection. Just as the latter is posthistorical, the former is prehistorical" (56). The fall ought, therefore, to be understood, "not as the action of an empirical individual, but as the total noumenal action of all humanity" (52). (Compare what we have said of the existential remembrance of paradise with this.) Hayd, therefore, as a consequence of this, rejects the rigorous opposition (*Beschränktheit*) of creationism and traducianism (60). Bergardes restores Gregory's theory to its Platonic (?) and Stoic (more accurately) surroundings, from which modern theologians try in vain to isolate it. The individual soul and the total soul of humanity are not at all separable like the concrete and the abstract. "Gregory . . . writes, too, of the soul's ability to be divided indivisibly because of her essence" (37). Indeed, Gregory says as much about the angels: "And being one essence they are reckoned as many" (*De hom. op.* 17; I, 189 B). And since Gregory establishes an analogy between concrete created nature and the concrete nature of God, we may apply to the former what he says of the Trinity: "that which is inseparably divisible" (*C. Eunom.* 1; II, 336 A). Whoever balks at entering into Gregory's philosophical views condemns himself to misjudging him forever. (See the Final Note.)

If, therefore, the whole question of the original state of humanity is reduced to the opposition between an earthly Adam and a celestial homeland for humanity in its entirety (a homeland that is at once "ideal" and "real"), the problem of an eschatological *return* to a primitive state poses no more difficulties. Some have maintained that the state of the risen body will be that of the first man. In Hilt's hypothesis, this body would need, therefore, to have sexual organs, despite its wholly spiritualized state (cf. Hilt, 231ff.). But Gregory pronounces himself explicitly against this hypothesis: "At the same time we doff the signs of this [sexual] difference along with the whole of the old man" (*In Cant.* 7; I, 916 B). Krampf's hypothesis finds itself excluded a fortiori. Must it therefore be said that the eschatological state has never existed? But would this not be opposed to the very letter of Gregory? What follows in the text will inform us in what sense the two assertions—cyclical return and evolution—are equally true.

produced green plants, that these green plants then bore seeds that, when scattered over the earth, reproduced the same plant."[60] But we, who know Gregory's *Hexaëmeron*, also know in what manner he interprets this account and how for him the "germ" precedes the "plant". This confirms us in the interpretation we had given of the "circle" of the spirit, which possesses its own end term but in which nonetheless there is inserted the diastema of real becoming. It is this that must be realized if we do not want to misjudge the quite vigorously expressed idea of a cyclical return to a primitive state. "For he who observes the marvels of nature knows there is no other way for the fruit to achieve fullness [οὐκ ἂν ἄλλως] than by buds and leaves and that nature always leads the fruit toward perfection by following the path of this artful order. It is not because the plant that is formed in advance is unfit to nourish us that it is useless and unnecessary."[61] "It is by necessary pathways that our nature journeys toward its proper end."[62] None of the stages of human life has a definitive meaning. "But all of them are merely a part of the journey we are making, a journey whose meaning and end term are none other than the reestablishment of the beginning, that is to say, the likeness to God."[63] Yet, once more, what is the meaning of this journey? It is revealed to us in the image of the "plant" and the "budding seed":

> The first man, Adam, was the first ear of wheat. But with the arrival of sin, which divided human nature into a multiplicity [εἰς πλῆθος ἡ φύσις κατεμερίσθη],[64] each one of us [οἱ καθ' ἕκαστον] loses the form of this first ear of wheat, just when it matures into the grains of wheat that were being prepared, and we are mingled with the earth. But with the resurrection, we shall be reborn one day to the ancient beauty, when we shall have become infinite myriads of harvests in place of the first single ear of wheat.[65]

---

[60] *De an. et res.* III, 156 C.

[61] *De mortuis* III, 517 D.

[62] Ibid., 520 C. (For the ἀποκατάστασις (reestablishment) in the primitive paradise, cf.: I, 188 C; II 33 B, 36 Bff., 40 C; I, 1197 C.)

[63] Ibid., 520 D.

[64] *De an. et res.* III, 157 A.—Cf. Augustine, *In Psalmum* 95, 15: "Adam symbolizes the whole earth. . . . He was scattered over the whole surface of the globe. He was in one single place, he sinned, and, in a way, was shattered into many pieces, filling up the earth. But the mercy of God gathered up the resulting fragments from everywhere and melted them in the fire of his love. Thus he reestablished in unity that which was broken."

[65] *De an. et res.* III, 157 AB.

This text carries a twofold interest in that it joins the cyclical aspect to the evolutionary aspect and affirms, under the image of the "first man", the participation of everyone (οἱ καθ' ἕκαστον) in primitive beauty. It is the expression, in a certain mythical way, of that fundamental intuition that Gregory could not express in abstract terms but that he endeavored to grasp with the help of Pauline images: namely, the transition from the "ideal" to the "real" is made without spacing (ἀδιαστάτως), on the plane of the spirit, but the transition is translated onto the "real" plane by the "necessary" pathway that leads it slowly toward its end term. Thus the "necessary road" (ἀναγκαῖος ὁδός)[66] is reconciled with the cyclical nature of the spirit, and "the impossible solution" (πόρος τοῖς ἀμηχάνοις) opens up.[67]

Thus there exists a certain immanence of death in life, for real becoming is a perpetual death of being. "At every moment, nature trains itself for death; life that progresses in time is radically inoculated with death. For, since transitory life is driven toward the future without ever finding a resolution vis-à-vis the past, death is what radically follows, in the strictest sense, life's energy."[68] True life must slowly extricate itself from this "dead life"[69] "as from a shell".[70] Real becoming consists of becoming conscious of this immanent death. And this consciousness is necessary for us, so that we might recognize by way of contrast the true good (ἵνα διὰ τῆς ἀντιπαραθέσεως τὴν τῶν ἀληθῶς ὄντων φύσιν νοήσωμεν).[71] It is "the necessary experience" of which Saint Irenaeus speaks so freely and which Gregory repeats (τῇ πείρᾳ μαθών).[72] Origen had also seen the fact that "first things" are completely abolished in the Bible in order to make way for "second things" as the fundamental law of the economy of salvation.[73] Gregory returns to one of these examples, that of the tables of the law that were broken and remade, in order to draw from it the same consequence.[74]

---

[66] *De mortuis* III, 520 C.
[67] *De hom. op. proœm.*; I, 128 B.
[68] *De mortuis* III, 521 AB.
[69] *In Cant.* 12; I, 1022 D.
[70] Ibid. 15; I, 1109 C.
[71] *In Eccles.* 8; I, 740 AB.
[72] *De mortuis* III, 524 B.
[73] *In Gen.* 9, 1; Baehrens 6, 88–89.
[74] *Vit. Moys.* I, 397 A–D.

Thus is resolved the anthropological paradox posed by the simultaneously spiritual and material nature of humanity. It is a bold solution, at least if we take the word ἀναγκαίως (necessity) in its modern, rationalist meaning. But we shall see, at the conclusion of this study, that this is not the meaning Gregory gives it. Then, but only then, we shall understand both the simplicity and boldness of Gregory's solution.

By this study of the ontological structure of twofold becoming, material and spiritual, two fundamental concepts of Gregory are clarified, and all their value is brought home to us. These are the concepts of divine "immanence" and of apocatastasis.

If Gregory places great emphasis on the immanence of life forces in the creature, in no way does he intend thereby to exclude from these forces the immanence of divine energy itself, which unceasingly creates them and gives them the impetus to surpass themselves. God "has given and always gives to beings the power of coming to be and also perseverance in being",[75] and, without this θεία δύναμις (divine power), matter would remain eternally inert.[76] The best image of this immanence is that of the soul in the body. For just as the soul shows her superiority over matter precisely by her power to touch it, not merely on the surface, but in all its depths and at each point of its substance,[77] so God shows his absolute transcendence precisely by means of a very intimate contact (ἐφάπτεσθαι) with things and a deep-seated immanence: "We do not hesitate to say that the divine Nature and Power are immanent in all things [Τὴν θείαν φύσιν τε καὶ δύναμιν ἐν πᾶσι τοῖς οὖσιν εἶναι οὐκ ἀμφιβάλλομεν]."[78] Even though there is no fusion of substances (οὐδεμίαν ἐπιμιξίαν . . .),[79] there is a union so intimate that Gregory calls it a mingling (ἐγκέκραται ἡμῖν . . .[80]; ἡ πρὸς τὸ πᾶν ἀνάκρασις).[81] If one can already say that the divine will is "the matter and substance of created works [ὕλη καὶ οὐσία τῶν δημιουργημάτων]"[82] or, better still, that it is "the matter and form and

---

[75] In Eccles. 7; 725 A; cf. Catech. 25; II, 65 D; C. Eunom. 12; II, 895 A.
[76] C. Apollin. II, 1256 A.
[77] De hom. op. 15; I, 177 BC.
[78] De an. et res. III, 44 B.
[79] C. Eunom. 8; II, 793 C.
[80] Catech. 25; II, 65 D.
[81] De an. et res. III, 73 A.
[82] In illud I, 1312 A.

energy of the world",[83] this will apply in a very particular way to the rational creature. Because of its spiritual character, the rational creature receives God's creative act as "its nourishment and drink".[84] By means of its freedom, it goes so far as to cooperate with this creative act itself. As far as God is concerned, "it finds itself always recreated in a certain way, through an augmentation of its goods [τϱόπον τινὰ πάντοτε κτίζεται διὰ τῆς ἐν τοῖς ἀγαθοῖς ἐπαυξήσεως]".[85] For its own part, it brings about its own birth to divine sonship by receiving God in itself.[86] It thus becomes its own father (ἑαυτῶν . . . πατέϱες) in a perpetual birth (ἀεὶ πάντως γεννᾶσθαι).[87] But this apparent emancipation of the all-powerful action of God is only the sign of a deeper immanence. On the one hand, this emancipation (ὡς αὐτοκϱατοϱική τις αὐθεντεία)[88] is described by Gregory as the supreme token of God's friendly confidence with respect to the soul. On the other hand, every command that God gives to a freedom is at the same time a grace, a gift of strength for its accomplishment.[89] It is, once again, on the spiritual plane, an identity of "word" and "energy": "The voice of the Word is always a powerful and active voice [πάντοτε ἡ τοῦ Λόγου φωνὴ δυνάμεώς ἐστι φωνή]."[90] Thus all the becoming of the material and spiritual world is sustained in its ascendant effort by divine being, to the point that it is imbued with divine being to the very depths of its freedom.

The other conception that can be derived as a conclusion from the study we have just undertaken is that of apocatastasis. This idea, so dear to Origen and discreetly enunciated by Gregory Nazianzen,[91] finds in Gregory of Nyssa an ontological foundation.[92] In the work of

---

[83] *De vita beat. Gregorii Thaumaturgi* III, 920 A.

[84] *In Eccles.* 8; 753 BC.

[85] *In Cant.* 6; I, 885 D.

[86] *In Eccles.* 6; I, 703 A.

[87] *Vit. Moys.* I, 328 B.

[88] *In Cant.* 10; I, 980 D.

[89] Ibid. 5; I, 868 BC.

[90] Ibid. 8; I, 945 D.

[91] *Oratio* 40, 36, the last phrase (PG 36, 412 AB); *Pœmata in seipsum* I, 543 (PG 37, 1010); cf. *Or.* 30, 6 (36, 112 AB).

[92] It would be absolutely idle to want to doubt that Gregory held the doctrine of apocatastasis. The endeavor of Germain of Constantinople (fl. 770), which is attested to by Photius, to see Origenist interpolations in the many passages where there is a question of apocatastasis is not only lacking in proof but is refuted by the very coherence of this doctrine with all

Origen himself, the real unity of human nature, or rather of all spiritual nature, keeps too many of the characteristics of a moral unity to constitute a philosophical basis for his theological and mystical idea of the suppression of all evil at the end of time. It is true that in Evagrius Ponticus this character of unity is affirmed more pointedly, even to the extent that individuation and number itself are seen as no more than a consequence of the initial fall.[93] Thus for Evagrius, as is demonstrated by his famous letter to Melanie, the unity of the created spirit merges almost completely with the uncreated unity of God himself. It is not within this line of thought that Gregory of Nyssa establishes his doctrine of apocatastasis. Although the scriptural proofs—above all the Pauline texts on the abolition of death and the complete subjection of the world to God—and the thought of the infinite superiority of divine (ontological) goodness over the malice and nothingness of sin do no more than repeat the ideas of

---

the rest of Gregory's system. Certain more recent authors (Tillemont, Oudin, Soultetus, Anatius, Ceillier) have judged it necessary to follow Germain in order to exculpate Gregory. Vincenzi (*S. Gregorii Nysseni et Origenis de æternitate pœnarum in vita futura omnimoda cum dogmate catholico concordia* [Rome, 1865], even though he conceded the integrity of the incriminated passages, tried in vain to interpret the texts so as to draw out of them the doctrine of hell. Krampf, in an attempt presented much more modestly ("it is not exactly necessary to exclude . . . ," 71), tried in his turn to defend an "objective" purification of κακία (evil) that would not exclude the notion of subjective punishment. The ἐξουδένωσις (contempt) that is an earmark of evil would be the fixation of the sinner in the nonbeing of sin (59). All these theories are definitively discarded by Hilt's treatise on Gregory's eschatology (cf. also Aufhauser, 204–5). As for the few passages where Gregory speaks of the "fire that lasts an age" (πῦρ αἰώνιον), of the "punishment that lasts an age" (κόλασις αἰώνιος), Hilt brings to our attention with good reason the very special meaning of the terms αἰών (aeon or age) and αἰώνιον (lasting an age) in Gregory's work, for, opposite as they are to ἀΐδιον (eternal), they refer precisely to a determined and completed lapse of time. Gregory, moreover, speaks even of the redemption of the devils (*In Christi resurr.* 1; III, 609 CD, 610 A; *Or. cat.* 26; II, 68 D). And let us not forget that, according to Gregory Nazianzen (*Or.* 27, 10; M. 36, 25 A) "resurrection" (ἀνάστασις), "judgment" (κρίσις), and "redemption" (ἀντίδοσις) count for themes, in which "being successful is not unprofitable and failure is not without danger [τὸ ἐπιτυγχάνειν οὐκ ἄχρηστον καὶ τὸ διαμαρτάνειν οὐκ ἀκίνδυνον]." For this whole question, refer by way of comparison to the following: E. Michaud, "Saint Gregoire de Nysse et l'Apocatastase", *Revue internationale de théologie* 37 (1902): 37–52; Wilhelm Vollert, "Hat Gregor von Nyssa die paulinische Eschatologie verändert?", *Theologische Blätter* 14 (1935): 106–12; and Petau's *De Angelis*, III, 7, 5 (the end of it).

[93] Cf. our articles on Evagrius in *Zeitschrift für Aszese und Mystik* (January 1939): "Metaphysik und Mystik des Evagrius Pontikus", and in *Zeitschrift für Katholische Theologie* (January 1939): "Die Hiera des Evagrius".

Origen,[94] the supreme and, for Gregory, evident proof on which he constantly bases himself is that of the unity of human nature.[95] We shall see later on that the theological unity of the Mystical Body of Christ is entirely based on this philosophical unity. The total Christ is none other than total humanity. In that case, how would the face of the total Christ be wholly radiant and turned toward God if certain features of that countenance, of that unique and indivisible image of the Father, remained deformed by sin?

> If such wrath on God's part appears intolerable, while in contrast a correction tempered by love for men appears tolerable, "make us understand your straight and narrow way", so that we may be capable of enduring it. In wisdom, not in vengeance, do you yourself, Lord, undertake our painful education! . . . And the phrase that follows is a beautiful one: The Psalmist wants to say that on account of the weakness of our nature we do not even grasp the magnitude of the anger that sin unleashes against us. But the fact remains that we have need of correction. Therefore may that which causes us to suffer be our return to a safe harbor rather than punishment for sin.[96]

---

[94] "Even if sin enjoyed infinite growth, the mercy of God would always outstrip it by virtue of his own greatness, a greatness that is higher than the height of the heavens" (*In Ps.* 14; I, 589 A).

[95] This gives him an assurance and a peacefulness that are disdainful of being concealed under the guise of a somewhat artificial esotericism. Cf. *In illud* I, 1514 A; *In Ps.* 8; I, 467 CD; 526 CD; 528 A; 14, 586 C, etc.

[96] *In Ps.* 7; I, 464 BD.

7

DESIRE AND KNOWLEDGE

Along with an ontological analysis of creation, the chapters on spacing and infinite becoming have given us the epistemological foundations that proceed from this analysis. We have seen in what way the knowledge of a temporal being is itself rooted in time. Not only does the formal movement of thought, which consists of analyzing and synthesizing,[1] follow the march of time, but the content itself, inasmuch as it is the thought of a finite being, is limited by the representation of spacing.

> The whole creature cannot go outside itself by means of a comprehensive knowledge. It always remains in itself. And whatever it perceives, it forms a perception of by itself. It is incapable of seeing a thing outside its own nature, even if it thinks it is glimpsing an object that goes beyond it. It does violence to itself in order to take flight beyond the notion of spacing in its contemplation of beings. But it does not achieve this goal. For in everything the spirit thinks and conceives, this notion is always included in the existence of the object that is thought about.[2]

But whence comes this need to break the bonds of the aeon? It is that the spirit by its nature surpasses material time and feels itself borne along by a natural kinship (συγγένεια)[3] toward the spiritual foundation of things. By its character as an image of God, it even surpasses the aeon and feels the desire to cast itself into the divine infinite. Between

---

[1] "How would our way of thinking, which travels through the diastematic dimension, lay hold of dimensionless nature, when, by means of an analysis of time, it is always closely examining matters that are greater than those that are currently being discovered?" (*In Eccles.* 7; I, 729 C; cf. *C. Eunom.* 12; II, 1064 CD).

[2] Ibid. BC.

[3] *De infantibus* III, 173 D, etc.

the original and its representations, there is this very connection of kinship.[4]

If this knowledge by kinship introduces us into a milieu of Stoic thought, the spiritual and personal character of the object immediately alters this appearance of Stoicism. The difference already appears in the realm of sensory knowledge. For the Stoic, as for Gregory, sensory knowledge, contrary to everything in Platonism, is at the basis of scientific certitude. We know, on the other hand, that for Gregory the body is nothing but a "con-cretion" of spiritual elements. But in that case, once these notions are grasped, the body seems to be well understood, and there is no further search to be made. On the one hand, Gregory will say that sensory qualities delimit the natural philosopher's field of investigation.[5] But, on the other hand, he assures us that we do not even know our own bodies, for, once we have stripped it of its qualities, we no longer grasp anything.[6] Would the "concrete" in this case be anything more than the sum of "qualities"? And if Gregory had established (as a Platonist) an idealistic theory of spiritual matter, in order to render it more comprehensible to the spirit,[7] would he not, by the same token, have rendered it precisely more incomprehensible? He declares to us, in fact (as a Stoic), that: "The sensory phenomenon, which is easy to grasp [διὰ τὸ πρόχειρον τῆς κατανοήσεως], is indispensable to the common knowledge of everyone, inasmuch as the decision of the senses [αἰσθητικὴ ἐπίκρισις] suffers no hesitation with regard to their object [ὑποκειμένου]." There is no cause here to discuss colors and the other sensations, for "all those who participate in an identical nature" are in agreement with respect to them. It is not the same for "the spiritual being, because it raises itself above the comprehension of the senses. Since thought has to make an ascensional [ἐπορεγομένη] and conjectural [στοχαστικῶς] effort toward that which escapes the senses, each one of us finds himself moved in a different way toward the object that is sought", and each of these ways is only an approximation (ἐγγίζοντες), "according to the distinctive character of the representation that each one makes

---

[4] "We have supposed that that which is perceived by the mind is kin to all such suppositions" (C. Eunom. 12; II, 1069 C).

[5] In Cant. 6; I, 885 C.

[6] C. Eunom. 12; II, 950 A.

[7] This was in fact the principal concern he had in establishing this theory: In hexaëm. I, 69 C; 77 C; De hom. op. 24; I, 212 D; De an. et res. III, 121 B.

for himself."[8] It really seems that there is, at least in the tendency of Gregory's thought, if not in the explicit contours of it, an assimilation of the idea of the "concrete", which goes beyond a purely analytical and static knowledge even in the realm of matter, to the idea of the "spiritual". For he draws a conclusion by a fortiori reasoning from the incomprehensibility of the body to the incomprehensibility of the soul and of God. We thereby rediscover an intellectual dynamism that is not limited to the formally (as "analysis") and materially (as representation of the diastema) temporal character of thought. Rather this dynamism includes, besides, an essentially dynamic relationship of the concept to the object and in this way has a radically "open" character. Here we find the place in Gregory's system for the idea of *epinoia*, which designates above all the aspect of subjective representation that does not reach the very essence (ἐπι). This aspect is not, for all that, purely subjective. It is an idea that is defined as "an inventive approach to the unknown".[9] We do not, however, understand the scope of this definition except when we compare it with the Stoic theory of knowledge, such as it was presented, in its most unfavorable light, in the work of Gregory's great adversary, Eunomius.

In a celebrated image, Zeno had described the comprehensive (κατά-ληψις) character of thought: The open hand is pure sensation (φαν-τασία); the hand half-closed is assent (συγκατάθεσις); the hand in a completely tightened grip is comprehension (κατάληψις); the other hand coming round to squeeze the already closed hand is systematic science. Intelligence is, therefore, above all a possession, and, for the Stoic, the degrees of thought are identical to the degrees of force and energy used in grasping the object. Eunomius had, in an analogous fashion, wished to grip God with his hand, even as he hemmed in his essence through the concept of agennesis.[10] Just as in the case of a certain quality of evidence, called "gripping appearance", (φαντασία καταληπτική), the Stoic possesses truth in sensation itself, so did Eunomius think to have a grip on the divine Truth itself through the idea of innascibility. Like Basil, Gregory is strongly opposed to this. His immense treatise against Eunomius has only one goal: that of

---

[8] *C. Eunom.* 12; II, 1101 D–1104 A.

[9] "For the power of thought [ἐπίνοια] is to my mind an inventive approach to the unknown" (Ibid., 969 C).

[10] "Like the palm of some child's hand, they enclose the incomprehensible nature of God with the few, paltry letters that make up the word 'agennesis'."

showing that our concepts are only remote analogies, approaches to
the infinitely rich reality of God, symbolic signs,[11] which point out
a direction[12] without ever reaching their object. There is, between
thought and its object, the same abyss that exists between word and
thought. Just as a word is only an imperfect and not very nuanced
sign of thought, so does thought remain eternally beneath its object.
A repetition of dots will never create a homogeneous surface.[13]

In this doctrine two things should be particularly noted. In the first
place, concerning the character of intellectual activity, it is clearly apparent that Gregory is in no way minded to set the Stoic conception
of "grasping" (κατάληψις), another idea of intelligence, in opposition
to the Platonic idea of a "gazing" toward the object, for example.[14]
To the contrary, Gregory stresses precisely this character of possession in the intelligence, its "mercenary sense".[15] The intelligence is
led in and of itself to consider its object as a "matter" of knowledge in a process that Gregory calls φυσιολογεῖν. But "the mystery of
Theology is one thing, physiology is another."[16] And it is precisely
this "manner of treating unapproachable and ineffable Nature as an
object of natural science that begets heresy".[17] There is indeed an
evidence that is immanent in the concept. But if the soul wishes to
retire within this evidence (φαντασία καταληπτική), she thereby loses
the living object itself[18] and adores her own concept as an idol.[19]
The "logos of creation", the essence of things, always escapes us.
God alone knows it.[20] Eunomius is like the child who would like to
grab hold of a ray of the sun. He wants to understand rather than to

---

[11] "Some kind of seals and distinctive marks, so to speak" (C. Eunom. 12; II, 965 C).

[12] "A name . . . that is indicative" (ibid., 968 D). "A way up" (Ibid. 1; II, 366 C).

[13] In Cant. 3; I, 821 AB. Cf. De beat. 1; I, 1197 AB; In Eccles. 1; I, 632 AD.

[14] Indeed, we meet this idea of "βλέπειν πρὸς . . ." (gazing toward) in Gregory, but not in
his polemical passages. Even in his mystical commentaries, the idea of "grasping" (κατάληψις)
is more dominant.

[15] "For knowledge has some kind of arrangement that is mercenary, as it were" C. Eunom.
12; II, 941 B. ("Mercenary" [ἐμπορικήν] is attested to by four manuscripts. Jaeger opts for
"empirical" [ἐμπειρικήν] in his edition, 1: 243.)

[16] C. Eunom. 3; II, 625 C; cf. Philo, De Mon. I, 6, end.

[17] In Cant. 11; I, 1013 C.

[18] "One who thinks that God is one of those things that come to be known: [He is] like
one who has, with his grasping imagination, turned aside from being to that which is thought
to be. And such a one does not have life" (Vit. Moys. I, 404 B).

[19] "Making an idol of their own concept" (C. Eunom. 12; II, 944 C).

[20] Ibid., 937 A.

adore.[21] Since the logos is forbidden to us, there remains only the ascensional ("ana") movement toward the logos: "By a certain ana-logy, one arrives at a knowledge of being [κατά τινα ἀναλογίαν εἰς γνῶσιν ἔρχεται τοῦ εἶναι]."[22] Knowledge through *epinoia*, therefore, holds the middle ground between knowing and ignorance.[23] It is useful only to those who do not misuse it.[24] To misuse it would be to misuse the divine mystery itself.[25] Human knowledge is therefore true only to the degree it renounces by a perpetual effort its own nature, which is to "seize" its prey.

Secondly, a remark is imperative on the nature of the object. If the latter is loath to be "captured", this is not because of its irrational character, since, in itself, it is a logos of God, but rather, as we have already noted, because of its interiority, its spirituality. The great, eloquent passages in which Gregory demonstrates to Eunomius that we do not know the essence of any thing, of any element, not even of the smallest little shoot of a plant, have no agnostic flavor to them. Rather they are atremble with the great mystery of the world[26] and end in silent adoration (σιωπῇ τιμᾶσθαι)[27] before the incomprehensible beauty of God. This attitude is fully manifested when Gregory comes to the incomprehensibility of the human soul. If, at first, a series of questions posed concerning her one and multiple nature, which is both spiritual and material, seems to evince more directly philosophical preoccupations,[28] Gregory holds in reserve a much more profound reason for this incomprehensibility of the soul, a reason that is theological and fundamentally Christian: namely, the soul's very likeness to God. The soul would be lacking an element essential to the fidelity of the "image" if God, who is "invisible in himself",[29] had not communicated his "incomprehensibility of essence" to her.[30]

---

[21] Ibid., BC: "They think that they hold sway through the inferences they devise." And *supra*, n. 17.

[22] Ibid., 916 A.

[23] Ibid., 1013 A.

[24] Ibid., 972 CD.

[25] "The one who is contentiously eager to draw this very matter into the category of reason offends God unawares" (*In Eccles.* 7; I, 729 A).

[26] *C. Eunom.* 12; II, 932 C–952 C.

[27] Ibid. 945 C.

[28] Ibid.

[29] *De beat.* 6; I, 1269 A.

[30] *De hom. op.* 11; I, 156 AB.

This is perhaps the first time a Greek thinker considered the incomprehensibility of a thing not only as a sign of its remoteness from us but as a perfection of the thing itself.[31] This discovery is none other than that of the freedom of the spirit to communicate itself and to *allow* itself "to be grasped".[32] Each spirit possesses an interior sanctuary,[33] which is "veiled and known by God alone".[34] Thus we get back to the prohibition against "treating God as a thing" (μὴ ἐκ τῶν κάτω φυσιολόγει τὰ ἄνω),[35] and we discover that the philosophy of spirit is perfectly identical to that "existential" philosophy we noted in our Introduction. As for the "feeling of presence" (αἴσθησις παρουσίας), spirit communicates it to us by its manifestations (ἐνέργειαι), and it is by them alone that it manifests itself. If it is true that our intellectual machinery is insufficient to conceive the "formal" aspect of God, because our machinery introduces time into it[36] and because in the realm of pure unity this machinery can no longer synthesize anything[37]—Aristotle had already understood this[38]—it is only, how-

---

[31] It is well enough known in our day and age that scholastic philosophy has not given this idea the deference it merited. Nevertheless, modern-day "personalism" is in its turn so imbued with dilettantism (not to say snobbery) that it is still far from having incarnated in a coherent and consistent system of thought that portion of truth that it contains. The discoveries of Max Scheler above all (*Der Formalismus in der Ethik, Das Ewige im Menschen*) should be compared seriously with scholastic philosophy, without prejudice on either side. At this point, let us cite a passage from Scheler: "It is not because of a flaw in the power of our intelligence or because there is a limit to this power, but rather it is because of the essential structure of the object . . . that the personal essence of God and even his existence (not as God in general, but as a personal God) is never given to us by an act of spontaneous knowledge but always by a free and revealing act of the person of God" (*Das Ewige*, 3d ed., 682).

[32] Cf., however, Origen: *C. Cels.* 7, 42–44; Koetschau 2:192–96; *In Luc.* 3; Raver 9:20–22. And already in Philo's *De mutatione nominum* 10, where God's incomprehensibility is deduced from that of the soul. The texts noted by Norden (*Agnostos Theos*) from Xenophon (*Memorab.* IV, 3) and Cicero (*Tusc.* I, 68–70, where the doctrine of Posidonius shines through) offer only very remote analogies.

[33] *Or. dom.* 3; I, 1149 C–1152 A.

[34] *In Cant.* 7; I, 920 D.

[35] *C. Eunom.* 4; II, 625 D.

[36] Ibid. 12; II, 1064 CD: "Inasmuch as our machinery of observation considers matters with a view to our own nature and measures off the eternal by means of past time and future time. . . ."

[37] "For we discern what is greater from the comparison of boundaries to each other. But with regard to the things for which there is no boundary, how could anyone come to understand what is out of the ordinary?" (*C. Eunom.* 1; II, 304 A; cf. 365 A).

[38] *Metaph.* Z, 15.

ever, the Christian attitude, that is to say, *faith*, that corresponds truly to the spiritual nature of God[39] and to the revelatory character of all of creation.[40] Faith is definitively the only knowledge that conforms to our condition (μόνον σύμμετρόν ἐστι τῇ ἡμετέρᾳ κατανοήσει),[41] a faith that is something completely other than a "conviction", which would still be only a form of knowing.[42]

---

[39] *De vita beat. Gregorii Thaumaturgi*; III, 901 AB.

[40] *C. Eunom.* 12; II, 945 Dff.

[41] Ibid. 10; II, 832 D.

[42] Note the play on words: "He has faith in the very fact of being beyond faith." If this faith were still merely a superior form of reasoning, "it would not differ in any way from Greek wisdom" (*De vita beat. Gregorii Thaumaturgi* III, 901 BC).

8

THE TWOFOLD MYSTICAL PARADOX

Up to this point we have studied knowledge by approaching it through its indistinct application to all objects: matter, soul, God. It still remains for us to specify its more intimate relationship with the object of supreme knowledge, the Divinity. Here we are approaching the more particularly "mystical" doctrine of Gregory. Our task, however, is facilitated in a certain way, at least, by the fact that Gregory does not distinguish different kinds of knowledge of God[1] but only degrees of *intensity* in one and the same epistemological structure. This structure is characterized by three elements: (1) representation (the Stoic φαντασία, ἐπίνοια), which is the static element; (2) its reference to the unknown subject (ἔφοδος, ἄνοδος, this is the Stoic ὁρμή), which is the dynamic element, the impetus, the tension; and finally (3) the third mysterious element that unites them by showing the insufficiency of representation, on the one hand, and by releasing, on the other hand, the movement that transcends image: the "feeling of presence".

As for representation, there is no doubt that, for Gregory, it makes up an integral part of all knowledge of God. Here again, he is more Aristotelian and Stoic than a disciple of Plato. The world is a whole, closed and limited by the aeon, and never will it go beyond these limits: "Everything exists only insofar as it remains within its frontiers. If it departed out of itself, it would depart from being at the same

---

[1] The radical distinctions that people are accustomed to making between knowledge by creatures (cosmological argument), knowledge by introspection of soul (knowledge through image), and knowledge by ecstasy (mystical knowledge) are certainly artificial. The first two are ways of seeing God in his creature (the first way being through the object, the second way through the subject). The third way, as we shall see in what follows, is only a transparency of God that is ever more intense through the medium of this veil. The proof of it is the commentary on the Song of Songs, where each stage in the mystical ascent, which appears to the soul as an immediate grasping of God, is always unveiled as a view, not indeed of God, but rather of one of his manifestations (ἐνέργεια). Cf. the end of our Introduction.

time."[2] This ontological law applies in all its rigor to knowledge: "Whatever the creature sees, it sees itself."[3] The world described by *De hominis opificio* resembles that great Stoic cosmos (ἡ τῶν ὅλων φύσις) that has no exterior fissures and that, on the inside, is a perfect harmony of all its parts, an organism. The knowledge of any part whatsoever of this world always maintains this cosmic imprint: "The limit of all motion and of all of man's intellectual activity is the aeon and what it contains."[4] The knowledge of God, says Gregory in an expressive image, is like a little air bubble that rises from the earthen bed at the bottom of a lake. It begins immediately to rise, attracted by its desire for a connatural milieu (ἄνω πρὸς τὸ συγγενές). But once it has arrived at the surface, it bursts and ceases to move.[5] But while, for the Stoic, the connatural was already the divine element itself, for Gregory this end-term designates the operation of God in his work.[6] This manifestation is constantly described as the limit of knowledge.[7] What is beyond it pertains to the domain of faith.[8]

It is here, at this limit of the world, that the infinite desire to fly beyond the frontiers of the created is inflamed, for every limit involves in its essence a beyond,[9] and the soul can rest only in the infinite. But the limit formed by cosmic representation is in no wise the limit that would be formed by an object with respect to the emptiness that surrounds it. On the contrary, the representation is, by comparison with that which hides behind it, "empty" and "dead". All the books in the world, says Saint John, could not contain the works of Christ. But this book which is the world, continues Gregory, contains the marvels of God even less, for they surpass it infinitely.[10] If it is thus true that representation transports us right to this last promontory,

---

[2] *In Eccles.* 7; II, 729 AB.

[3] Ibid.

[4] *C. Eunom.* 1; II, 365 C.

[5] *In Cant.* 11; I, 1009 BC.

[6] "It cannot advance farther through curiosity. But it marvels at and honors the one who is perceived to exist only through the things in which he acts" (Ibid., C).

[7] *De an. et res.* 3; III, 25 AB. *De beat.* 6; I, 1268 B–1269 A. *C. Eunom.* 12; II, 913 D–916 A. *In Christi resurr.* 3; III, 665 C.

[8] *In Cant.* 3; I, 821 A.

[9] "For if the divine were observed to be bound up in any kind of limit, it would be categorically necessary as a consequence for it to be contemplated in unison with this limit" (*Vit. Moys.* I, 401 B).

[10] *C. Eunom.* 12; II, 949 D–952 B.

this "pinnacle" of the world, where an abyss opens up beneath our feet and vertigo lays hold of us,[11] this vertigo proceeds, as the soul knows, from the fact that *she* is powerless to understand an infinitely rich object.[12] But if it is so, if the character of representation is only the subjective limit of the object that is in itself limitless, there is a possibility, within the very interior of this limitation, of indefinite progress. The manifestations of God, even though they never yield him to us without a veil, are not, for all that, in opposition to him, as if they were the detached result of an action. They are this action itself and, thereby, God himself. In other words, we cannot say either that we see God or that we do not see him.[13] Only one thing can be affirmed categorically. As soon as the intelligence falls back on the evidence of the representation, it no longer sees. "Seeing" therefore is the very *movement* that surpasses the intelligence, whereas the (static) *content*, on the basis of which desire surges up, is precisely not the vision. And these terms are essentially relative. Each vision is, in relation to a superior vision, a nonvision. Gregory is inexhaustible in his employment of images to denote this dynamism: each vision, compared to the next one, is only an audition;[14] each time the soul has laid aside her veil by means of a new purification, she finds herself enveloped again with regard to the next.[15] Each time God calls her, she rises, even though she has been running a long time.[16] Each time God gives her a kiss, it is as if she had not yet received any.[17] She is ever refashioned by the divine goldsmith.[18] Always the fragrance that intoxicates her is only the tiny remainder of nard in a vessel that has been overturned.[19] And each time God seems to have entered her, she finds herself still outside.[20] From a static point of view, it must always be said that the soul does not see God. Since God is not his

---

[11] *In Eccles.* 7; I, 729 D–732 A.

[12] Cf. *De beat.* 6; I, 1264 B–65 A.

[13] "[Human thought] is not so sharp-sighted as to see distinctly what is invisible or so utterly incapable of making a close approach to it as not to be able to grasp a likeness of what is being sought" (*C. Eunom.* 12; II, 956 D).

[14] *In Cant.* 5; I, 860 A.

[15] Ibid. 12; I, 1029 C.

[16] Ibid. 5; I, 876 C.

[17] Ibid. 1; I, 777 C.

[18] Ibid. 4; I, 832 AB.

[19] Ibid. 1; 781 C–784 A; 3; I, 821 D–824 B.

[20] Ibid. 11; I, 997 C.

representation, the soul is each time "as if she had not even begun" to see,[21] and God on his part remains always at "the same distance above" her.[22] The vision is found in its entirety in the very impetus that outstrips every representation: "He who does not search will not find what is granted only to those who search",[23] because the search itself is the vision: "There is only one way of knowing transcendent power: it is in not ever stopping at what one has understood but rather in tending ceaselessly to what is beyond the known."[24] Desire, indeed, is a grace that is quite superior to enjoyment, for in desire alone do we see God, insofar as we can.[25]

At this point, let us recall the phenomenology of twofold desire, which was developed above. Origen, in his myth of the fall, had confounded these, believing that the soul could at a given moment turn from God in disgust, on account of a sense of surfeit. But this in itself is the sign of a material desire. As for spiritual desire, it is of a wholly different nature. It increases to the extent that it participates in the beloved thing. It expands at the same time as its thirst is quenched.[26] Now the concept of God that we can form for ourselves is necessarily limited in a certain way. If, therefore, the creature were to understand God by way of such an idea, it would be able to rise above him by its infinite desire, something that is clearly impossible: "Through all eternity you are the highest of all [ὕψιστος]", exclaims David, "you can never appear lower than those who ascend, for you will always be equidistantly higher and more exalted than the impetus of those who go beyond themselves."[27] We see things, therefore, insofar as we go beyond what we view, and it is at once true that "he who has

---

[21] Ibid. 8; I, 941 D–944 C; 6; I, 891 CD.

[22] Ibid. 8; I, 941 B; cf. Philo: *De post. Cain.*, 18; *De somn.* 1, 66.

[23] *De beat.* 3; I, 1229 A.

[24] *In Cant.* 12; I, 1024 BC; cf. Plotinus: "For seeing is the desire for sight" (*Enn.* 5, 6, 5). Philo: "The knowledge of God is therefore the result, not of a logical reasoning, but of a fervent desire" (Brehier, *Philon* [1925], 197); cf. *De post Cain.* 4 (I, 228ff.).

[25] *In Cant.* 2; I, 801 A.

[26] "With the truly beautiful, no surfeit is possible, and, since no feeling of surfeit intervenes to trouble the relationship of love with the beautiful, the divine life is an ever-operative love" (*De an. et res.* 13; III, 96 C). "[It is] always being filled and never delimiting the fullness with surfeit. For the fastidiousness of the mind is not a burden, and, always insatiable, the mind overflows unceasingly with longings for the things that are fellow partners to it" (*De mortuis* III, 505 A. Cf. *De beat.* 4; I, 1233 BC).

[27] *In Cant.* 8; I, 941 B.

a pure heart sees God, according to the certain words of the Lord"
and that "no eye has seen that supreme goodness, even though it is
always busy seeing. For he does not see God as great as he is, but
rather he sees him as great as his eye allows him to grasp him."[28]

The "true view" is, therefore, that mysterious step that goes beyond "view". Wherefore we grasp how, for Gregory, the dynamism
can plainly be infinite. On the one hand, in fact, the "*true* view" of
desire is translated immediately (inasmuch as it is a "*view*") into a
representation to be surpassed, so that each beginning engenders a
new beginning.[29] On the other hand, since this object that is to be
surpassed is not a material object but the very objectivization of spiritual desire, desire can never be subject to distaste but is bound to
be inflamed more and more: "For those who have tasted and experienced how gentle the Lord is, the taste they have of him is in itself
already a stimulation for more. Thus excitement for what is beyond
never leaves the person who ascends, and it draws him toward ever
greater things."[30] But in that case, what, in this ascent, reveals God to
us most profoundly is not the "view", it is desire. This is the reason
why the soul, after having given God all the names she was able to
devise, finally calls him no more than: "You whom my soul loves."
"Thus I wish to name you, since your name is above all names . . . ,
the proper name of your goodness to me is the love my soul bears
toward you."[31]

This first phase of the mystical paradox is expressed perfectly in
the emblem of Moses' vision. He has seen God face to face, Scripture tells us. But how, then, can he entreat the Lord for the favor of
seeing him, as if he had not yet seen him? It is because "the vision
of God consists, in all truth, of the fact that it never grows weary of
the desire to lift its eyes toward him."[32] "Veritably this constitutes
the view of God: never to find satiety in desire."[33] And when God
refuses Moses the favor and allows himself to be seen only "from be-

---

[28] Ibid., AB.

[29] "And the one who goes up never stands still, exchanging beginning for beginning, nor
is the beginning of ever-greater things ever completed within its own frame of reference . . .
he always advances through higher things toward that which is boundless" (ibid., C).

[30] Ibid., 944 A.

[31] Ibid. 2; I, 801 A.

[32] *Vit. Moys.* I, 404 A.

[33] Ibid., D.

hind", "God concedes the favor by his very refusal [δίδωσι τὸ αἰτηθὲν δι' ὧν ἀπαναίνεται]."[34] How is this? "This great lover of beauty took each apparition [τὸ ἀεὶ φαινόμενον] as an image of the desired thing [εἰκών] and desired to enjoy an impression of the archetype itself."[35] But if Moses was right in going beyond each apparition, inasmuch as each of them was only a representation (this is the twofold meaning of φαινόμενον), he himself did not understand the meaning of his desire, for he wished to end up at a supreme "vision". In order to see an object "face to face", one must place oneself "opposite" it. But to wish to be opposite to God is to wish to be opposite to good. It is to be evil. Only one thing remains: in order to see the face of God (πρόσωπον), we must follow him "from behind". In order to see him frontally (πρόσω), we must go forward (πρόσω).[36]

> "If anyone wishes to walk behind me", says Christ. He does not say, "before me". Similarly he bids the man who wished to acquire eternal life: "Come, follow me." But he who follows sees his back. Thus Moses, who burned to see the face of God, learns how one sees God: to follow God wherever he leads, this, indeed, is what it means to see God. . . . He who follows cannot leave the right path, inasmuch as he sees the back of his guide. On the other hand, whoever makes his way along the side of the road or puts himself in a position that faces his guide devises a route to his own liking, not the one indicated by his guide. That is why God says to the person who follows him: You will not see my face. By this he means to say: Do not oppose yourself [μὴ ἀντιπρόσωπος γίνου] to him who leads you.[37]

But if this following behind God is the sure way, it is no less so because at every moment it renounces the vision of the "apparition", because it is the obscure way. What does Scripture say to us concerning Abraham, when God called him from his homeland? "He

---

[34] Ibid., A.

[35] Ibid., 401 D.

[36] *In Cant.* 12; I, 1028 A.

[37] *Vit. Moys.* I, 408 D–409 A. "Who knows?" asks Rilke in one of his letters. "I ask myself sometimes whether we do not approach the gods only from behind, so to speak, separated from their lofty and radiant faces by nothing other than themselves, so that we are quite close to that facial expression we are desirous of, except that we are behind it. But what does this mean, except that our countenance and the divine face both look at the horizon from the same direction, that there exists between them a secret conspiracy; and consequently how could we approach God from the space that stretches out in front of him?" (Rilke, *Briefe*, 1914–1921, 87).

left, not knowing where he was going." "But this was precisely for him the sure course toward what he was seeking: not to be guided by any of the current [προχείρων] representations of God that were presented to his mind." Not that he did not avail himself of them, but he took them as "his provisions for the voyage" (ἐφόδια), on which he relied (ἐπερειδόμενος) so that he could go beyond them (καὶ τοῖς ἔμπροσθεν ἐπεκτεινόμενος).[38] Saint Paul gives us an example that is no different. He who was favored with the highest of visions "does not boast of having grasped" but "is always rushing toward what is in front of him".[39] Thus true knowledge is produced outside of all light, in the night, but in a "divine night" (θεία νύξ),[40] in a "dazzling dark-ness" (λαμπρὸς γνόφος).[41] This night is faith, in which all knowledge is reached and which alone "links and joins together the searching spirit and the ungraspable nature . . . , and there is no other way to approach God."[42] Seized itself by the presence of being,[43] faith, and faith alone, in its turn, seizes being.[44]

There is no doubt that, for Gregory, the structure of knowledge we have just analyzed is the only possible one and therefore definitive and eternal. The infinity of the created spirit is an infinity in the pro-cess of becoming. It is an infinity "of endless growth",[45] "an infinity that, in all the eternities piled on eternities, draws near him . . . who is The-Always-Greater."[46] "The sight of his face is ceaseless progress toward him."[47] There is no need to look beyond (as does Diekamp). Gregory gives us formal notice of the situation. The desire itself is the joy, the search itself is the view. But must we not in that case say that there is a secret and unacknowledged sadness in this desire?

---

[38] C. Eunom. 12; II, 940 CD–941 A. Cf. De vita beat. Gregorii Thaumaturgi III, 901 AB, In laudem fratris Basilii III, 792 BC. The one who inspired this interpretation is evidently Philo: De Abrahamo, de migratione Abrahæ. Some reflections on Gregory's text in Endre von Ivánka, "Ein Wort Gregors von Nyssa über den Patriarchen Abraham", Studia Catholica, Nymwegen, 1935, 45–47.

[39] In Cant. 8; I, 940 D–41 A.

[40] Ibid. 11; I, 1001 B.

[41] Vit. Moys. I, 377 A.

[42] C. Eunom. 12; II, 941 B.

[43] "The belief that God is greater and loftier than any cognitive sign" (ibid., A).

[44] "Having left behind all ways of direct apprehension, I found my beloved through faith" (In Cant. 6; I, 893 BC).

[45] De an. et res. III, 105 C.

[46] In Cant. 8; I, 941 B.

[47] Ibid. 12; I, 1025 D–18 A.

And truly it is here that we find the most significant meaning of *beati lugentes* (blessed are those who mourn) . . . ! There is a sadness in the creature, who knows that it will never see God as he is for himself: "And to the extent we understand that this Good surpasses all our intelligence, sadness ought to grow in us, on account of the fact that this Good is so immense. . . ."[48] It is true that what Gregory has in view in the passage cited is above all "the present life".[49] But the reasons he enumerates are quite as valid for the future life. Even if this eternal desire *is* the highest joy to which a creature can have access, is there not something in this metaphysics of becoming that leaves us dissatisfied? This desire, even though it is ceaselessly appeased by God, is *in itself* "like a thirst, which makes us very dry and scorchingly hot".[50] From a certain perspective this appeal to God, even though God ceaselessly responds to it, remains unheard, precisely *insofar* as it is an appeal: "*Vocavi ipsum et non audiit me* [I called him and he did not hear me]."[51] It is a strange thing. We are dissatisfied with this metaphysics that erects into an absolute that part of us that is more radical: namely, dissatisfaction. However, this metaphysics is merely the result of a rigorous analysis that has been conducted precisely on the ontological constitution of the creature: diastema, time, becoming, indefinite progress. Or does the fault, indeed, lie in that rigorous

---

[48] *De beat.* 3; I, 1225 CD. (See the whole passage.) The German Idealists will resume this theme, but on a more sombre note, construing the sadness of the creature as the sadness of not being God (Schelling, *Untersuchungen über das Wesen der menschlichen Freiheit* [1809]. *Œuvres Completes:* 7:399, 465–66). Father Lippert (*Der Mensch Iob redet mit Gott* [1934], 274–75) resumes it with a note of abandonment and love, which has affinities with the spirit of Gregory of Nyssa: "Now and for all time, as far as I can see, my eyes are going to wander, forever and ever, as if blinded, here below, beneath the steps of your throne. It is only from very far away, from below, that I find it possible to raise my gaze toward your countenance. It is only from an invisible height, as it were, that your tenderness descends on me, and it is always like a sound that fades off, coming from far away. . . . So I should very much like to weep because of this burning desire and this nostalgia. . . . Therefore I am always and for all eternity across from you on the other side of you, and always there lies between us an infinity, and always there is need of a bridge! To speak this way is the mark of a fool, Lord, I know it. (But it is all the same true.) So pardon me. I want to disavow these words of mine (even though they are true!). You who are good, behold, I am not weeping any more now because of this abyss between you and me. But I am smiling at you above it. Yes, I am smiling at you, my Great Beyond! I well know that you are doing all that your love can do: my unworthiness—it is your desire to make me forget it."

[49] I, 1225 A.

[50] *De beat.* 4; I, 1241 A.

[51] *In Cant.* 6; I, 893 A–C.

logic itself, which claims to establish a metaphysics of the creature by proceeding from the creature itself? The parts of this study that follow will give us the answer to this question, which looms inevitably at the end of this examination of the "metaphysics of becoming and desire".

The question becomes more pressing if, from this first mystical paradox, we detach a second one, which renders it more paradoxical but is, to be sure, merely its logical continuation. Up to this point, religious knowledge has been presented as a continual overstepping of the acquired given, where the "intelligence" resided precisely in the nonconceptual part of the approach, in the motion. But then it would be necessary to speak not only of an overstepping but of a self-negation of intelligence. The latter, as we have seen, is characterized essentially by a "taking possession", a seizure. And by διάνοια Gregory means the human intelligence in its entirety, making no distinction between an inferior reason (*Verstand*) and a superior reason (*Vernunft*), in order to reserve for the latter a faculty of vision that is other than a "grasping" (κατάληψις). The nature of the intelligence in its entirety resides in this embrace of the object (περί-ληψις),[52] whereas the object, by its nature as well, escapes any kind of embrace (ἀπερίληπτον). There is thus a true contradiction, and intelligence must deny itself, must renounce itself, if it wishes to assimilate itself to the nature of the object. The intelligence will see exactly to the extent the object escapes it (παριέναι): "The greatness of the divine nature is understood, not in comprehending it, but insofar as it escapes all evidence and all intellectual power [καταληπτικὴ φαντασία καὶ δύναμις]."[53] Just as the wind slips through the mesh of a net, God escapes all grasping (δια-διδράσκων).[54] The "night of intelligence" is thus, strictly speaking, "the view of that which cannot be seen".[55] And God is not only "always beyond" (ἐπέκεινα), but he is—inasmuch as the motion of desire includes a knowledge—"above the beyond": ὑπὲρ ἐπέκεινα.[56] In this regard, the usage of a term that returns constantly to Gregory's pen, that of πολυπραγμοσύνη, becomes very instructive. For it is evident that, on the one hand, this term connotes a certain feverish agitation

---

[52] *Vit. Moys.* I, 404 C.
[53] *In Cant.* 12; I, 1028 AB.
[54] Ibid., B.
[55] Ibid. 6; I, 892 C.
[56] *In Eccles.* 7; I, 732 C.

of the intelligence as it searches for its object and that, in this respect, it has a pejorative note. On the other hand, it is noticeable that Gregory treats this agitation with that indulgence which is directed toward inevitable things: it is the very nature of the spirit to be agitated. Furthermore, it is the case that the spirit has true knowledge only when it reaches the end of its agitation, just as it has true knowledge when it reaches the end of its own self, when it emerges, fatigued by its movement, into eternal life: ἐπειδὰν ἐμπελάσῃ τοῖς ἀνεικάστοις ἀργὴ μένει.[57] It is here that we find that failure of "essential" thought, a failure that, having been ceaselessly repeated, comes to augment the "existential" knowing of the Presence, about which we spoke in our Introduction: "It is necessary that the knowledge of things that exceed all grasping [κατάληψιν] should be exempt from the agitation of thought [ἀπολυπραγμόνητον], in a testimony to the existence of that which this knowledge seeks. . . ."[58] The measuring intellect capsizes in this Sea, "whose measure is infinity".[59] All our happiness is in this failure. In shattering our desire to possess, it gives us eternal hope: "That which one possesses like a thing can no longer be hoped for."[60] In removing from us the whole hermeneutics of infinite nature (ἑρμηνείαν τῆς ἀορίστου φύσεως), which resembles "a grasping of the sea in the hollow palm of one's hand",[61] it opens up our eyes to the vista of infinite existence: "This is what it means to see: not to see."[62] The soul who has not been able to find God in anything that is possessed "presently leaves all objects found and thus comprehends what she seeks: she comprehends it, comprehends that it Is, and by the sole fact that she does not grasp what it is."[63]

In the first paradox, representation played the role of a "point of departure" (ὑπόβαθρα),[64] while here it is an "impediment" (ἐμπόδιον πρὸς τὴν εὕρεσιν).[65] In the first paradox, the joy of love had as its

---

[57] *In Ps.* 9; I, 485 A.

[58] *Vit. Moys.* I, 388 A; cf. ibid., 315 D–318 A.

[59] *C. Eunom.* 12; II, 933 A.

[60] Ibid., II, 941 C.

[61] Ibid. 7; II, 761 A.

[62] *Vit. Moys.* I, 377 A. Pseudo-Dionysius will take up these formulas again: "To see in blindness, the very act of not seeing" (PG III, 1025 A).

[63] *In Cant.* 6; I, 893 B.

[64] *C. Eunom.* 12; II, 940 D.

[65] *In Cant.* 6; I, 893 B.

basis a "complaint" (ὡς ἐνδεὴς ... ἀποδύρεται),[66] while here it has "despair" (ἀνελπιστία) in the very depths of itself.[67] And God is not only the eternally desired object. He truly is "desperate beauty" (τὸ ἀνέλπιστον κάλλος).[68] This despair is merely the adequate expression of the total negation of the intelligence, which is at the same time its supreme act: it is precisely in *accepting* this despair that the soul "receives in herself the chosen arrow of God in her heart's mortal flesh. . . ."[69] She is terrified (θρόησις) by it.[70] But this terror is merely the heart jumping at the approach of the Bridegroom (ἡ δὲ κοιλία μου ἐθροήθη ἐπ' αὐτόν).[71] And the paradox is not merely the effect of a moment. It is perpetuated in the realm of becoming by a mysterious and parallel growth of ignorance and knowledge: "To the extent that it approaches the vision of God, the mind sees ever more clearly the divine nature's invisibility."[72] You do not know whom you are adoring, Jesus said to the Samaritans. As for us, we know him whom we adore. We know he is the Unknowable. You wished to grasp him on Mount Gerizim. We know he is the Ungraspable[73]: *docta ignorantia* (learned ignorance).

The last sound yielded up by this metaphysics of becoming is a Bergsonian sound. The intelligence is made for grasping. It is essentially practical: "How could he who does not understand himself understand what is beyond him? . . . The only way we understand the elements of the world is through the senses, precisely to the degree this is useful to us for our practical lives."[74] Life eternally outstrips Ideas: "For what exists in truth is Life, and it is life that is Truth, and the latter cannot be transposed into knowing."[75] Fichte gave voice to these beautiful words: "It is not death that kills, but life when it is more alive."[76] This is the thinking of Gregory himself:

---

[66] Ibid., 892 A.
[67] Ibid. 12; I, 1037 B.
[68] Ibid., C.
[69] Ibid.
[70] Ibid. 11; I, 1012 B.
[71] Ibid.
[72] *Vit. Moys.* I, 376 D.
[73] *C. Eunom.* 3; II, 604 BC.
[74] Ibid. 12; II, 949 B.
[75] *Vit. Moys.* I, 404 B.
[76] *Über die Bestimmung des Menschen* (*Sämtl. Werke* 2:317).

God says: "You shall not be able to see my face, for it is impossible for a man to see my face and live." But this is not so in the sense that this face should be a cause of death for those who contemplate it—for how could the face of Life ever be deadly to those who approach it?—but rather it is true inasmuch as God is in his essence vivifying, and the proper sign of the divine nature is to remain beyond all signs, so that he who believes that a known thing can be God thereby turns away from Being itself toward that which for him has the semblance of intellectual evidence—and by doing so he does not have Life.[77]

What attitude should we espouse then? By what means should we enter into that Life which does not allow itself to be either seen, or grasped, or comprehended?

Let us suppose that there is someone who is journeying in the full heat of noonday. His head is broiled by the rays of the sun; all the moisture in his body is being sucked up by it. His feet tread on rough ground; the road is difficult and barren. But behold now, he suddenly hits upon a fountain whose waters are limpid and clear-flowing. Its abundant streams offer him the prospect of a gentle quenching of his thirst. . . . Is he going to sit down by this wellspring and begin to philosophize on its nature, examine where it comes from, and the how and the why, and so on and so forth? . . . Or will he not rather dismiss all this and stoop down to touch his lips to the living waters and give thanks to the One who has made a gift of these waters to him?

You also, therefore, in your turn, ought to imitate this thirsty man.[78]

---

[77] *Vit. Moys.* I, 404 AB.
[78] *Or. in suam ordin.* III, 552 D–3 A.

PART TWO

The Philosophy of Image

THE DEFINITION OF NATURE

All the philosophy developed up to this point has arisen from one single principle: namely, the principle that characterizes the creature inasmuch as it is opposed to Being. This philosophy is deduced from a structure that is formal and, so to speak, "void" of becoming. But without abandoning this acquired base, should we not ask ourselves whether principles as abstract as "Being" and "becoming" really suffice for the construction of a religious philosophy, whether, on the one hand, there might not be occasion to consider the analogy of being in a more concrete light, one less "mechanical" and more "organic", and whether, on the other hand (and this is perhaps only another way of viewing the same concretion), created "nature" is truly nothing but that "opposition" to God[1] that seemed to constitute it inasmuch as it is a creature. In departing from this pure opposition, was it not, in fact, fatal when we ended up in "sadness", indeed, in "despair"? If it remains true that the creature can never "*have*" God, could one not, all the same, try a different path and ask oneself whether, within the terms of the analogy itself, this path could not, in a certain fashion, "*be*" God? "The health of the body is a great good for human life. But happiness does not consist of the fact of *knowing* what health is, but of *living* healthy. . . . The Lord does not call blessed those who know God but those who possess God."[2] There exists a possession of God that is antecedent to all efforts of the intelligence: it is the image of God in the soul, the *concrete* form of the analogy of being, which at the same time leads us outside of "nature" (inasmuch as it is pure creature) and carries us into that intermediate domain that can be called, not without anachronism, the domain of "created grace". It is a domain that is essentially labile, dynamic, and transitory, and it

---

[1] Cf. Part One, Chapter Two, n. 15.
[2] *De beat.* 6; I, 1269 BC.

will detain us only briefly, a necessary stage, as it were, for thought. It is a frontier domain between philosophy and theology, where the paths of Greek exemplarism and those of the Bible cross, a difficult domain to delimit and one that is essentially dialectical.

In the present chapter we shall study the matter of image, and from it we shall draw consequences for the concept of nature, comparing the doctrine thus acquired with the doctrine of Part One. The following chapter will lead us farther on into the dialectic of image.

In Gregory's principal passage on this subject, his commentary on the sixth beatitude, "blessed are the pure of heart, for they shall see God", he feels overcome by "vertigo", as it were, at the sight of this paradox. Does Saint John not say: "Nobody has seen God"? And does not Saint Paul say: "Nobody can see him"? "But does not eternal life consist of the vision of God? . . . This casts human hope into distress and disarray!"[3] Christ's promise seems to pull us out of this dilemma. But at this point we find "a new feeling of vertigo, for I fear that purity of heart pertains to things that surpass our nature".[4] Yet even so, no! "Do not let your hope fail [μὴ ἐκπίπτετε εἰς ἀνελπιστίαν], as if you were incapable of seeing what you desire! For you carry in yourselves a certain measure of knowledge of God, since, from the beginning, he who has formed you has made a part of your very nature from this immense good [κατουσιώσαντος τὸ τοιοῦτον ἀγαθὸν εὐθὺς τῇ φύσει]. He has imbued your constitution with semblances of his own connatural goods."[5] This treasure lies at the bottom of your spiritual soul. Disencumber it of the debris and filth of sin, and this image will appear in all its purity: "And he who thus contemplates himself perceives in himself the object he desires. In this way whoever possesses a pure heart achieves beatitude. In gazing upon his own purity, he contemplates the archetype in the image." "You are, it is true, too weak to grasp the light in itself. But if you return to that beautiful grace [χάρις] of the image that was deposited in your nature at the beginning, you will possess within yourselves what you are looking for." Those who see the sun in a pure mirror "do not see it any the less [οὐδὲν ἔλαττον]" than it is in itself.[6] (Let us take

---

[3] Ibid., 1264 D.
[4] Ibid.
[5] Ibid., 1269 D–1272 A.
[6] Ibid. 1272 AB.

particular notice of this twofold affirmation: "too weak", on the one hand, "not any the less", on the other. Herein lies the whole problem of the image!)

What then is this image? It is, Gregory tells us, participation in all the goods of divinity,[7] in that infinity which is the lot of the spirit. In the first place, it is Spirit and Reason (Νοῦς καὶ Λόγος), which are divine, "and from which human nature is not estranged", and then it is Love (Ἀγάπη), of which Saint John says that it is God and which "our Creator has given us as the expression of our human countenance" and "whose absence alters the character of the whole image".[8] Love includes all the virtues and brings about through their harmonious interaction the brightness of the image.[9] Spirit includes that ability to see through everything, an ability that is properly divine.[10] The two of these together bestow on the creature that "light" which caused the Prophet to say: "The light of your face, Lord, has shone upon us." It is "the face of God expressed in human features [Θεοῦ πρόσωπον ἐν χαρακτῆρσι θεωρούμενον]."[11] It can be seen how little this image is added exteriorly to a nature that is already constituted. It is rather the very constitution of it,[12] inasmuch as the spirit possesses this grace (χάρις),[13] which is the brightness of its divine kinship. Nor is this a dead image and separated, as it were, from the archetype. On the contrary, we have seen that for the spirit the term "creation" came to be analogical and that it was necessary rather to speak of "participation". This is therefore a living image, which for this reason bespeaks a very close union as well. It is that connaturality (συγγένεια)[14] that is so dear to Gregory and that is merely the concrete form of the analogy. The intimacy of the connections that were already created

---

[7] *De hom. op.* 16; I, 184 A.

[8] Ibid. 5; I, 137 BC; for intelligence: *C. Apollin.* II, 1145 C.

[9] *De hom. op.* 5; I, 137 A; cf. *In Ps.* 4; I, 446 BC.

[10] *De hom. op.* 5; I, 137 C.; cf. *In Ps.* 6; I, 451 C: "And it comes to be admitted to the highest of mysteries and surveys the nature of all things that be."

[11] *In Ps.* 4; I, 446 BC.

[12] "So that nothing beautiful is superimposed on us from outside. Rather it is in us—which is what we desire to be the case."

[13] *De hom. op.* 16; I, 185 C.

[14] *Or. dom.* 2: "With a view to a certain connaturality with the nature that is superior to it . . .": I, 1137 B. *De beat.* 7: "He does not promise any sameness of worth through connaturality": I, 1280 D. *De an. et res.*: "united with that which is kin to it . . .": III, 89 B. Cf. *Or. cat.* 5; II, 21. *De infantibus* III, 173 D–176 A.

by the Platonic structure of "participation" is increased by the Stoic contribution of kinship with the divine nature, on the one hand,[15] and by the contribution of the gospel on the other hand.[16] In this sense, Gregory limits the idea of man as a "microcosm" to the human body alone,[17] in order to proclaim it, in its totality, as a likeness, not of the world, which was created, like he was, but of God.[18] This parallel is significant, for it shows that, just as the "microcosm" moves in the world as if in its natural milieu, the spirit waxes strong in the milieu that is proper to it, the divine milieu: "Just as, in irrational nature, each animal that lives in water or in air is constituted according to the demands of its kind of life . . . , similarly man, destined to enjoy divine goods, had to receive in his very nature a kinship with that in which he was bound to participate."[19] Plotinus' famous image of the "heliomorphic" eye[20] is taken up by Gregory. The eye attracts light by the active brightness of its nature (διὰ τῆς ἐγκειμένης αὐτῷ φύσικῶς αὐγῆς . . . τὸ συγγενὲς ἐφελκόμενος).[21] Our insistence on this point is intentional: the vital and living character of kinship through image is in fact the foundation of all the doctrine proposed in this scheme. It raises us, right from the beginning, above that irreducibility of life and knowledge that marked the end of Part One. As things stand at present, the life of the soul, that is to say, her spiritual activity, is in itself already a "view", even though rudimentary and implicit: "A certain idea of God [ὑπόληψις] is rooted in the nature of all men [φύσικῶς ἔγκειται]",[22] and the expansion of this "idea" ("innate" because it is none other than spiritual nature in its entirety) appropri-

---

[15] Although this idea of "kinship" with God was already widespread in Greek philosophy before Stoicism: in Pythagoras (*Diog. Laertius* VIII, 27), Sextus Empiricus (*Adv. Mathem.* VII, 92), in Plato (*Timæus* 90 a, *Laws* 899 d. 24), Julian the Apostate (Letter 89, Bidez ed., 167), Cicero (*De leg.* I, 24ff.; *De nat. deorum* II, 133ff.), Philo (*In Exod.* II, 29, p. 488 A).

[16] Acts 17:28–29; 1 Pet 1:4; 1 Jn 3:1.

[17] *In Ps.* 3; I, 440 C; 441 CD; *De hom. op.* 16; I, 177 D.

[18] *De hom. op.* 16; I, 180 AB.

[19] *Or. cat.* 5; II, 21 CD.

[20] "For the eye would never have seen the sun if it had not become sun-like, nor would the soul see if she did not first become beautiful" (*Enn.* I, 6, 9). The groundwork for this idea is laid as early as Plato: the "god-like" (θεοειδής) soul (*Phaedrus* 95 C) "having kinship with the divine" (συγγενὴς τῷ θείῳ) (*Rep.* X, 611 E), "most like the sun" (ἡλιοειδέστατον) (ibid. VI, 508 B). Cf. Philo (*De præm. et pæn.* 7; M. II, 415).

[21] *Or. cat.* 5; II, 21 C; cf. *De infantibus* III, 173 D.

[22] *De beat.* 5; I, 1249 D.

ately constitutes the life of the soul: "To contemplate God is the life of the soul."[23]

Gregory formally distinguishes this new form of knowledge from the first.[24] But a more attentive comparison of the two shows us that the new form is merely a transposition of the first into the mode of the spirit. In fact, we rediscover within it the three constituent characters: φαντασία, ὁρμή, and συγγένεια. But while in Part One, these elements were merely psychological *actions* (representation, desire, feeling of presence), we rediscover them here as *states* of nature itself. In the case of the third term, ontological kinship, which establishes the link between representation and motion, the proof of it has just been established. The same holds true of the first two terms.

In fact, in this mode of knowledge, representation is the soul herself. It is no longer, properly speaking, a fantasy that must simply be "denied" in order to see its truth. It is a living image and, more than that, a pure mirror. It is no longer God himself, who cannot be seen without a veil. The law that a creature will never go outside itself remains in full force: "It ought not to transgress its own limits, and the knowledge of itself ought to be sufficient [ἀγαπᾶν] for it."[25] But within the terms of this restriction, Gregory strives to render the partitioning wall that separates the created spirit from God thinner and thinner. It is characteristic of him that almost always when he speaks of "image", he immediately substitutes for it the example of the "mirror".[26] But this is not a passive mirror that would receive only an external imprint. It is a "free and living mirror",[27] whose interior activity is entirely "surface". There is in the word ἔμφασις, which occurs in connection with this, a significant ambiguity. On the one hand, it connotes the "reflection" of light and of divine features on the surface of the "water" or the "mirror".[28] But this reflection or this "appearance" is produced quite as much by what is within

---

[23] *De infantibus*, III, 176 A. Compare, however, with n. 9 in Part One, Chapter Two.

[24] *De beat.* 6; I, 1269 B: "But the other one. . . ."

[25] *In Eccles.* 7; I, 732 C.

[26] *In Cant.* 15; I, 1093 CD (εἰκὼν-κάτοπτρον [image-mirror]). *De an. et res.* III, 41 CD ("an image in a small fragment of glass"). *De mortuis* III, 504 C ("an image in a mirror"). Similarly *De beat.* 6; I, 1272 B. *In Cant.* 3; I, 824 AB. *De an. et res.* III, 98 C: "Gazing on an image in a mirror toward the archetype through the beauty that is kin to them both. . . ."

[27] "A free and living mirror": *In Cant.* 15; I, 1096 A.

[28] Ibid. 15; I, 1093 D.

and is thus its "expression".²⁹ Here we rediscover the doctrine of the identity of the divine λόγος with the internal δύναμις of creatures. Image—mirror—life: these three terms, therefore, designate the whole created "medium" that allows the soul to see God in it.

It is not otherwise for the second element of knowledge: "desire" (πόθος), "impetus" (ὁρμή). Inasmuch as Gregory's idea of "nature" is essentially dynamic and open, he is opposed to any doctrine that would like to "intermingle" all natures in order to establish metempsychosis,³⁰ even as he is opposed to every prospect of fusion between the nature of God and the nature of man.³¹ Part One demonstrated his idea of nature to us: becoming is the very nature of created spirit, and becoming is a movement, "not by local displacement, for nature does not depart outside of itself, but by alteration".³² Now the alteration by which nature is defined (ὁρίζεται) is none other than assimilation to God.³³ This definition (ὅρος) does not transgress the measures of nature (τὰ μέτρα τῆς φύσεως),³⁴ because the final end (ὅρος) of man consists of this assimilation.³⁵ If, therefore, from a static point of view, nature was an initial view of God (ὑπόληψις), it is, from a dynamic point of view, an "affinity" (σχέσις)³⁶ and an "impetus" (ὁρμή).³⁷ Only this assimilation is a thing so unprecedented that the person who approaches God in this manner "is scarcely still within the limits of hu-

---

²⁹ "Mankind, which is transformed according to the reflections that arise from its free choices, is truly like a mirror" (ibid. 4; I, 833 B). Cf. De beat. 1; I, 1197 B: "The reflections of the characteristics of blessedness" is a phrase that is redolent at once of an "impression" and an "expression".

³⁰ "To commingle the properties of nature" (De an. et res.) III, 109 B; σύγχυσις (a commingling) (ibid., 113 B).

³¹ Ibid. III, 41 C; De beat. 1; I, 1200 CD.

³² De an. et res. III, 141 A.

³³ De prof. Christiana III, 244 CD. Consequently it is easily understood with what irritation Gregory must have received news of the sola fides of Eunomius (". . . that for man heretical faith alone is sufficient for perfection" [C. Eunom. 1; II, 281 A]). For Gregory, faith ought to expand quite naturally into the dynamic activity of works.

³⁴ Ibid. Cf. In Ps. 2: 12; I, 557 C: "The characteristic that is peculiar to man is assimilation to the divine."

³⁵ "The end of human blessedness is assimilation to the divine" (In Ps. 1; I, 433 C).

³⁶ "In all men there is some kind of natural relationship to the beautiful" (De mortuis III, 497 B).

³⁷ "The impetus of desire toward the best and the beautiful, an impetus that is joined essentially to man and is united to him . . ." (De prop. sec. Deum III, 288 A). Cf. C. Eunom. 1; II, 340: "The attractive force [of God] . . . who implants it naturally."

man nature [οὐκέτι σχεδὸν ἐν ἀνθρωπίνης φύσεως ὅροις].³⁸ It is none
other than a complete ontological ecstasy toward God: "Man leaves
behind his own nature [ἐκβαίνει τὴν αὐτοῦ φύσιν ὁ ἄνθρωπος]; . . . to
sum up everything in a word: from being man, he becomes God."³⁹
Thus the mystical appeal to Abraham that he should leave his homeland was already being defined, for this homeland was his nature.⁴⁰
These two affirmations, namely, transgressing nature and remaining
in it, are correlative. Their unity defines the dynamic character of this
nature. If we place ourselves at the end term, in the true man (ὁ ὄντως
ἄνθρωπος),⁴¹ "who has fully realized the reason in his nature",⁴² or if
—which amounts to the same thing—we place ourselves at the ideal
outset of humanity, then the state of man, his "nature" (φύσις), is the
realization of assimilation to God. If, by way of contrast, we place
ourselves in the actual state of humanity, this perfection appears to us
so inconceivable "that human nature seems to be something other".⁴³
And in spite of all this, the two are the same nature, for if Christ exhorts us to tend toward this first perfection that has been lost, "is he
asking something that would surpass the limits of human power?" No,
"nature is not violated in any way [οὐδὲν ὑπὲρ τὴν φύσιν βιάζεται]":
no more than one would ask birds to fly if they did not have wings
would Christ give us this law if we were not fit to launch ourselves
forth into the divine milieu.⁴⁴ And the law (νόμος) of Christ is such
that it gives us strength (δύναμις) at the same time. It is therefore not
perhaps without reason that Gregory did not accept the distinction
between "image" and "likeness", which he must, nevertheless, have
known about.⁴⁵ According to this distinction, "image" (εἰκών) would
designate the natural, ontological similitude of the soul, while "likeness" would connote the perfection acquired by her free and moral
assimilation. For Gregory, this distinction loses its validity, since the

---

³⁸ *Or. dom.* 5; I, 1177 A.

³⁹ *De beat.* 7; I, 1280 C.

⁴⁰ "Having raised his thinking as far as possible beyond the common boundaries of nature"
(*C. Eunom.* 12; II, 940 B).

⁴¹ *In Ps.* 16; I, 605 A.

⁴² "For whom the reason in his nature is fully realized" (*In Eccles.* 6; I, 704 A).

⁴³ "So great was that inconceivable good in our nature that human nature seemed to be
something other" (*De beat.* 3; I, 1225 D).

⁴⁴ Ibid. 6; I, 1265 D.

⁴⁵ Cf. Dr. Arnold Stucker: *Die Gottebenbildlichkeit des Menschen in den ersten zwei Jahrhunderten*
(Münster, 1913). In particular the text of Origen: *Peri Archon* III, 6, 1 (Koetschau 5:280–1).

image is itself essentially dynamic, just as the likeness is essentially ontological.[46]

---

[46] Moeller (*Gregorii Nysseni doctrinam de hominis natura et illustravit et cum Origeniana comparavit* [E. G. M. Halis, 1854]) accused Gregory of Baianism: "Continetur igitur hac rationali natura Deo cognata facultas Deum recipiendi . . . [Therefore the ability to receive God is contained in this rational nature that is known by God]", (27). By means of sin "non peculiare aliquod donum amisit, sed ipsam naturam corrupit [it did not lose any particular gift, but corrupted its very nature], (ibid., 58, n. As for original grace, "prorsus aliam esse rem quam Romanorum donum superadditum nemo non videt [nobody, indeed, fails to see that it is something other than the superaddition of the gift of the Romans]", (ibid.). Against this accusation, the distinctions of Krampf, Hilt, Diekamp, and Aufhauser certainly have their value. It is only too clear that Gregory understands the term φύσις to apply to concrete nature, thus nature elevated to a supernatural state, and that he describes the gift of grace constantly as a gift that is purely gratuitous. The image cannot be given by "Prâkriti". It comes from on high. It is the gift of God, χάρις (F. Hilt, *Des hl. Gregor von Nyssa Lehre vom Menschen systematisch dargestellt* [Cologne, 1890], 76ff.; J. B. Aufhauser, *Die Heilslehre des hl. Gregor von Nyssa* [Munich, 1910], 54ff.; A. Krampf, *Der Urzustand des Menschen nach des Lehre des hl. Gregor von Nyssa* [Würzburg, 1889], 64ff. Notice especially the diverse meanings of φύσις in Gregory: Krampf, 65–66). It is true that the authors cited, in order to prove the gratuity of grace, enumerate many texts concerning the restitution of the Image by Christ, texts that prove only very indirectly the thesis in question. But the passages of *De hominis opificio* are largely sufficient to dispel all suspicion of Baianism. There is, however, a graver objection against these authors. None of them succeeds in making out the exact role of nature and grace in the texts of Gregory. Operating with scholastic and modern concepts and supposing, therefore, the hypothesis of a pure nature, they try in vain to show that *nous*, Freedom, and Love are not, as such, a free gift. Schwane admits openly: "What is missing here is a precise distinction between the natural image and the supernatural assimilation to God" (*Dogmengeschichte* IIa, 453). In fact, for Gregory, the gratuity of grace is in no way linked to the hypothesis of a pure nature. It is defined, not on the basis of man as the starting point, but uniquely on the basis of God as its starting point: through participation (μετουσία) in his intimate life. The true proof of the complete gratuity of grace is glimpsed by Krampf, when he shows that Gregory ceaselessly affirms *two* things: divinized man's proximity to God and the absolute transcendence of this same God, who remains eternally unapproachable and infinitely distant (Krampf, 67). On the other hand, the frequently developed proof that argues from the starting point of nature that is fallen, but that has nevertheless remained spiritual and free, would not prove to be conclusive in its full rigor, since this nature is in no wise a "pure nature", but a nature contained in a total supernatural order. Thus Gregory can say: "Speculative thought and the making of distinctions are peculiar to the God-like soul, inasmuch as we apprehend the divine by these qualities" (*De an. et res.* III, 89 B), since the depths of the human being are forever and ever *specified* by the human being's supernatural final end. Henceforth there will be no need to say with Stigler (*Die Psychologie der hl. Gregor von Nyssa* [1897]) that the supernatural life of the soul is "the normal activation of the two powers that are constitutive of the soul" (the powers of intelligence and will) (19). If the principle itself is not "supernatural", how would its activity be so? (For this whole question, see the Conclusion of our current study.) The idea of a purely dynamic conception has been perfectly realized by Max Scheler, who takes it right to the extreme in terms of its conse-

If, however, we do at present grasp the ontological structure of the image, its exact relationship with spiritual activity, with its "second act", has not yet been clarified. It is this act that we must now study to see in what sense, whether definitive or not, the philosophy of "desire" and "despair" finds itself truly liberated and definitively transfigured in it.

---

quences: "The error of all the anthropologies of the past has been that of wishing to interpolate between 'life' and 'God' an intermediate stage, a stage, however, that is indefinable in essential terms: 'man'. But this stage does not exist, and it is quite essential to man not to be definable. He is only an 'in-between', a 'limit', a 'transition', a 'theophany' in the stream of life and a perpetual movement of life's self-surpassing transcendence" (*Vom Umsturz der Werte* [1919], 1:296). Scheler repudiates any definition of man that takes its point of departure from below "nature" (ibid., 309). For him monophyletism holds no theological or philosophical importance for the true unity of mankind. All properly human unity comes from on high: "The natural unity of man does not exist. Nothing essentially and specifically new begins yet with *homo naturalis*, but only with 'historical' man, who is ordered toward the divine. This man receives his unity only through what he *ought* to be: an image of God, to be precise, and of an infinitely perfect person" (ibid., 309–10). We have demonstrated elsewhere the profound error of this conception of Scheler's (see *Apokalypse der deutschen Seele* [1938], vol. 3, the chapter on Scheler's personalism). Gregory of Nyssa is less radical. His conception of the unity of human nature is situated, as we have observed, beyond "real" unity and "ideal" unity, beyond creationism and traducianism. But it cannot be denied that Gregory of Nyssa prepares the ground in some ways for that gnostic dynamism of the Byzantine philosophies, which end up logically in the gnosis of Dostoevsky, Soloviev, and Berdyaev. And we know the influence that Dostoevsky had on Scheler.

MONAD, MIRROR, AND WINDOW

The problem posed is always the same: How is an immediate contact, a view without the veil, possible through a "medium", a veil? What should the spiritual activity of the soul be, in order that she might bring reality to this contradiction?

A preliminary path opens up for us. If created nature is limited (τοῖς ἰδίοις μέτροις),[1] there remains to it nonetheless the dimension of its own depth. The bride, in her mystical ascent, was moving "ever more toward that which is within" (πρὸς τὸ ἐνδότερον),[2] and it is there that we find the proper dimension of the spirit: a return to self (νόησις νοήσεως). In this sense, the spiritual movement will tend in the first place, by a successive elimination of all that we "have", to constitute what we "are": "Our surest refuge is not to fail to recognize ourselves, not to believe that we are seeing ourselves when we are seeing only something that surrounds us", our body, our faculties, the idea that others have of us. For anything unstable is not us.[3] We have already seen that the soul is purified in this way, as she lays aside garment after garment.[4] Thus the ideal will appear as that supreme instant wherein the soul, having been disencumbered of all her "corporeal [veils], presents herself naked and pure in spirit to the vision of God in a divine vigil".[5] This vision (ἐμφάνεια) would therefore constitute only the soul's taking possession of her own spiritual purity, a "reflection" of that deepest depth of herself, where the *scintilla animæ* (spark of the soul) burns. Thus "the soul, freed from the movement of the passions, comes to no harm by them . . . , she withdraws into herself [πρὸς ἑαυτὴν ἐπανελθοῦσα] and is able to know herself in her

[1] *C. Eunom.* 1; II, 365 B.
[2] *In Cant.* 13; I, 1036 A; "ever toward that which is within": *Vit. Moys.* I, 377 A.
[3] *In Cant.* 2; I, 804 AB.
[4] Ibid. 12; I, 1029 C.
[5] Ibid. 11; I, 993 D.

depths [ἑαυτήν ἀκριβῶς εἰδοῦσα], such as she is in her very nature,
and she contemplates the archetype in her own beauty as in a mirror
and in image."[6] This would therefore be, as Gregory affirms in certain passages, first and foremost that reflexive faculty that would express the divine image,[7] or, what amounts to the same thing, it would
be that independent freedom that is possession of self (ἀδέσποτον καὶ
αὐτεξούσιον . . . αὐτοκρατικῶς).[8] "For virtue is a sovereign and voluntary thing; constraint and violence cannot be virtuous."[9] "The Creator who made man in his image deposited the seeds of all the virtues
in the nature of the being that he molded, so that there is no need for
any good to be instilled from outside; rather he made it so that all
that we desire should be within our reach [ἐφ' ἡμῖν] . . . , and there
is no other means of achieving what we desire than that of bestowing
the good on ourselves."[10] Thus the interior world seems in some way
to be closed in on itself, like a windowless monad.

To this perspective there is added the eschatology given to us by
De anima et resurrectione. It is the eschatology of an interior sanctuary,[11]
where the spirit "leaves desire behind" and reaches that stage "where
there is no longer place for hope and remembrance. Everything the
soul hoped for, she presently possesses, and, occupied fully, therefore,
in the enjoyment of every good, she excludes remembrance from her
spirit."[12] But this restful repose is not the soul's solitary withdrawal
into herself. It is nothing less than her highest possible assimilation
to God: "By the purity she has acquired, the soul enters into a close
relationship with God, with her own proper milieu [τῷ οἰκείῳ], as it
were. She no longer needs, then, the movement of desire that guides
us toward the beautiful. It is true: the one who lives in the shadows
has a longing for the light, whereas for the one who is already entering into the clearness of light, joy follows on desire."[13] In this perfect
assimilation to God, who, to be sure, "does not know desire, because
no good is lacking to him, the soul also, in coming to be without

---

[6] *De an. et res.* III, 89 C.
[7] Ibid., 57 B.
[8] *De hom. op.* 4; I, 136 BC (cf. *De virg.* 12; III, 369 CD).
[9] *De hom. op.* 16; I, 184 B.
[10] *De beat.* 5; I, 1253 D–1256 A.
[11] Cf. *Or. dom.* 3; I, 1149 CD.
[12] *De an. et res.* III, 93 B.
[13] Ibid., 89 BC.

needs [ἀνενδεεῖ], will be obliged to leave behind the movement of desire and even the disposition to it, since desire only has a place when
the thing desired is not present".[14] There remains a place only for
the "movement and activity of love conforming itself to the object
that has been grasped and found eternally [ἀεὶ]".[15] At the moment,
therefore, when the soul is completely unified (ἁπλῆ καὶ μονοειδής)
in herself, she is also deiform (ἀκριβῶς θεοείκελος). She embraces the
tranquillity of God in himself, who is pure love without desire. "In
a certain way she becomes God [ἐκεῖνο γίνεται τρόπον τινά]."[16] This
is the metaphysics of the monad: the pure interiority of the soul who
has closed all the "windows" of the passions is found to be the pure
exteriority of love, because it is pure assimilation to God, who loves
only himself.[17] This dialectic that identifies the pure interior with the
pure exterior is found justified by Plotinus' theory of light, which
was adopted by Gregory. Indeed, for Plotinus, the view is effected by
an *actio in distans* (action from a distance) of the sun on the interior,
"heliomorphic" power of the eye.[18] Similarly, for Gregory, the eye
"possesses in itself that natural gleam that permits it to comprehend
what is homogeneous to it".[19] And, according to him, this is what
the image of our knowledge of God consists of.

But is this Gregory's last word on the subject? In that case, there
would be an opposition between this metaphysics of the monad and
that of desire, and the synthesis we were looking for would not be
operative here. And is there not a secret illusion in this monadology, insofar, precisely, as it involves an *unmediated* identity between
love of self and love of God, because it rests on an identity between
knowledge of self and knowledge of God? Also, in order to arrive at
the supposition that these two loves coincide in a supreme harmony,
should we not distinguish between them before we unite them? In
this "assimilation" to God, the final law is no longer that of *analogy*
but that of *identity*. The structure of this metaphysics, if taken in isolation, would no longer be Platonic, not even Aristotelian (where God
remains the eternal beyond: κινοῦν ὡς ἐρώμενον), but Stoic. In this

---

[14] Ibid., 96 A.
[15] Ibid., 93 C.
[16] *Or. dom.* 5; I, 1177 B.
[17] *De an. et res.* III, 96 C–97 A.
[18] *Enn.* I, 6, 9.
[19] *De infantibus* III, 173 D.

scheme, the soul would be a "divine particle",[20] the world would be "a single movement",[21] and the ideal, for which all spiritual beings are destined, would be perfect unity in perfect distinction.[22] "How do you possess in yourself the inexhaustible wellspring?" asks Marcus Aurelius. "At all times make yourself grow in independence."[23] In order to make this wellspring bubble forth, one must know how to isolate it from all that is not identical to it,[24] one must know how "to limit oneself",[25] "to close oneself in on oneself",[26] in order to arrive, by way of this very isolation and impassibility, at the great, universal love. In the contemplation of itself,[27] the full possession of self,[28] in that ideal "of purity and nakedness",[29] this wellspring acquires the transparency of love: "Penetrate into the soul of everyone, and let everyone penetrate into your soul!"[30]

In the last analysis, this perfect equilibrium between what is within and what is without presupposes an identity between the soul and God. And it demonstrates to us quite obviously that this monad, even though it considers itself to be outside itself, is in reality without windows. In a Christian metaphysics, the excess weight of *amor-pondus*, which is none other than analogy, remains definitive. Saint Thomas deduced from this very analogy that, before loving itself, the creature, by its very nature, had already to have been loving its Creator.[31]

---

[20] Marcus Aurelius: *Meditations* II, 1: "divine particle".

[21] Ibid. IV, 40: "single movement".

[22] Ibid. IX, 9: "For as much as it is greater in comparison with other things, to that extent is it more fit to be intermingled and united with that which is kin to it . . . even in things that are separated."

[23] Ibid. VIII, 51.

[24] Ibid. X, 38.

[25] Ibid. VII, 55: "It is the peculiar function of rational movement to impose limits on itself."

[26] Ibid. VIII, 48: "The which has a ruling function is . . . gathered together into itself."

[27] Ibid. XI, 1: "It sees itself, it perceives itself distinctly."

[28] Ibid.: "I possess that which is my own."

[29] Ibid. XI, 27: "purity and nakedness".

[30] Ibid. VIII, 61.

[31] 1a 2æ, 109, 5: cf. *Quodl.* 1, 8; *Comm. in Dionys.* c. 41, 10; 1a, 60. 5, *ad* 1. One cannot therefore deduce a pure idealism from Christian principles, even in the sense that it would be only an *ideal* of the created spirit. That an angel (who is an intelligent, subsisting *species*) should receive "elements" "from without" is not *merely* an imperfection. The finality of being does not end in total intelligence (νόησις νοήσεως) but only in love. The Trinity is the truth of extraposition.

Now Gregory understands this excess weight, and up to now we have managed to isolate only a partial aspect of his doctrine. It will be total only at the moment we rediscover the truth of such a monadology in the broader context of a philosophy of love. If it is true that in all knowledge the creature sees only itself,[32] there is an opposite principle that in a single stroke ruptures this whole, closely knit monadology: "What nature has done for the eyes of the body, which, when they see other things, never see themselves, it has done also for the soul: the soul explores all other things, she exercises her inquisitive and sagacious activity on all that is outside her, but it is impossible for her to see herself." But in that case, what should the soul do? Let her imitate the eyes of the body. Just as the eyes "do not have the power to reflect onto themselves the power of sight [τὴν ὀπτικὴν δύναμιν ἀναστρέψαι] but are able to perceive their form [τὸ εἶδός τε καὶ τὸ σχῆμα] in a mirror, thus it is with the soul: let her turn away from herself [ἀπιδεῖν] and turn toward her image [εἰκών]." Except, Gregory goes on, this parallel is not quite exact: "As for that which concerns the form in the mirror, the image is elaborated according to the archetype.[33] For the expression of the soul, it is the opposite: it is from divine beauty that the soul is copied. Thus, when the soul turns her gaze toward her archetype, then she is truly contemplating herself."[34]

But, it will be replied, the two formulas are equivalent. In seeing God, the soul sees herself. In seeing her own purity, she sees God. She has no other means of seeing him. What we have here is simply the two faces of "appearance" (ἔμφασις)! But what we have is nothing of the sort. The text we have just cited postulates a priority for a detour of self, and it is only through this detour that spiritual reflection is produced. In this way it establishes again a priority of "impetus" (ὁρμή) over "representation" (φαντασία), which reintroduces the theory of desire in the monadology.

---

[32] *In Eccles.* 7; II, 729 AB.

[33] Of what archetype is Gregory speaking? Of the exterior object reflected by the mirror or of the eye itself (as the Latin translation supposes)? This last hypothesis would be the most interesting and would render the comparison more exact.

[34] Texts gathered together in Endre von Ivánka, "Vom Platonismus zur Theorie der Mystik. Zur Erkenntnislehre Gregors von Nyssa", *Scholastik*, 11 (1936): 186–87. Josef Stiglmayr, S.J., "Die Schrift des hl. Gregor von Nyssa 'Über die Jungfräulichkeit'", *Zeitschrift für Aszese und Mystik*, 1927, no. 4, 346–47.

It seems, however, at first sight that this activity is, in spite of everything, only a *means* for definitive action, just as the mirror is a means for the eye to see itself. Indeed, a whole part of Gregory's work seems to consider Christianity and the exercise of the virtues as the way that rids the soul of the filth of sin, in order to discover the image, the mirror, the pure eye at the bottom of her.[35] "Hidden beauty becomes transparent"[36] as soon as the soul washes herself clean of the defilement of sin,[37] as soon as she is freed from those "garments of skin" with which the original transgression has clothed her, in order to present herself "naked" once more before her Creator.[38] The manner in which God works at his image in us is that of the sculptor. By an ever finer and more subtle chipping away, he disengages a mysteriously preexisting statue from the formless stone.

Yet it would be wrong to isolate this aspect. We have seen how Gregory does not make a distinction between εἰκών (image) and ὁμοίωσις (likeness). For him, the static image, the point of departure for moral dynamism, is confounded with this very movement. It is for this reason that he can say that through sin we have lost the image itself.[39] The obscured image is no longer an image. It is, Saint Augustine will say, worn out, as it were, by the flux and reflux of the billowing waves of this world.[40] Its restoration is therefore less a work of discovery, which, once achieved, would render useless the working tools, than the effort of the work itself. The image is nothing other than the knowledge and love of God. It is the Christian life in its entirety that is the distillation of that precious "nard" offered to the Bridegroom.[41] Only that lived and experienced purity, condensed like a drop of honey distilled from a whole meadow,[42] will help us to understand and to taste the divine purity. In this sense, "all the virtues

---

[35] "To clear off completely the beauty that has been covered up" (*De virg.* 12; III, 372 D).

[36] Ibid., 368 D.

[37] Ibid., 374 C. *De beat.* 6; I, 1272 AB.

[38] *In Ps.* 11; I, 541 D–544 B; *De beat.* 1; I, 1197 BC.

[39] "He lost his being an image of the imperishable God" (*De virg.* 12; III, 372 B). "Having fallen to earth, it will be crushed" (*Vit. Moys.* I, 398 B). "The fact of their having been destroyed" (*Vit. Moys.* I, 381 B).

[40] *Enarr. in Ps.* 129, 1; "Imago ipsius, quod est homo . . . in hoc profundo tamquam assiduis fluctibus exagitata, detrita est [His image, which is man . . . was destroyed, after having been tossed about the ocean depths by unrelenting waves]" (PL 37, 1696).

[41] *In Cant.* 3; I, 821 D–824 B.

[42] Ibid.

are intimately coherent, and all of them pursue a unique goal",[43] a goal, indeed, that also has nothing fixed about it. Saint Paul, in drawing all at once from the flowers of all the virtues that fragrance of his life that he called the fragrance of Christ, spread it at the same time throughout the world. "He gave himself up like a divine libation."[44] Spirit and water are two related things, but the spirit was hardened and "frozen, as it were", by assimilation to the idols of stone that it adored. Christ came to reheat it, "so that man might become water again, a water that springs forth to eternal life".[45] It was precisely by way of this characteristic of liquidity that he passed beyond the rigid opposition between himself and the object. "Christ does not make men mere spectators [οὐ θεατὰς μόνον] of the divine majesty. To be sure, he makes participants [κοινωνούς] of them . . . , and he gives us water that does not come from strange, far-off streams but which springs from our own depths."[46]

Thus the monad is dissolved in this penetrating element that has the capacity to resolve in a more marvelous way the paradox of being at once "in self" and "outside self". The movement of desire is so far from being abolished by ascetical purification that, to the contrary, it is this ascetical purification that truly liberates it: "If the human soul is once truly swept clean of all this attachment to heavy, earthly life, and if she can by virtue lift her eyes toward that which is homogeneous to her, which is to say, the Divine, from this moment on she no longer takes any rest in researching and investigating the first beginning of things."[47] But it is precisely this disquiet that is the sign of a Presence in her. In becoming supple and flowing, the soul is assimilated to the Eternal Ocean, which is not either, to be sure, an "image" one can contemplate without being engaged by it. The prophecy made to those who have a pure heart is not meant "to show God to the interior eye as a kind of spectacle facing it [ὡς ἀντιπρόσωπον τι θέαμα τὸν θεὸν προτιθέναι]"[48]—we already know God's refusal to let himself be seen "face on": μὴ ἀντιπρόσωπος γίνου![49]—but this prophecy exhorts

---

[43] *De beat.* 8; I, 1293 B.
[44] *In Cant.* 14; I, 1065 B.
[45] Ibid. 5; I, 865 D.
[46] *Or. dom.* 2; I, 1137 AB.
[47] *In Cant.* 11; I, 1009 B.
[48] *De beat.* 6; I, 1269 C.
[49] *Vit. Moys.* I, 409 A.

them to reenter into themselves: "You possess in yourselves what you desire. God is purity . . . , if, then, this purity is in you, God is very much in you."[50] This ethereal transparency of the heart (καθαρὰ τῆς καρδίας αἰθρία) is itself the blessed spectacle (τὸ μακάριον θέαμα).[51]

Thus the philosophy of desire and that of the monad are recovered. And, on the one hand, the "sadness" of not rejoining the object is assuaged, for God is present within the desiring act itself. On the other hand, the independence of the monad, which leaves behind it all desires in order to close itself up in the impassibility of pure love, it, too, is made supple: the taking hold of self always presupposes a movement toward the Other. And, in the last place, all this purification of the soul by way of virtue is effected only by the immanence of the grace of God in us. If the eyes of the Bride are wholly pure and if they contemplate God, it is because "the image of the dove" is in them, that is to say, the Holy Spirit who *gives* them purity.[52] The bridal gown the soul puts on is none other than Christ himself.[53] The holiness she acquires for herself is the Lord.[54]

But it is precisely at this point that a question is posed, a question that concerns this whole philosophy of image. Is this identity of "virtue" and "grace" that we have just established as absolute as all that? Have we resolved in its entirety the question that was posed concerning the monad, with a view to learning whether the persons therein were distinct enough to be united and to render love possible? Does not the soul in this case love, unconsciously perhaps, her own virtue, her own beauty? In this chapter we have set aside Christianity in its historical guise. We have remained in the realm of a mystical morality. Will this morality free us definitively from the specter of "solipsism", or, if you will, "pantheism"? Is the "pure mirror" truly a "window"? We find, in fact, at the end of this philosophy of image something that resembles a kind of *resignation* and that could only be a mitigated form of "despair" and "sadness". Indeed, without any doubt, Gregory considers this form of knowledge a "compensation" for what is inaccessible to us. This is the hidden meaning of that verb ἀγαπᾶν, which at once signifies "to find oneself happy" and "to be

---

[50] *De beat.* 6; I, 1272 BC.
[51] Ibid., C.
[52] *In Cant.* 4; I, 833 D–863 A.
[53] Ibid. 9; I, 1005 A.
[54] Ibid., 1008 C.

content": "The soul should ἀγαπᾶν to see itself" without aspiring to that which is impossible.[55] And again, the nard-like purity of the virtues must be "a compensation" for the soul, "which cannot fix her gaze on the sun itself [ἀντ᾽ ἐκείνου ἡμῖν γίνεται]".[56] Certainly we shall no longer employ the term "mediate" vision here any more than the term "immediate" intuition. We have gone beyond these contrasting opposites since Part One of our book. But will the desire of the soul that "tends to migrate to God himself",[57] "in order to enter into God",[58] not hold good for as long as the soul is conscious of this compensation? There is, in the *Commentary on the Song of Songs*, something like an obsession on the part of the soul, as she seeks to *leave*: First the Bridegroom is behind the wall, then he lies in wait on the other side of the iron grille; a light pierces through by way of the window, "evoking a deep yearning to see the sun in the open air".[59] Indeed, the virtues appear as beautiful "images that imitate truth [εἴδωλα . . . πρὸς μίμησιν τῆς ἀληθείας]", as "statues of truth [τὰ τῆς ἀληθείας ἀγάλματα]".[60] But the statues "represent", they are not the Presence itself. There is an "as if" (ὡς παρὸν κατανοήσας . . .),[61] which impedes the full Presence. Virtue is a "vestige" of God.[62] It is "the shadow of God's wings", the shadow he casts on the earth of our soul.[63] It is "the forecourt" of the temple[64]—but no more.

Is this, therefore, the soul's highest beatitude, or will the soul succeed in "issuing forth beyond it"?

---

[55] *In Eccles.* 7; I, 732 C.

[56] *In Cant.* 3; I, 824 B.

[57] "The soul migrates to God" (*In Cant.* 6; I, 889 D).

[58] "To come to rest in God himself" (*De an. et res.* III, 152 A).

[59] *In Cant.* 5; I, 864 D.

[60] *In Eccles.* 3; 637 C.

[61] *In Ps.* 6; I, 453 A.

[62] *Or. in suam ordin.* III, 545 B.

[63] *In Ps.* 14; I, 586 CD.

[64] *In Eccles.* 7; I, 721 A.

PART THREE

The Philosophy of Love

I

HUMAN NATURE AND INCARNATION

If up to this point Gregory has distinguished knowledge by desire and knowledge by image, nothing in his texts seems to indicate a third way of knowing. Let us, however, recall two things. First, these diverse ways of knowing are strictly only modalities of one sole and unique epistemological structure. If, therefore, we attempt to take a last step that goes beyond knowledge by image, we are, despite this, holding fast all the while to the self-same *interior* of this unique structure, by *intensifying* it, not by going beyond it. In the second place, it is a priori probable that Gregory, who is above all a Christian theologian and not simply a religious philosopher, finds, in the contribution of Christianity as a historical revelation, a means to raise himself above an epistemology inferred in its entirety from a general similarity between God and the soul, an epistemology whose principles were admitted by pagans as well as by Jews (Philo). What Gregory in fact developed *exercite* (in a disciplined fashion) in his theology, we shall endeavor to become conscious of *reflexive* (reflexively), in order to compare it to the first two parts and impart the stamp of its development on them.

Now Christianity brings to religious philosophy a complete reversal of its point of departure. It is no longer a question of knowing how the soul can approach God but of learning how, indeed, God has approached us. Through a historical fact that is exterior, Christianity teaches us a historical fact that is interior. For metaphysics, it substitutes metahistory. In a more profound way, these two facts are, to be sure, but one sole event. The interior approach of grace is produced by the Incarnation. Just, therefore, as no philosophy was able to foresee the exterior fact, no ontological analysis of the soul, as preoccupied as it may have been with "image" and "created grace", could have calculated on the basis of its own givens the fact of God's sensory approach to the heart, the fact of "Uncreated

Grace".[1] The μετά of φύσις, its open dynamism, does not attain this "fact". It is, at the very most, its place of action. In theology, the point of departure—and this is quite as true for the exterior fact as for the interior fact—is that which is beyond the limits of the cosmos.

To this reversal there corresponds a second one. The point of departure of religious "metaphysics" is necessarily of an individual nature: it is an analysis of desire and the aspirations of the soul. Whatever there was of a social nature in the mysteries of the pagans was merely the expression of a gregarious instinct whose aim it was to assure the individual salvation of the members of the group. The theological fact, by way of contrast, is radically social. For if the exterior fact and the interior fact constitute one solitary history, the social character of the exterior fact (the Church) demonstrates thereby the social character, as well, of the interior fact (the Mystical Body). Already we have a presentiment of the importance that the doctrine of the common nature is thus going to assume here. In Part One of our treatise, this doctrine seemed to be only a long *excursus* without any value for a religious philosophy. And if, in that section of our work, we established that the image was given only to the common nature as such, it is exceedingly significant that in dealing with the "philosophy of image" we were able to set aside this assertion completely, even though it is in itself of capital importance. What remained up to this point an unutilized theorem becomes the very center in the case of "metahistory".

For the theology of the Incarnation, the task is facilitated for us by the penetrating study of Father L. Malevez.[2] We fully accept the results of it,[3] and we should like merely to add a few details. The following is the essential outline of these results: in the first place,

---

[1] That she should have to look on God in order to see herself—an experience of this kind undergone by the soul was very much a beginning of this reversal. But the soul availed herself of God as of a "nature", taking him almost like an object (mirror) without reckoning on the absolute freedom of God in his communications. There was not yet that unique word of God and that gaze "which penetrates so far as to separate soul and spirit and which pierced [Magdalen] through, right to the depths" (*In Christi resurr.* 2; III, 640 A).

[2] "Eglise dans le Christ", *Recherches de science religieuse*, 1935, 257–91; 418–40.

[3] We can set aside his attempt at theological interpretation in the second part of his study. As for the identification of Gregory's theory with Platonism, see Part One of our book. We believe that our interpretation of God's "power of foresight" (προγνωστικὴ δύναμις), which must seem to Father Malevez a "clumsy expression" (*expression maladroite*, 262), has provided a more positive justification for it.

Christ assumed[4] an individual[5] and concrete nature, a nature that was in no wise "the" human nature as such. Yet what is more, by means of this partial contact, he touched nature in its entirety, a nature that is indivisible[6] and continuous[7]. And by this vital unity,[8] he transmits grace,[9] resurrection,[10] and divinization[11] to the entire body,[12] thus uniting all men[13] and, through them, all creation[14] to himself.

This doctrine therefore yields to us in an unexpected way that "fissure" in the monad, through which "God comes to live in the soul and the soul migrates into God."[15] It presupposes, on the one hand, the real and organic unity of nature, a unity that is antecedent even to the Incarnation.[16] On the other hand, it presupposes the ontological unity of the divine and the human in Christ.[17] It is this latter aspect that now concerns us. It implies, in the first place, a veritable immersion of the eternal in duration: the phrase *hodie genui te* (today I have begotten you) is a reference, according to Gregory, to the birth of the Logos in time.[18] Christ was like a man "who perceives a weak person carried away by a raging current. He knows that he himself will

---

[4] "Having taken up" (ἀναλαβών): *De perf. Christ. forma* III, 280 A.

[5] "His own man" (τὸν ἑαυτοῦ ἄνθρωπον): ibid., 277 C; "the divine man" (τὸν θεοδόχον ἄνθρωπον): *In Cant.* 13; I, 1056 A.

[6] "Absolutely one and not divided into parts" (ἀδιάτμητος ἀκριβῶς μονάς): *Quod non sint tres dii* II, 120 B.

[7] "Continuous" (συνεχής): ibid. *Or. cat.* 32; II, 80 C; "continuity of substance" (συμφυΐα): *C. Apollin.* 11, 1165 A.

[8] "His whole nature being something alive" (ibid).

[9] "He drew together all of nature toward his grace" (*C. Eunom.* 12; II, 889 C).

[10] "The beginning of resurrection stretches out to all of humanity through one man" (*Or. cat.*, 16; II, 52 C).

[11] "All of human nature, with which was mingled the divine" (*In illud* I, 1313 B; 1320 B; *C. Apollin.* II, 1165 C).

[12] *C. Eunom.* 12; II, 889 C.

[13] *In illud*, etc.; I, 1320 A.

[14] Ibid., C.

[15] *In Cant.* 6; I, 889 C.

[16] See Malevez, 275.

[17] "Just as divine power extends equally through the whole nature of the union, in the same way I maintain that it does not have a share in divinity without the divine element being, suitably enough, in both body and soul" (*C. Apollin.* II, 1256 B; cf. ibid., C: "The divine nature [is] . . . implanted . . . and has become one with respect to each of the two [parts]." The best analogy for this unity remains that of the soul and the body: *Or. cat.* 11; II, 44 AB.

[18] "Birth in time" (Χρονικὴ γένεσις): *In Ps.* 8; I, 428 C; cf. ibid., 415 B.

by sucked up by the whirlpool, wounded and lacerated by the rocks swept away by the water. But pity for this man in danger stimulates him. He does not hesitate to throw himself into the current."[19] He enters, therefore, without reservation into the flow of duration. But in order to save the one who is drowning, he must "jump" *from on high*, that is to say, he must bring us the integrity of our nature. It is very much a necessity that he not be born of a mortal man who is subject to the "passions"[20] but that he bring us that nature that is *antecedent* to the "passions" (which, indeed, as we know, are linked in a mysterious way to sin).[21] It is equally necessary that Mary should be a virgin, so that in this pure relationship the prodigy of the burning bush might be fulfilled: unity without blemish.[22] It is a "new birth",[23] a "new order of nature",[24] finally a "new creation",[25] "the beginning of a world".[26] It is, in the final analysis, the day "when the true man is created [κτίζεται ὁ ἀληθινὸς ἄνθρωπος], he who is in the image and likeness of God".[27]

"We are thus aware of a twofold creation of our nature, the first, by which we were formed, and a second, by which we were re-formed. . . . Of old God fashioned man . . . , now he clothes himself with him; of old he created, at present he is created. Of old the Word made flesh, now he is made flesh."[28] This "new man",[29] Gregory insists on this point, is such only because he comes to us from a transcosmic region, a region that is not blemished by the contagion of sin.[30] He can come, we shall see, only from that celestial region that is our ancient homeland, paradise, the place of the true image. If,

---

[19] *In Pascha* 3; III, 656 C.

[20] *Or. cat.* 13; II, 45.

[21] "Inasmuch as it is only flesh, it is sin" (*In diem nat. Chr.* III, 1136 C); cf. *C. Eunom.* 12; II, 889 C.

[22] *In diem nat. Chr.* III, 1136 BC.

[23] Ibid., 1137 A: "new birth" (καινὴ γέννησις); cf. *In Pascha* 1: "Birth is one thing, life is another . . .": 604 C.

[24] *In diem nat. Chr.* 1136 A.

[25] *In Pascha* 1; 605 AB (cf. 606).

[26] Ibid., B.

[27] Ibid.

[28] *C. Eunom.* 4; II, 637 AB.

[29] Ibid. 12; II, 889 C: "that new man who has been brought on the scene by the favor of God".

[30] *In Pascha or.* 1; III, 616 B: "Therefore it has been said of this new man that he was brought to us by the favor of God, not according to the habit of men. . . ."

therefore, humanity, through sin, has lost the image,[31] and if sin has entered into humanity as a condition of its nature, only the presence of a "true" and pure man effects in humanity as a whole a "change in our very nature [αὐτῆς τῆς φύσεως ἡμῶν μεταστοιχείωσις]",[32] and that "by a simple and incomprehensible coming of life, by the presence [παρουσία] of light".[33] Through this interior change we possess the first condition of nature's dynamism. It is rendered possible only because Christ is at once "nature" and "more than nature" (μείζω τῆς φύσεως).[34] This is the reason Gregory insists so much on the moment of the Resurrection. Without excluding the Incarnation[35] or the life of the Lord in its entirety, which was necessary for the transformation of all of human life,[36] the Resurrection denotes, however, that precise point at which the deepest roots of sin are extirpated, roots that sink themselves down, as we know, by means of the πάθη and death, into corporeality, indeed, into time itself. The human soul was a spiritual and living synthesis of this ever-shifting diversity, but, being herself subject to the aeon, she was not able definitively to dominate the temporal domain. Dying at every moment on account of time,[37] she was not fit to dominate death. What was necessary was divine power itself, supremely free of all constraint, in order to realize this radical healing through a truly supernatural synthesis:

> Since man is a twofold being, and divine nature by contrast is simple and without composition, it follows that, while the soul is separated from the body in death, the indivisible does not, for all that, follow the soul. On the contrary, by the very unity of the divine nature, which is found equally united to the two parts, the divided can once again be united. Thus death is effected by the division of the united parts, and resurrection by the union of the divided parts.[38]

The important thing, therefore, is that this death should be an expression of the very freedom of Christ,[39] that his mystical immola-

---

[31] *De virg.* III, 372 B.
[32] *In Pascha* 1; III, 604 C; cf. 617 A: "It was God who transformed the whole man."
[33] *In Pascha* 1; 609 B.
[34] *Or. cat.* 13; II, 45 D.
[35] Ibid. 26; II, 69 B.
[36] Ibid., 69 C, and the very formal text of the third Letter (III, 1020 D–21 B).
[37] *De mortuis* III, 521 AB.
[38] *In Pascha* 1; III, 17 B.
[39] "Voluntarily" (ἑκουσίως): ibid., A.

tion should be achieved before his real immolation. This is indeed the meaning of the Last Supper: Christ "anticipates in its economy . . . the unjust judgment of Pilate, in a mode of sacrifice that is secret and invisible to men. . . . How is that? In giving to his apostles his flesh as food and his blood as drink. . . . In accomplishing this, his body was already secretly immolated."[40]

We see, parenthetically, the capital role (and a role very different from that in Origen) that eucharistic communion is going to play in the work of Gregory. This role is entirely based on his idea of human nature. The entry of Christ into this nature, the diffusion of divine grace through the whole body of humanity, constitutes in itself alone already a kind of ontological communion, which has only a remote likeness to the communion of Origen, which is also ontological, but purely spiritual and much more individual.[41] For Gregory, ontological communion happens through the sameness of human nature:

> God the Only Begotten himself revived [individual] man, with whom he had mingled himself, by dividing the body from the soul and then uniting them again. And in this manner the universal salvation of nature is accomplished. Thus he is also called the author of life . . . , for he has saved us by that blood that is akin to ours [διὰ τοῦ συγγενοῦς ἡμῶν αἵματος], he has, indeed, saved all of us who are in communion with him through the identity of flesh and blood [πάντας τοὺς κεκοινωνηκότας αὐτῷ τῆς σαρκὸς καὶ τοῦ αἵματος].[42]

This is an ontological communion, of which the sacrament will merely be the efficacious sign, but a communion that is essentially corporeal as much as spiritual. The place where intimate communication is effected is "nature", not the "spirit". It is therefore quite as much the body as the soul. When the Divinity immolates the two parts of man by separating them, it is precisely to the body that the more immediate role of *contact* falls, whereas the soul instead has the role of acquiescing to the divine will: θέλων μὲν διὰ τῆς ψυχῆς, ἐφαπτόμενος δὲ διὰ τοῦ σώματος.[43] Hence we find that apparent dualism introduced by Gregory into the doctrine of the Eucharist. As for spiritual nourishment,

---

[40] *In Pascha* 1; III, 612 CD.
[41] Compare our study on Origen's *Mysterion* in *Recherches de science religieuse*, 1936, 548ff.
[42] *C. Apollin.* II, 1156 D.
[43] *C. Eunom.* 2; II, 548 CD; cf. *In Pascha* 1; III, 616 C: "For the body . . . through touch . . . but the soul by that mighty will . . . the soul makes an act of the will and the body [is touched]."

he accepts in full Origen's idea.[44] Only "how would an incorporeal thing become nourishment for the body?"[45] The body also demands its "eternal nourishment" through a "participation in and a mingling with the Savior [μετουσίᾳ τε καὶ ἀνακράσει τοῦ σώζοντος]".[46] In a celebrated chapter of his *Great Catechesis*, Gregory describes this assimilation for us. But has he not, in this doctrine, brought together in an overly exterior way two incompatible conceptions of communion? Is sacramental communion not reduced to a purely corporeal effect? No, for this sacrament is precisely the sacrament of the union of body and soul through a separating immolation and thereby the sacrament of primitive wholeness. The Hebrews, during their mystical journey across the desert, continue to be purified of all their attachments to earthly things in order to become worthy of the manna,

> in order to receive nourishment from on high in a totally pure soul, this manna that no sowing or agriculture produced for us. . . . You recognize this true nourishment that is denoted beneath the historical enigma, you know that this bread come down from heaven is not an incorporeal thing. . . . Except the substance of this bread has been harvested without laboring and without sowing: the earth, even while it remains intact, finds itself full of this divine nourishment . . . , a miracle that reveals to us in advance the mystery of the Virgin.[47]

Thus we see that the redemption as the restitution of the entire, intact man (ὁ ὄντως ἄνθρωπος) is joined together with the Eucharist: Christ in his entirety, flesh and soul, is the bread of life.[48] The most striking proof of this is the idea Gregory conceives of the glorious Christ, whose whole humanity is, as it were, absorbed by divine unity. And it is with this Christ that we are in contact, since the Lord prohibits Mary Magdalen from touching him before he has ascended into heaven: "But when I shall have ascended to my Father, it is then that you will be able to touch me [τότε σοι ἔξεστιν ἅπτεσθαι]."[49] To this contact there corresponds on the part of Christ the action of unification, which Gregory describes, according to the Gospel (John 12:32),

---

[44] *Or. cat.* 37; II, 92 D, and many analogous passages.
[45] *Vit. Moys.* I, 368 C.
[46] *Or. cat.* 37; II, 93 A.
[47] *Vit. Moys.* I, 368 C.
[48] *In diem nat. Chr.*, III, 1144.
[49] *In Pascha* 1; III, 625 D (cf. 2; 640 AB).

as attraction[50] and in that way as the centralization[51] and crystalliza-
tion of all of nature around the Mediator.

There are thus two times, as it were, in this work of redemption.
There is a first, which is the contact, through the taking on of manhood, with the indivisible unity of nature: "The Word . . . , in taking
on flesh, involved himself with man and took on himself our nature
in its entirety [πᾶσαν ἐν ἑαυτῷ τὴν ἡμετέραν φύσιν δεξάμενος], so that
the human might be divinized by this involvement with God [ἵνα
τῇ πρὸς τὸ θεῖον ἀνακράσει συναποθεωθῇ τὸ ἀνθρώπινον], the stuff
of our nature being cosanctified in its entirety by these first fruits
[συναγιαζομένου]."[52] The Incarnation is in itself like a taking possession of all humanity, both juridically and ontologically. If evil seems
not to have disappeared yet, the same principle applies here as with
the death of a serpent: Christ, "slayer of the serpent . . . , has cut off
its head . . . without paying any more attention to the rest of its body.
He has permitted these contractions of a beast that is already dead in
order to give those who would come after him the opportunity to
exert themselves."[53] "Once the head is separated from the body, it is
already potentially dead [τῇ μὲν δυνάμει ἤδη νεκρός ἐστι]."[54] It is no
more than a question of time (ἐπειδὰν δὲ παρέλθῃ ὁ χρόνος) before the
death of this serpent is made manifest. This is yet the period of time
that finishes the interior work of the mystical leaven, such as Gregory
describes it to us in his beautiful treatise entitled *In illud: Tunc ipse
Filius subjicietur.* "When good will be widespread everywhere, then
the whole body will be subject to vivifying power, and thus such
a submission of this body will be called the submission of the Son
himself, who can only be at one with his own body, which is the
Church. . . . Then Christ will cease building himself up . . . , then
all of creation will be none other than one single body."[55]

---

[50] "He drew together along with himself . . . all that is kin . . . and all that is of the same
stock" (*De perf. Christ. forma* III, 280 A); ". . . so that through him he drew to himself everything that is of like kind . . . and he attracted all of creation in which man had a share
through the flesh that is mingled with man's flesh" (*In Pascha* 1; III, 628 A). *C. Eunom.*, II,
889 C: "he drew together with himself" (συνεφειλκύσατο). This is the word that had served
to designate the active power of the eye (Part Two).

[51] Gregory recurs to Plotinus' image of the "leader" (κορυφαῖος): *In Eccles.* 2; I, 636 C.

[52] *C. Apollin.*, II, 1152 C; cf. *C. Eunom.* 4; II, 637: "co-sanctifying the whole mass".

[53] *In diem nat. Chr.* III, 1133 A.

[54] Ibid., B.

[55] *In illud* I, 1317 AB, C, 1320 A; the slow expansion of grace should follow the creature's

If, in itself, this eschatology is merely a repetition of Origen,[56] it nonetheless draws a profound originality from its philosophical base, since nature and its unity postulate such an eschatology much more rigorously than in Origen's system. According to Gregory, as we know, there is in the order of nature only one man, but in several persons.[57] He is the lost sheep: "The Savior takes him wholly on his shoulders . . . , for having been utterly led astray, he is utterly taken back."[58] This inference from the restoration of a member of "man" to the restoration of his totality (τῇ γὰρ μερικῇ ἀποδείξει καὶ τὸ καθόλου συναποδείκνυται) seems for him to have the force of a syllogism: συλ-λογιστικῶς συναναγκάσας.[59] It receives its rigorous character through its comparison of Christ with the primitive man in paradise, the ideal Adam.

Indeed, we must remember here the whole doctrine that has been enunciated concerning the primitive state and the fall. If this state has never been realized in an individual man, but if right from the beginning sexual generation, an efficacious sign and a "sacrament" of sin, has had a place in humanity, we understand why Gregory can with so much force lay claim to the title of Πρωτότοκος πάσης τῆς κτίσεως (First-born of all creation) for the humanity of Christ.[60] He is indeed the first and the only one (πρῶτος καὶ μόνος) of all men who has realized in himself the mode of birth that is ontologically antecedent to sin.[61] If, therefore, for profound reasons that touch on the economy of salvation, he was obliged not to appear as the first man on

---

diastema. Gregory expressly puts this becoming of the new creation in parallel with that of the first creation: *In Pascha* 1; III, 609 D. The aeon enters into the service of him who "reigns over the aeons": ibid., 613 CD. On this rests the idea of tradition (*C. Eunom.* 4; II, 654 B) and the evolution of dogma, which is part of the economy of salvation (*De Spir. Sancto* III, 696 B–697 B). After the revelation of the Father (Old Testament), the Son was shown to us by the Gospel: "And finally we receive the perfect nourishment of our nature, the Holy Spirit, in whom there is life." As for that life that saves us ("for that which saves us is life-creating power"), which is God in his entirety (ibid., 697 A), it is the vigor of this life that is diffused through the members of Christ: "life-creating authoritative power" (I, 1317 A). "The distribution of the glory of the Spirit over all that is of like kind comes to pass" (*In Cant. h.* 15; I, 1117 B).

[56] *In Lev.* 7; Baehrens 6:370–80.

[57] *De comm. not.* II, 177 Bff.

[58] *C. Apollin.* II, 1153 A.

[59] *In illud* I, 1312 CD. Cf. *De hom. op.* 25; I, 216 D.

[60] *C. Eunom.* 4; II, 633 C–640 A.

[61] Ibid., 636 D. *De Occ. Dn.* III, 1157 BC.

earth,[62] he is even so, in spite of this, by the manner of his coming, really the first man: "There are three generations by which human nature finds itself vivified. The first is according to the body, the second according to the mystery of regeneration, and lastly, the third, according to the resurrection of the dead for which we hope. And, in terms of all three, Christ is the first-born."[63] In terms of the first generation, he is such by his virginal birth; in terms of the second, by his baptism in the Jordan ("he himself introduced this kind of birth [τόκος] by his own baptism, in drawing down the Holy Spirit over the water"),[64] in terms of the third, by his Resurrection. The name Πρωτότοκος is thus applied to both his natural generation and his supernatural generation, "so that Christ may reign over the dead no less than the living".[65] "He took our sinful nature"[66] in order to render "our own nature upright [τὸ ἄμωμον τῆς ἀνθρωπίνης φύσεως]"[67] and "perfect"[68] from the imperfect (ἀτελεῖς ἐν τῷ λόγῳ τῆς φύσεως)[69] and abortive[70] state that it was in up to that point. By him alone men become true sons of God,[71] at once perfecting and surpassing their nature.[72]

But while Christ as the first *real* and perfect man remains posterior to "ideal", perfect "Nature", of which he is only one part, a secret kinship of these two perfections tends to introduce the priority of Christ into the priority of Nature itself. We know already in fact that the unity of the latter is ἀδιαστάτως (continuously) that of the beginning and purpose (or "end" [τέλος] of humanity and thus is governed quite as much by teleological considerations (προγνωστικὴ δύναμις) as by the order of time's passing. Besides, we were saying that these considerations were lifting the unity of Nature (by the very implication of real becoming) above and beyond the categories of the

---

[62] *In diem nat. Chr.* III, 1129 B–1133 C.

[63] *C. Eunom.* 4; II, 336 CD.

[64] Ibid. 2; II, 501 C.

[65] Ibid., 4; II, 657 B.

[66] "Bringing under his aegis our sinful nature" (*Vit. Moys.* I, 336 B).

[67] *In Pascha* 2; III, 640 BC. Cf. *In diem nat. Chr.* III, 1136 B.

[68] *De Occ. Dn.* III, 1152 BC.

[69] *In Ps.* 15; I, 596 B.

[70] "Having been aborted through evil" (ibid.).

[71] *In Pascha* 2; III, 640 B.

[72] "So that they become sons, while their nature remains principally within its own boundaries" (*C. Eunom.* 3; II, 608 A).

real and the ideal. In this sense, it goes without saying that Christ, from the point of view of the real becoming engendered by Nature, achieves, by the fact that he becomes the center of Nature, a (real and ideal) superiority over it: "He is that tall palm that has shot up in the middle of the forest of our nature, but he becomes in his turn a mountain on which cedars shoot up, cedars that, through faith, sink their roots into him."[73]

It is not by chance that Christ should appear to Magdalen in the guise of a gardener. Nor is it any less by chance that in the Song of Songs he descends into the garden of the bride: "By the symbol of the garden, we learn that the true gardener cultivates anew his own garden, which is none other than us men. . . . Since, to be sure, it is he who, in the beginning, had cultivated human nature in paradise, that nature planted by the heavenly Father. It must have been he, too, who, when a savage beast had ravaged our garden and ruined what had been planted by God, descended in order to reestablish the devastated garden."[74] This great body *of which* Christ is merely a member becomes in its entirety the body *of* this member. The entire batter is leavened again by his holiness: ὅλον ὥσπερ ἀναζυμώσας εἰς ἁγιασμὸν τῆς ἀνθρωπίνης οὐσίας τὸ σύνκριμα.[75] There is a word that recurs constantly in the work of Gregory, when it is a question either of paradise or of the Incarnation: φιλανθρωπία, love of men.[76] It joins together in a symbolic way those two unique moments in the economy of salvation. Through Christ we are "regenerated to our ancient make-up",[77] "we return to our true homeland, the heavenly Jerusalem."[78]

This replacement of "Nature" by Christ finds a moving expression in the sermons on the poor. The first great cause for mercy is in fact our common nature.

> Do not consider all goods as belonging to you personally. Let a portion be given to the destitute and to the friends of God! Everything belongs to God, our common Father. As for us, we are brothers because we are

---

[73] *In Cant.* 14; I, 1081 C.

[74] Ibid. 15; I, 1092 C.

[75] *De Occ. Dn.* III, 1165 B.

[76] *In Ps.* 15; I, 596 BC; *C. Eunom.* 4; II, 637 C; *C. Eunom.* 12; II, 889 B; *In Pascha* 3; III, 661 C.

[77] *In Pascha* 3; III, 661 D: "to restore to its ancient make-up".

[78] "Let us return to our true homeland, the heavenly Jerusalem" (*In Occ. Dn.* III, 1181).

of the same stock [ὡς ὁμόφυλοι]. . . .[79] Are you, who have the same nature as this sick man, fleeing someone who springs from the same stock
as you [τὸν ὁμογενῆ]? My brother, let this odious decision not prevail
over you! Recognize who you are and about whom you are musing,
recognize that you, a man, are considering men, you, who have received
nothing privately outside of our commonly shared nature. . . . Like all
the others, you participate in that nature. Let it be a question of something held in common, as it were [ὡς ὑπὲρ κοινοῦ τοῦ πράγματος ὁ λόγος
ἔστω].[80]

And it is well known what vigorous emphases Gregory is capable of
drawing from his philosophy when he comes to speak of slavery.

> As for him who is made in the likeness of God, who holds dominion
> over the whole earth . . . , who, tell me, will buy him, who will sell
> him? . . . Where, then, are the titles by which you claim superiority?
> . . . Neither time nor any privilege gives them to you. You were born
> of one same source, your lives resemble one another, the same passions
> of soul and body dominate you both, both you who make yourself out
> to be the master and he who is under the yoke of your domination:
> tears and self-assurance, joys and sorrows, pain and pleasure, anger and
> fear, sickness and death. . . . Do they not breathe the same air, do they
> not look on the same sun . . . will they not end up as the same bit of
> dust after death? Is their judgment not the same? Will they not share a
> common kingdom or a common hell?[81]

But all this does not constitute the ultimate argument, for it is in
this way, through the countenance of the poor man, that the countenance of Christ becomes transparent: "Consider who they are, and
you will discover their value. They have taken on the countenance
[πρόσωπον] of our Savior."[82] "Stranger, naked, hungry, sick, and in
prison—all that is said in the Gospel is for you. . . . You can make
the Lord your debtor in all things, if you want to show yourself
as humane toward this man. Why then struggle against your own
life?"[83]

The poor take shelter "behind the image of the king in order to turn

---

[79] *De paup. amand.* 1; III, 465 B.
[80] Ibid. 2; III, 476 CD.
[81] *In Eccles.* 4; I, 665 A–668 A.
[82] *De paup. amand.* 1; III, 460 B.
[83] Ibid. 2; III, 484 AB.

aside the attacks of persecutors".[84] Thus they lead the procession of all humanity. In order to appropriate its new "nature", transformed as it is by Christ (μεταστοιχείωσις),[85] humanity must become conscious of its new center and effect in him and through him that supreme synthesis of death and life. Just as Christ saved the world by that divine power that had, in its unity, endured the rupture between body and soul,[86] thus the Christian should, by his supernatural assimilation to Christ, cooperate in this synthesis, while enduring the same death: "For this reason we die the same death with him who died for us. And I am not speaking of that mortal death that is common to our nature, for it comes to us without our wishing it. Rather I am speaking of the fact that it is necessary that we ourselves of our own free will [θέλοντας] should die with him who died voluntarily [ἑκουσίως]. . . . For that which occurs under constraint cannot be called an imitation of what is done freely."[87]

It would seem at first glance that, according to Gregory, the work of Christ on its own has already attained everything. For he compares death, which is common to all of nature, to a stem that has been broken into two pieces. Christ has through his own humanity reestablished unity, "and this unity has, through the Resurrection and because of the continuity of human nature [πᾶσαν κατὰ τὸ συνεχὲς τὴν ἀνθρωπίνην φύσιν], effected the link with the whole of this nature."[88] By the union of the two extremes, the whole finds itself unified. However, this image loses sight of the fact that each man must pass individually through death. But since Christ has placed himself at that "frontier between the two, death and life [αὐτοῖς γένοιτο μεθόριον ἀμφοτέρων θανάτου τε καὶ ζωῆς]",[89] the Christian should himself pass away by way of Christ, through his attitude of free acceptance: "The Resurrection would not have efficacy, if it were not preceded by a

[84] Ibid. 1; III, 460 C.
[85] Vit. Moys. I, 336 A.
[86] C. Apollin. II, 1253 C–1206; cf. In Pascha 1; III, 613 C–616 C. In the work of Macarius the Egyptian, the mysterious power of divinity that holds together the separated body and soul becomes a mystical fire that at once effects resurrection and transfiguration (Homiliæ II, 4).
[87] C. Apollin. II, 1260 B.
[88] Ibid., A; cf. Or. cat. 32; II, 80 BC: "The resurrection of the part passes through to the whole in accordance with the continuity and unity of nature."
[89] Or. cat., 16; II, 52 D.

voluntary death.''[90] "Man cannot arrive at life except along the path of death.''[91] This death is understood above all as being like baptism,[92] the "commencement and cause of resurrection''.[93] But baptism is still only a symbolic death: "The need is for the person who is engaging in this imitation of Christ to go the whole way to complete death and not merely to an imitation of Christ's death, so that our act of dying might come to coincide with Christ's act [ταυτότης . . . ἦν] and evil might be eliminated completely from our nature.''[94] Baptism is merely the foundation (ἀρχὴ τε καὶ ὑπόθεσις) and the introduction (ἐντὸς τοῦ θείου γενέσθαι χοροῦ)[95] to that death which is the work of our whole lifetime and which ought to become more and more complete in us.[96]

If we suppose, in fact, that death is not the sole consequence of sin, but that our whole animal structure coheres with sin in a mysterious manner, the necessity of a voluntary death seems even more striking. There is in us an internal contradiction that we must go beyond. It constitutes the twofold natural movement of our being (ἐξ ἐναντίου τοίνυν γινομένης αὐτοῖς φυσικῶς τῆς κινήσεως . . .).[97] It can be resolved only by an attenuation (ἀτονία), by the mortification of one of these tendencies, so that the soul possesses her death within the confines of her very own nature. Death is none other than the secret contradiction at the heart of this nature: "Thus, therefore, we live by means of death, so that the Word, of whom it is said, 'It is I who kill and who vivify', kills one part of ourselves and vivifies another. . . . And if the soul does not die, she remains dead forever and incapable of receiving life. By the very action of dying, she enters into life.''[98]

Here the immense symbol of the Cross stands before Gregory's

---

[90] *In Cant.* 12; I, 1016 D.

[91] Ibid., 1017 C.

[92] Ibid., 1016 D; *C. Apollin.* II, 1260 BC; *Or. cat.* 35; II, 85 D–92 C.

[93] "Commencement and cause" (ἀρχὰς καὶ αἰτίας): *Or. cat.* 35; II, 92 A (Gregory specifies that it is a question of a glorious resurrection, since he considers resurrection as such to be a natural fact, just like the rebirth of seed). Baptism is a birth: *Or. cat.* 33; II, 84; cf. *In Cant.* 8; I, 944 B, D.

[94] *Or. cat.* 33; II, 89 B.

[95] Ibid. 34; II, 92 CD.

[96] *In Cant.* 12; I, 1017 B.

[97] Ibid. 12; I, 1017 C.

[98] Ibid., 1020 AB.

gaze, the Cross, which, with its four arms, embraces the universe in order to center it around the divine, redemptive action, a symbol to which he loves to return.[99] But it is in this center that man himself is also nailed and, as it were, "immobilized" (ἀκίνητον) with his Savior.[100] It is here that he enters into the spirit and vocation of Christ. He becomes a "priest" of his own life,[101] by the very fact of being with Christ on the Cross.[102] Finally he becomes a mediator, as together with God he distributes graces and intercedes for those who are like him (τοῖς ὁμογενέσι).[103] And just as Christ by his death had become "the limit [μεθόριος] of death and of life", the Christian, when he in turn places himself on this frontier,[104] becomes "in a certain manner the limit [μεθόριος] between mobile nature and immutable nature. He makes the transition between the two poles [μεσιτεύει καταλλήλως τοῖς ἄκροις]".[105] But it goes without saying that all this mediation is possible only in Christ, "who has sanctified the totality of our nature and who has rendered it capable of being offered to God".[106] It is he who "distributes to all those who wish it the common grace of the priesthood".[107]

We can now summarize this whole study by means of three assertions: (1) The immediate communication between God and creature, impossible though it be on the level of the individual, is rendered accessible by the fact that in the Incarnation God and creature make up only one Person. (2) This fact is a social fact. The place where it is realized is common "Nature", which is made central by the God-Man.

---

[99] *C. Eunom.* 5; II, 695 B; *Or. cat.* 32; II, 80 C–81 D; *In Pascha* 1; III, 621 C–624 C. Gregory says that he received this symbolism through tradition (II, 80 C). It is already recognizable in a fragment from Origen (*In Ephes.*, edited by Gregg in *The Journal of Theological Studies* 3, [1903]: 411–12). Gregory parallels it with Eph 3:18–19, which will end up being the point of departure for the brilliant interpretation of Saint Augustine: *Epist.* 140, 64; PL 33, 566; *Serm.* 53, 15; PL 38, 371; *Serm.* 165, 3; PL 38, 903–4.

[100] *Vit. Moys.* I, 413 D.

[101] *Or. dom.* 3; I, 1149 CD.

[102] Ibid., 388 D; *De virg.* 24; III, 413 C–416 B. Cf. *In St. Steph.* III, 712 A. Gregory considers that Christ himself is also a "sacerdos in æternum" inasmuch as he is a man: *C. Eunom.* 6; II, 718 BC.

[103] *Vit. Moys.* I, 332 BC. *In Ps.* 7; I, 457 CD.

[104] "The one who comes to be in the middle between the two ways of life mediates between these two ways of life" (*In Cant.* 12; I, 1024 D).

[105] *In Ps.* 7; I, 457 B.

[106] *De Occ. Dn.* III, 1168 B.

[107] *Or. dom.* 3; I, 1149 A.

(3) But the invasion of nature by grace is a dynamism that requires a free assimilation on the part of man to the death of the Redeemer.

Since the "place" or "field of play" of the Incarnation is Nature, and since Nature is transformed by the Incarnation into the Mystical Body of Christ, the "place" of this individual assimilation can be none other than the *Church*. The Bride of the Song of Songs, who is a figure, in the first place, of the individual soul, is revealed at the end of the commentary as being a unity of all these individual souls in "the unique one, the dove, the perfect one",[108] the body of Christ and thereby Christ himself: "He who, from the state of being a little child, grows to perfect manhood and who, arriving at the full measure of age and maturity, is the son, no longer of the maidservant and the concubine, but of the queen . . . , this son, indeed, is the perfect dove whom the bridegroom regards when he says: There is only one who is my dove."[109]

Yet this unity is essentially eschatological.[110] It is to this unity that souls *tend* under the figurative guise, in the Song of Songs, of young girls, concubines, and queens. All of them sing the praises of the one and only, "for only one course toward this blessed state is proposed to souls of every degree". "Thus when the virgins bless the Dove, they express the fact that by all manner of means they themselves desire to become doves . . . , they show that their ardor pushes them toward the object of their praise, to the point, indeed, that they all become one."[111] Not that the Church does not exist before this is achieved, for it is the Church who throughout the Song of Songs teaches souls to see Christ. But just as Christ's possession of a common nature retains a "juridical" aspect (but a *jus ad rem* that does not exclude— which rather presupposes—an ontological and "physical" relationship through the "continuity" of nature), so the distance that separates the vision of Christ possessed by souls from that enjoyed by the Church lends an "abstract" character to the Church's teaching, since souls are not yet able to see things as the Church does.[112]

But here there reappears (and it is a sign that we are on the right track) the whole dynamism of the "philosophy of desire" and of "im-

[108] *In Cant.* 15; I, 1117 B–C.
[109] Ibid., B.
[110] Cf. *In illud* I, 1320 A.
[111] *In Cant.* 15; I, 1117 CD.
[112] Ibid. 13; I, 1048 D, 1049 B.

age". Ecclesiology is nothing but its resumption on a higher plane. The paradox seems to be even more accentuated. To souls that are desirous of being assimilated to the eternal Word, the Bride shows a way that has the appearance of being opposite: precisely that of assimilation to the death and kenosis of Christ: "Since all the other qualities we perceive in God transcend the measure [μέτρον] of human nature, but since humility and humiliation are innate, as it were, and connatural to us, who crawl on this earth, who draw our substance from it and who sink back into it, begin, therefore, to imitate God in whatever responds to your nature and in anything of God's that it is fitting that you should imitate. In this way you will dress yourself with the form of beatitude."[113] It is thus the humbled Christ, veiled by flesh, whom the Bride teaches souls to see. Is this not an instance of an even more obscure mirror than even the mirror of desire and of image? Let us be careful here! Gregory does not linger on the individual flesh of the Savior. What the Bride shows souls is ever and from the beginning the mystical flesh of Christ. In this flesh, "the constitution of the world of the Church, God's Invisible One is contemplated intellectually in his work. The constitution of the Church is in fact the creation of a world . . . , and whoever contemplates this new world, contemplates in it Him who *is* and *becomes* all in all in it. By belief in things that are accessible and comprehensible to us, we find ourselves guided toward the knowledge [γνῶσις] of inaccessible things."[114] Assimilation to the Church and her teaching [γνῶσις] by faith is therefore none other than the edification of the Mystical Body of Christ himself, its growth, its intimate life: "If, then, someone looks toward the Church, he sees immediately [ἄντικρυς] and without differentiation Christ, who, by admitting his saved members, is edified and increases in glory [μεγαλύνοντα]."[115]

"The beginning of its teaching is therefore something that is near and familiar to us. It is from this body that catechesis takes its rise."[116] The young girls learn to desire the bridegroom, to run after his fragrance.[117] But the veil of this "new world", which vaguely reveals to them the forms of the beloved object, is no longer the same as that

---

[113] *De beat.* 1; I, 1200 D.
[114] *In Cant.* 13; I, 1049 B–1052 A.
[115] Ibid., 1048 C.
[116] Ibid., 1052 B.
[117] Ibid. 1; I, 784 BD.

thick veil of the first creation. This new veil is itself a part of the object. It is his body. And the love that inflames them is no longer a desire that is eternally opposed to the object. It is the very substance of this body: "His crown is the Church, for on all sides she encircles his head with living stones. It is love that has fashioned this crown. She can be called Mother or Love. It comes to the same thing, for God is Love."[118] The veil that the soul puts on is Christ himself.[119] But Christ (as Severus of Antioch explains, inspired no doubt by Gregory) has left behind him the shroud of death. He is risen without any clothes, "which shows the restoration of Adam to his primitive state, for he was naked in paradise and was not embarrassed."[120] According to Gregory, the soul, in casting off her garments one by one, imitates Christ.[121] Only this divine nakedness with which the soul is presently endowed does not, for all that, cause her to abandon her own proper substance. Here again, it remains true that "the creature will always see itself." The progress that has been accomplished consists rather in the fact that *her* love, which permits her to see Christ, has become identical to the love of Christ for her. "*Se dicit sponsum, se sponsam* [he calls himself bridegroom and bride]", Saint Augustine will assert, summarizing magnificently what Gregory had said about the Dove. *Amabile in actu est amor in actu* (actual love is actually lovable), one may say, in imitation of the scholastic adage concerning intelligence.

What this presupposes is that this love remains quite entirely movement, becoming. Indeed, Gregory presented the genesis of the Church to us as an essentially dynamic process. On the one hand, the members of the Church are incorporated by their very tendency to love. On the other hand, the Church herself grows and is made perfect by her teaching, which is a perpetual act of love and imitation of Christ.[122] Thus, the view of the Church, to which souls are moving in order to be assimilated, is not itself a stable possession. The "nuptial bed" where "divine nature and human nature are mingled" is, according to the Song of Songs, "shaded".[123] The love in which the Church

---

[118] Ibid. 7; I, 916 D.

[119] Ibid. 1; I, 764 D; 11; I, 1005 A.

[120] *In Pascha* 2 (Severus of Antioch); III, 637 B.

[121] See above, Part Two.

[122] *In Cant.* 7; I, 917 B: "having approached God through love for neighbor".

[123] Ibid. 4; I, 836 C.

initiates souls is the love of this God "who does not respond to any
appeal, who is not reached by any particular course". And if souls beg
the Church, saying, "Lift the veil from our eyes, just as the wardens
of the town lifted it from you",[124] they still do not know that the
veil that had fallen from the eyes of the Church was none other than
the recognition of God's incomprehensibility.[125] Thus, true initiation
is merely participation in the gaze of the Church, in the good and
laudable direction of this gaze, which alone meets the gaze of the
Bridegroom: ὅπου δὲ ἀποβλέπει διδαχθεῖσαι, οὕτω στήσωσιν ἑαυτάς.[126]
It is for this reason also that the lips of the mystical Christ, which
is to say, the words of the Church, are called "pure desire" by the
Song of Songs.[127] "It is the very definition, as it were, of the Church's
beauty." Therein lies the true meaning of the "tradition of grace",[128]
which remains an "ineffable tradition [ἄῤῥητος διάδοσις]".[129]

By way of this love, the Church is substituted at last for the image
of God, which is, as we know, spiritual human nature, just as Christ
was substituted for this nature as the second Adam. Thus the Church
becomes the "truth" of the image just as she was the "truth" of desire. She is this truth in so absolute a way that the angels themselves,
as Saint Paul attests, have received a new revelation of God through
her.

> Through the Church, indeed, the celestial powers have learned to know
> the many-colored wisdom of God, who realizes his great miracles by
> things that are opposites. How then has life arisen from death? Justice
> from sin? Blessing from a curse, glory from shame, strength from weak-
> ness? For, up to that time, the celestial powers had known only a simple
> and uniform divine wisdom. . . . As for this new form, this many-colored
> wisdom, it is only now at the present time that it has been revealed to
> them by the Church, so that they might know how the Word became
> flesh, how life is mingled with death . . . , how the invisible becomes
> visible. . . . If, then, the Church is the body of Christ, and Christ is the
> head of the body, shaping the countenance of the Church according to
> his own expressive features, it is possible that the friends of the Bride-

---

[124] Ibid. 13; I, 1045 A.
[125] Ibid. 12; I, 1037 BC.
[126] Ibid. 15; I, 1092 A.
[127] Ibid. 14; I, 1084 CD.
[128] Ibid. 1; I, 785 B.
[129] Ibid., C.

groom, in contemplating the Church, may see the Invisible One in a more penetrating way.[130]

These oppositions, indeed, contradictions, which constitute the form of the Church, place the Church once more at that precise point where Christ himself was placed and where each Christian in his turn was bound to follow him: the "limit", the μεθόριον. The Church, in being the "limit" between death and life, glory and ignominy, God and the world, is thereby the very point of contact between opposites and therefore the true mediatrix. She is the truth of the image, the window through which the flood tide of divine life penetrates into the creature.

---

[130] Ibid. 8; I, 948 C–949 B.

2

TRANSPOSITION OF BECOMING

This is the immense revelation that has been granted to us by the Incarnation: God is Life. Most certainly he had appeared to us, from the time our desire had its first awakening, as that Ocean of Being that our thought would never be in a position to capture. His own life, his pure infinity, his repose, his light, would never be our life, which would eternally remain a life of movement, of struggle, and of desire. We believed that becoming and Being were opposites, two forms, as it were, analogous without a doubt, but irreducible. Through the Incarnation we learn that all the unsatisfied movement of becoming is itself only repose and fixity when compared to that immense movement of love inside of God: Being is a Super-Becoming. In constantly surpassing ourselves, therefore, by means of our love, we assimilate ourselves to God much more intimately than we could have suspected.

In order to understand love, it was necessary for our desire to become love. But our desire could become love only through the initiative of divine love. Indeed, knowledge through desire could only grasp in God his very incomprehensibility. This knowledge turned on this paradoxical limit: to understand is not to understand God (to know that the object is ungraspable); not to understand is to understand God (in the self-negation of the intellect, to grasp the object). The impenetrability of the object stimulated the intellect to be broken and to fail constantly, again and again, when ranged against it. Only one thing was necessary to substitute the quiet movement of love for this movement, broken and irregular like flashes of lightning that succeed each other: that incomprehensibility, while remaining ungraspable, should be clarified, so to speak, by what is within, that it should be revealed. There is only a shade of difference between the two movements, for it is no more a matter of understanding afterward than before. But while, beforehand, we were incapable of reflecting on this incomprehensibility, at present we cannot grow weary as we cast our gaze toward it. It is the *miracle* par excellence. It is as if God had become liquid: "Christ was, as the Apostle says, the rocky crag, barren and very hard for unbelievers. But for those who approach the authority of faith, he becomes a drink for their thirst and flows forth [εἰσρέων] into them."[1] For faith gives us a sense of the *positive quality* that incomprehensibility represents. It is no longer only the perfection, understood abstractly, of being ungraspable as a free person, but what is more, the perfection, seen concretely, of being able freely to reveal this freedom. This revelation then produces in the contemplating being that kind of dazzlement and ecstasy that comes, no longer from the transcendence of desire with respect to representation, but from the transcendence of the object, which appears as such through the revelation:

> Never does sight amount to a vision of the object such as our eyes have reproduced it in the soul. But these eyes of ours are always busy looking, as if they had not yet begun to see, and we are always in a state of ignorance about what our senses have perceived. Sight cannot plumb the depths of color. It derives its field of play from what is presented to it [προφαινόμενον] on the surface of things. This is why it is said: The eye will not be satiated with sight, and the ear will not be filled with hearing. For hearing as well is incapable of being filled to satisfaction as it receives all its words.[2]

The image is good. It does not, however, suffice. Even in just revealing its "surface", the object should cause its "depths" to be seen. Here is a more perfect image:

> Let us suppose that someone is standing up, close to a wellspring . . . , he will admire [θαυμάσει] that endless [ἄπειρον] gush of water that is always rising from within and spilling out. He will never say, though, that he has seen the water entirely. For how could he see that which is still hidden in the bosom of the earth? And even if he remained a very long time beside these bubbling waters, he would always be at the outset of his view of the water. For the water never becomes weary of flowing, and it is constantly beginning to gush forth again. The same applies to the one who looks toward this divine and infinite beauty. Since what he finds at each moment is always newer and more paradoxical [καινότερόν

---

[1] *Vit. Moys.* I, 368 A.
[2] *In Eccles.* 1; I, 632 CD.

τε καὶ παραδοξότερον πάντως] than what his sight had already grasped, he can only admire what at each moment is presented to him [τὸ ἀεί προφαινόμενον]. But his desire to look never tires, for the revelations he awaits will always be more magnificent and more divine than all he has already seen.[3]

The inexhaustible depth of the object appears on its very surface. To the eternal movement of desire there corresponds that of the source. There is no longer an opposition, but one and the same form of Being, Life, unites God and his creature. Thus the creature has found that "chariot of Elijah" that raises him into an inaccessible dimension.[4] Indeed, the creature has no more need "to leave" its "becoming" or its "image", for there is a radical continuity from it to God, who is a Life beyond all spacing: "[God is] not that spaced life that runs from a beginning to an end, since he does not enter into life through the participation of another life, in such a way that it would be necessary to fix a limit and a beginning to the participation. But God is that which he is, a Life that is active in itself, as it were [ἐν αὐτῷ ἐνεργουμένη]."[5] Through this communication of Life, the soul "walks beside God on the heights" (συμμετεωροπορεῖν).[6] In a very mysterious way, the soul's return back into self is now immediately a leaving of self:

"My well-beloved has passed by." It is not that he has forsaken the soul that follows him, but rather he is drawing her to himself. "My soul goes forth toward his word." O happy going forth, in which the soul that follows the Word goes forth! "May the Lord watch over your coming and your going", says the Prophet. It is here that we find, in truth, the coming and the going that God reserves for those who are worthy: our

[3] *In Cant.* 11; I, 1000 AB; cf. Didymus the Blind: "so that he is ever satiated and ever hungering" (PG 39, 1649 C).

[4] This is the image to which Gregory loves to recur in order to indicate the paradox of approaching God: *C. Apollin.*, II, 1177 C; *De beat.* 2; I, 1212 BC; ibid. 6; I, 1272 D–1273 A; *In Cant.* 10; I, 980 C: "If what we hear about Elijah were to happen to our soul, and our understanding, having been taken up by the flaming chariot, were to be lifted high in the air toward the beauties of heaven . . . , our drawing near to these stars, sacred as I say they are, will not occur apart from hope."

[5] *C. Eunom.* 12; II, 933 B. Gregory hesitates, because of this characteristic of infinite life, to apply to God the symbol of a closed circle: *C. Eunom.* 1; II, 456 C.

[6] *In Cant.* 8; I, 945 B. It is this that Philo the Jew could not attain. It would be necessary, said he, to become God himself in order to grasp God (Fragm. Mangey, II, 651).

going beyond the things in which we are situated becomes an entering
into the goods that surpass us. It is thus that the soul goes forth, led
by the Word who says: "I am the Gate and the Way. If anyone enters
by me, he will enter and he will go forth", for he will never weary of
entering and will never rest from going forth. But he will be at rest by
means of an ever-new entry into things that are ever greater.[7]

The ontological "comparative" of the created spirit is now no longer
inferred by the transcendence of God as much as by the immanent
wellspring eternally gushing forth in the spirit:

Just as the wellspring of all goods flows without ever stopping, it follows that the nature that participates in it . . . becomes more capable of
attracting greater goods toward itself and of receiving more of them into
itself. The two increase together: the power nourished by the abundance
of goods grows, and the abundance of nourishing goods is perfected by
the augmented capacity for reception.[8]

The wellspring of all goods always attracts those who have a thirst for
it, as the Source himself explains in the Gospel: If anyone is thirsty, let
him come to me and drink. And in this way the Wellspring allows no
end either to thirst or . . . to the desire to drink. The inexorable rule
eternalizes the invitation to desire it, to drink of it, and to come to it.
Since for those who have already tasted and experienced how gentle the
Lord is, the experience itself serves them as an invitation to more.[9]

This eternal desire of the creature is thus freed from all the distress it
might have found in the (Bergsonian) opposition between "Knowledge" and "Life". The anguish of becoming is identified with the
tranquillity of Being. It is the richness of the divine *Presence* in the
soul and not the abyss between God and the soul that constantly creates that *space* (beyond all spacing)[10] in which love accomplishes its
necessary course:

Once again the Word says to the soul, which has already stood up,
"Arise!", and to the soul that has already come, "Come!" For he who
truly rises can never stop rising, and he who runs toward the Lord will
never have exhausted the great space of this divine journey. . . . Thus

[7] *In Cant.* 12; I, 1024 D–1025 A.
[8] *De an. et res.* III, 105 C.
[9] *In Cant.* 8; I, 941 D–944 A.
[10] See the following paragraph.

each time he repeats the words "Arise!" and "Come!", he confers at the same time the possibility of ascent.[11]

Thus God spoke to Moses: "See, there is room in my house. I am going to place you on a steep rock."

But in saying "room", he does not intend to circumscribe in terms of quantity he is denoting (since there cannot be dimensions of measure in what is not quantitative). . . . Here, rather, is what this word means, it seems to me: since your desire impels you toward what surpasses you and since there is no feeling of disgust to arrest your progress . . . , know, therefore, that in me there is space in such abundance that he who traverses it will never be able to arrest his flight. But this flight, from another point of view, is tranquil rest: "I am going to place you on a steep rock." Here, indeed, is the full measure of the paradox: rest and movement are identical [τὸ αὐτὸ καὶ στάσις ἐστι καὶ κίνησις]. . . . And the more someone becomes firmly established in good and immobilizes himself, the more rapid his flight becomes: rest itself serves him as a pair of wings.[12]

The same mystery is proclaimed by the Song of Songs in the guise of the sealed fountain:

Purity seals this fountain, so that it may be reserved for its Possessor and so that no blemish of troubled thoughts may come to sully and ripple the transparent and ethereal surface of the water of the heart. . . . Here the Bride receives the highest of praise. For whereas everywhere else Holy Scripture applies the image of living water to Vivifying Nature . . . , here it proclaims infallibly that the Bride is "a fountain of living water. . . ." This is truly the summit of paradox. For while all other wells contain their water in tranquil quiet, only the Bride possesses it flowing within herself, so that it has both a well's depth and a river's perpetual movement. Who could properly describe the marvelous work of assimilation accomplished in this way? Perhaps, in truth, there remains nothing more for the Bride to achieve beyond herself, since she has been assimilated in everything, to beauty of the first order. In her minute way, she imitates the Fountain in becoming a fountain, Life in being life, Water in becoming water. The Word of God is alive. So also is the soul that receives this Word in her. And this Water flows from God (for the Fountain itself says: "I emanate from God and I am coming"), and the soul welcomes

---

[11] *In Cant.* 5; I, 876 BC.
[12] *Vit. Moys.* I, 405 BCD.

it as it enters her basin, and the soul thus becomes a reservoir of living Water.[13]

In this text the transposition of becoming within the Eternal appears with the highest possible clarity. The life that is movement is that of God himself. Without leaving herself, the soul possesses this life in the very depths of her heart. This contact is the perfect realization by means of *love* of the first ontological contact worked by the Incarnation and the revelation of God's intimate one. The image of lips in the act of kissing constitutes the expressive image of this contact:

> The fountain is none other than the mouth of the Bridegroom, from which the words of eternal life gush forth, words that fill the mouth that brings them (as the Prophet says: "I opened my mouth and brought the spirit"). Since, then, he who wishes to drink ought to bring his mouth to the fountain, and since the Lord is himself this fountain . . . , the soul that wishes to put her lips to this mouth from which Life springs forth says the following words: "May he kiss me with a kiss from his mouth."[14]

Only, since this mystery of contact is accomplished on the foundations of the Incarnation, and therefore of kenosis, of the death of Christ as well as of the soul, the mouth of the Beloved is none other than the wound of his heart: "I want to run to You, O Fountainhead, and to drink deep drafts of the divine flood that You pour out on those who are thirsty. It is from your side, whose vein the lance opened wide like a mouth, that this water rushes out, transforming him who drinks into a fountain."[15] But the soul, too, in letting herself be struck by the rod of divine authority, imitates the Rock, of which the Prophet said: "He struck the rock and the waters flowed."[16] The "window" by which the soul is able to make her escape and touch God is the wound of crucified love: "I am wounded by love. . . . The Bride, by loving in her turn him who had loved her first, makes show of the arrow of love that found its way right to the center of her heart. This is another way of saying that she participates in his

---

[13] *In Cant.* 9; I, 977 AD. Cf. *De virg.* 7; III, 352 AC.
[14] *In Cant.* 1; I, 780 A.
[15] Ibid. 2; I, 801 B.
[16] Ibid. 12; I, 1036 B.

very divinity. For love, as it is said, is God."[17] In this way everything is confounded, love and sorrow, remoteness and proximity to God, tranquil rest and flight:

> Thus the soul praises the expert bowman who has been able to direct so well his arrow at her. For she says: "I am wounded by love." In this way she demonstrates the nature of this arrow that is fixed in the inmost depths of her heart. The bowman is Love. We have learned from Sacred Scripture that God is Love and that he sends his chosen arrow, his only Son, to those who need to be saved . . . , so that this Love may introduce into the one it pierces the archer himself, together with the arrow—as the Lord says: "The Father and I are one, and we shall come and dwell in him. . ." O lovely wound and gentle injury by which Life penetrates within, forcing its way through the tearing of the arrow, as if it were a door and a passageway! For scarcely does the soul feel herself struck by the arrow of love, when already her wound is transformed into nuptial joy. It is well known how a bowman's hands ply the bow, how they portion out their respective roles. The left hand takes the bow, while the right hand stretches the string toward itself, drawing the arrow with it into the hollowed cavity that is formed. The arrow in its turn is directed toward its target by the left hand. Here suddenly we have the soul, then, who was just now supposing herself to be the target of the arrow, in the hands of the archer, whose right and left hands have gripped her, each in a different way. But since the ideas that follow are expressed in the form of a nuptial song, the object that has been gripped by the left hand is no longer the point of the arrow (whereas the right hand held the rest of the arrow, and the soul was an arrow in the hand of a powerful man, an arrow skillfully directed at the highest of targets); it is under her head and no longer around the arrow that he puts his left hand, while with his right hand he embraces her body. (For thus says the Bride: "His left hand supports my head and his right hand holds me fast.") The Word therefore describes to us the ascent of the soul under a twofold series of symbols. It shows us that our Bridegroom and our Archer are one and the same, and that for him the pure soul is Bride and Arrow. As an Arrow he directs her toward the blessed target. As a Bride he takes her up into intimate communion with incorruptible eternity. . . . Thus she says: His left hand rests under my head and through it the bolt is directed toward the target. Conversely his right hand pulls me toward himself, it draws me to him, it renders me light for my journey toward the heights, me, who, once I am launched toward these heights, do not,

---

[17] Ibid. 13; I, 1044 CD.

for all that, leave the archer. All at once I am launched through space, and at the same time I rest in the hands of the Lord.[18]

On this summit, where all contradictions are resolved, all the audacities of love become possible: the soul thus leaves behind her own nature,[19] she welcomes the Infinite in her finitude, "she lodges that which cannot be sheltered."[20] In her turn, she presents her fruits to her guest. She spreads the table for him who had been her eternal banquet.[21] She is, as it were, dissolved with him into one same nature (συμφύεται τρόπον τινὰ τῷ θεῷ).[22] She possesses in her own right this Nature over which, however, nobody has mastery: ἰδιοποιουμένων τὴν ἀδέσποτον φύσιν.[23] Now God is everything for her: "nourishment . . . and drink, clothing and shelter, air, place, wealth, sensual delight, beauty, health, strength, wisdom, glory, beatitude".[24]

The mystical level achieved by the soul has definitively gone beyond the "philosophy of desire".[25] Of old her nostalgia seemed eternal to her, and her inability to be fulfilled seemed to be beatitude itself.

---

[18] Ibid. 4; I, 852 A–853 A.

[19] "The soul, having gone out of its nature": ibid. 12; I, 1028 B; "come out of the coverings of nature": ibid. 7; I, 916 A.

[20] Ibid. 14; I, 1085 C; "She lodges in herself that which cannot be sheltered." There is a subtle play on words here: πανδοχεύω signifies "to lodge" but evokes the idea of welcoming "completely".

[21] Ibid. 10; I, 985 BD.

[22] In Ps. 6; I, 456 AB.

[23] C. Eunom. 1; 427 AB.

[24] In illud I, 1316 D–1317 A.

[25] There is an important idea founded on this dynamism: that of the positive, albeit preparatory, role of "passion" and natural love in spiritual ascent. In fact, without this natural passion, "would there be anything that could still stimulate us to look for celestial things?" (De an. et res. III, 65 AB). Divine pedagogy will tend therefore to transform interiorly the sensuality of the soul and replace it with its gentleness ("The senses of the soul are sweetened by the Word" [In Cant. 4; I, 844 D]). "Do you understand now why this sensory appetite has been given to you?" (In Cant. 4; I, 844 D). Certainly the spiritual senses are not identical to the ordinary senses of the soul (In Cant. 1; I, 780 CD). But there is a continuity between them and not a break: thus the Song of Songs uses sensual symbols to initiate the soul into divine things ("the passion of love . . . a guide-post for beliefs" In Cant., 1; I, 773 C), in order to give her "impassible passion" (ἀπαθὲς πάθος [In Cant. 1; I, 772 A]), so as to bring about her maturation into spiritual puberty (In Cant. 1; I, 784 C). Thus, the extinguishing of natural passion is not produced by violence but by an excess of that which is spiritual (Or. dom. 3; I, 1157 A). Sensuality can disappear. "We no longer have the need to be led toward the beautiful" (De an. et res. III, 89 C).

There is in fact a moment when the soul is weary of seeing only through symbols (In Cant. 5; 880 AB), when she is no longer content with the "milk" of doctrine that is full of

But is this inability not therefore imputable to God? No, for God, who seemed to be "hopeless beauty", τὸ ἀνέλπιστον κάλλος, knows how to find a hope beyond hope: ἐλπίδα τοῖς ὑπὲρ ἐλπίδα.[26] What he has devised surpasses all that the creature could hope for: κρεῖττον ἢ κατ᾿ ελπίδα ἐστίν.[27] The God who is "above God"[28] thus remains the God who is *semper maior* (always greater), even with respect to the most "supernatural" aspirations of his creature: "The soul thus calls on the Word with all her strength. But she cannot do as much as she would like. For her desires outstrip her capabilities, and her very ability to desire cannot match what the Word actually is but rather matches only what her vigor allows her."[29] "We are permitted a happiness that surpasses our desire, a gift that surpasses our hope, a grace that surpasses our nature."[30] What madness it is, then, to believe "that God can do only what we can imagine"![31]

There is behind all this only one fundamental mystery, that of the divine wellspring that at every moment is something else and can never be seen in its entirety. It is the mystery of the *Presence* that has never finished *coming*: "Here is something that would be worth lengthy research, namely, understanding how he who is always present comes: πῶς ἔρχεται ὁ ἀεὶ παρών."[32]

---

imagery (ibid. 14; I, 1001 C; 9; I, 956 A), but she wishes to grasp the truth. And the truth of passion is pure desire (καθαρὰ ἐπιθυμία: *De virg.* 6; III, 349 C).

[26] *De hom. op. proœm.*; I, 128 B.

[27] *In Ps.* 9; I, 485 A.

[28] *C. Eunom.* 5; II, 884 B: "that very [God] who is beyond God".

[29] *In Cant.* 12; I, 1028 D.

[30] *De beat.* 7; 1, 1277 C.

[31] *De an. et res.* III, 152 C.

[32] *De paup. amand.* 2; III, 472 C.

3

TRANSPOSITION OF THE IMAGE

But have we already fully integrated the essential progress that constituted the philosophy of image as it relates to the philosophy of desire? The intimate dealings between God and the soul have up to this point been described only as dealings, a communion of *Life*, not yet as a communion of *Spirit*. On the other hand, the communion of Spirit in which the philosophy of image ended up was in danger of foundering in a kind of mystical solipsism. There, too, is a question that has remained open.

But the solution of this twofold question is no longer difficult: the revelation of the Presence, that is to say, the depths, of Divine Being is in concrete terms nothing other than the revelation of the Trinity by the Trinity. The infinite life of God is a personal life. The divine archer, the Father, has sent his Only Begotten into the world, and the latter, wounded by love and united to the Son as his mystical body, recognizes himself in turn through his archetype, the Father. But the spirit that unites them is far from confounding them. This spirit is himself a Person, the Holy Spirit. He is union as a Person. The "heliomorphic" (ἡλιοειδής) character of the eye is now confounded with the presence of this Spirit in the soul:

> The glory of the eyes is to be the eyes of the Dove. To me this appears to signify that in the pure pupils of these eyes is perceived the countenance of the things that have been gazed upon. The natural scientists claim that eyesight is activated by the impression of the images that flow from objects. Thus, then, the image of the Dove, which appears in the pupils, becomes the glory of well-formed eyes. . . . It is the character of the Spiritual Life that is illumined in the visual power [τῷ διορατικῷ] of the soul. And in virtue of its capacity to receive the imprint of the Dove, the purified eye is rendered capable of also seeing the beauty of the Bridegroom. It is only now that the young girl fixes her gaze on

the form of the Bridegroom. . . . Indeed, nobody can say "Lord Jesus" except in the Holy Spirit.[1]

Yet again, the mystery of the ἐμφάνεια as both "impression" and "expression" is repeated. For the Holy Spirit, the "perfect nourishment of our nature",[2] enters into our nature—such as Saint Irenaeus conceived it—as a condition of internal integrity: "Once again the Spirit mingles [κατεμίχθη] with men, that Spirit who distanced himself from our nature when man became flesh."[3] On account of this fact, the Spirit is also an internal condition of our vision of God:

> According to the Prophet, light can only be seen in light. For he says: "In your light we shall see light." If, therefore, there is no vision of the light except if one is in light—for how would a person see the sun if he were not bathed in its rays?—if, therefore, the only begotten light can be seen only in the light of the Father, that is to say, in the Holy Spirit who proceeds from him, it is only when we are illumined in advance by the glory of the Spirit that we can enter into a knowledge of the glory of the Father and the Son. Otherwise, how would we salvage the truth of the words of the Gospel: "O God, nobody has seen you"? . . . If the glory of the Father and the Son were accessible to human nature and human power, these words would certainly have been false and lying words. . . . It was only when caught up [ἀνακραθείς] in the grace of the Spirit that Saint Stephen saw God, elevated by it to the comprehension of God.[4]

Thus we see that Gregory's mystical theology ends up logically and necessarily in a trinitarian theology. We do not have to expound on it here or even give a broad summary of the Eunomian and Macedonian controversy. It will suffice for us to choose a few of its salient traits that show the link between Gregory's religious philosophy and his trinitarian theology.

The dogma of the Trinity is essentially that of Life within the Eternal: "This is what the Word of God affirms of the Father: to know him is eternal life. And of the Son: whoever will believe in him will have eternal life. And of the Holy Spirit: he who receives grace will be a gushing fountain unto eternal life."[5] There cannot be loneliness

---

[1] *In Cant.* 4; I, 835 CD–836 A.
[2] *De Spir. Sancto* III, 697 B.
[3] Ibid., B.
[4] *In St. Steph.* III, 717 ABC.
[5] *C. Eunom.* 10; II, 836 B.

(ἐρημία) in God. Without his Son, God would be without Light, without Wisdom, without Life, without Truth,[6] since all these things are affirmed of the Only Begotten. "A glory without this radiance would be dark and blind, closed in on itself [ἀλαμπὴς καὶ τυφλὴ ἐπ' ἑαυτῆς ... δόξα]."[7] All these goods of the Father are already Someone— and this Eunomius does not want to understand. "When the Father wants something, the Son who is in the Father knows what the Father wishes. Or rather, the Son is himself the wish of the Father."[8] They do not have "a life of their own [κεχωρισμένην καὶ ἰδιάζουσαν ζωήν]". The ἐξ αὐτοῦ (from him) of the Son is from all eternity a σὺν αὐτῷ (with him).[9] It is a perfectly mutual inclusion: "He who is in the Father is evidently in him with all that he possesses in the way of being, and he who has the Father in him includes in himself the totality of the Father's power."[10] This is what is meant by the term, "unity of nature". With respect to every other quality, which is merely an attribute of nature (ἐπιθεωρεῖται), there can be unity between God and creature. By an assimilation to the divine will, the creature becomes one with him (ἕν πρὸς τὸν θεόν). But there will never be unity of nature, coincidence (ἐν πᾶσι ταὐτό). The latter is possible only if a "natural" unity precedes (προσλαβούσης φυσικῆς συναφείας) "free" unity (τὴν κατὰ προαίρεσιν ἑνότητα).[11] Not through a temporal priority, for, from a certain point of view, "free" unity and "natural" unity coincide completely. Just as, in the case of the eye, "seeing" and "wishing to see" are simply one, so is generation in God. The two things are τρόπον τινὰ μετ' ἀλλήλων. "Natural activity accompanies free activity", and inversely.[12] What we have in this inseparability is merely the expression of God's perfect spirituality. The difference between persons is in no way synthetic (ἀσύνθετος),[13] but it is perfectly analytic (ἀγεννησία ... Μονογενοῦς ἀϊδιότης γεννητῶς συνεπινοεῖται).[14] This is an inexpressible difference "such as accords with the majesty

[6] Ibid. 3; II, 594 D.
[7] Ibid. 2; II, 514 A.
[8] Ibid. 12; II, 984 A.
[9] Ibid. 1; II, 361 CD.
[10] Ibid. 2; II, 485 D.
[11] Ibid. 1; II, 405 AB.
[12] Ibid. 8; II, 775 CD–778 A.
[13] Ibid. 1; II, 336 A.
[14] Ibid. 369 C.

of nature".[15] This difference radically excludes that which forms the foundation of all distinctions in the world: spacing. God is ἀδιαστάτως μεριζόμενον.[16] In this way, again, any of nature's closed characteristics that would prevent knowledge of self from being immediately (ἀδιαστάτως) knowledge also of another are found to be excluded: "The Only Begotten who is in the Father sees the Father in himself."[17]

Regarding the dynamic structure of the three Persons, Gregory, the Greek theologian, is, at least at first glance, partial to that "linear" schema that calls for the Son to be born of the Father and the Spirit to proceed from the Son (and thus mediately from the Father).[18] "Just as it is impossible to grasp the Father without the Son, so the Son is ungraspable without the Holy Spirit. For just as it is impossible to rise up [ἀνελθεῖν] toward the Father without being raised to him by the Son, similarly it is impossible to say Lord Jesus except in the Holy Spirit."[19] The Spirit is the anointing of Christ. But in order to touch the skin, the oil must first be touched (προεντυγχάνειν διὰ τῆς ἁφῆς τῷ μύρῳ).[20] Thus "vivifying grace takes its rise from the Father as from a fountain from which life gushes forth, then [continues] through the Son who is 'true life' and achieves its end [τελειοῦσθαι] for those who benefit from it by the operation of the Holy Spirit."[21]

But already this "achievement of its end",[22] counter to a conception that, if pushed too far, would lead to subordinationism, proclaims a "reversal of values", as it were. It is continued by the essential ambiguity of the idea of "glory" (δόξα), which is adapted quite particularly to the Spirit. For if the δόξα is like the radiance of divine majesty in its glory, it is in its turn that which actively glorifies it. The Spirit

is glorified and already possesses glory, inasmuch as it is clear that he who confers glory on another himself possesses a superabundant glory. For

[15] Ibid. 336 A.

[16] Ibid. 2; II, 469 B. "There is no diastema between the Son and the Holy Spirit" (C. Mar. II, 1321 A).

[17] C. Eunom. 12; II, 1041 B.

[18] Ibid. 1; II, 464 BC: "For just as the Son is united to the Father . . . thus in turn the Holy Spirit clings fast to the Only Begotten. . . ." Letter XXIV (III, 1092 A): "Faith, which begins with the Father, ends up going through the Son, who is in the middle, right to the Holy Spirit."

[19] C. Maced. II, 1316 B.

[20] Ibid., II, 1321 A.

[21] Ibid., II, 1325 AB.

[22] Ibid., II, 1317 B.

how would he who lacks glory glorify? If he were not himself light, how would he demonstrate the grace of light? . . . It is thus the Spirit who glorifies the Son and the Father. But truly does he speak who says: "I will glorify those who glorify me." "I have glorified you", says the Lord to his Father . . . , and the divine voice responds: "I have glorified and I will glorify again." Do you see this circular movement of glorification between equals [ἐγκύκλιον τῆς δόξης περιφοράν]?[23]

The straight line of processions curves back to its beginning (πάλιν ἀνακυκλούμενος ὁ λόγος).[24] The divine life is an infinite circle.[25] But in that case one might just as well begin at the end: after having risen from the Spirit to the Son, and from the Son to the Father, "we can, at the summit of the 'theognosis' [θεογνωσία], retrace our course [δίαυλον ἀνακάμνοντες] and begin with the supreme God [τὸν ἐπὶ πάντων θεόν], traversing what is at present near and familiar to our thought, in order to reach the Holy Spirit from the Father through the Son [ἀναχωροῦμεν]."[26] In a true sense, this "return" is an "ascent" (ἀνα-χώρησις), even while being a "retreat" into the intimate heart of God. For everything "is perfected in the Spirit who effects all in all".[27] "Just as each person is all of nature, so is the Spirit nature in its entirety. It is in the Spirit that nature comes to an end and is closed: "For truly he is one, he who without spacing is comprehended in the One, the first in the First, the alone in the Alone. And in the same way that a man's spirit, which is in him, and the man himself are one, unique man, so God's Spirit, which is in him, and God himself ought with good reason to be considered one, unique God."[28] And since the Spirit is the place that unites the Father and the Son, he is, one may say, in an eminent fashion the very unity of God.

This doctrine finds an unexpected and magnificent echo in the economic aspect of the Trinity. Whereas Origen's subordinationism prompted him to consider the mystical ascent as passing from the virtually multiple domain of the Word to the absolutely solitary kingdom of the Father, Gregory forms a conception of supreme unity, not in the sign of the Father, but in that of the Spirit. And this is quite

---

[23] Ibid., II, 1329 A.
[24] Ibid., B.
[25] C. Eunom. 1; II, 456 CD.
[26] Ibid., 416 A.
[27] C. Maced. II, 1329 B.
[28] C. Eunom. 2; II, 564 D.

expressly the case—the idea will be found surprising, perhaps, in the
case of a Greek Father—insofar as he is the mutual love of the Father
and the Son. In fact, when the Son asks the Father for the unity of his
Mystical Body, he asks for that unity that holds sway *between* them:
sicut nos unum sumus (just as we are one). We cannot therefore be
perfectly unified without possessing that unity which is the unity of
the Father and the Son and which is the identity of the Spirit.[29]

> When perfect charity will have cast out fear . . . and when fear shall
> have been changed into love, then all that is saved will be one unity, a
> unity that increases in consonance with the unique good, and all will be,
> mutually, one in the perfect Dove. . . . So that, encircled by the unity
> of the Holy Spirit as by a "bond of peace" . . . , all will be one body
> and one spirit. . . . But it is more worthwhile to repeat here the exact
> words of the Gospel: "So that all may be one, like you, Father, and I in
> you". . . . The bond of this unity is glory and that this glory is the Holy
> Spirit anyone who is familiar with Scripture will agree, if he reflects on
> the word of the Lord: "The glory you have given me I have handed on
> to them." For in all truth he gave them this very same glory when he
> says: "Receive the Holy Spirit."[30]

Therefore it is not by chance that the Dove should be at one and the
same time the perfect, eschatological Church and that little "image"
(εἴδωλον)[31] that had shone in the pupil of the Bride. The little *image*,
principle of unity between God and creature, is at the same time, as
a grace of the Spirit, a *power* (δύναμις) that tends to integrate itself
into the entire world in its ever-growing unity (πάσης τῆς κτίσεως
ἐν σῶμα γενομένης)[32] and that forms from it the perfect, eschatological *Image* that is the total Christ. The solution of the dilemma of
the image is thus the elevation of the created image to the plane of
the uncreated Image and its integration into it: "It is impossible to
contemplate archetypal goodness except through its appearance in the
Image of the Infinite One [μὴ ἐν τῇ εἰκόνι ἀοράτου φαινόμενον]."[33]
But what integrates us into this Image is Love, the Spirit who is more
than Thought, who is Holy: "Just as the person who piously receives
the Spirit sees in the Spirit the glory of the Only Begotten, [so the

---

[29] *In illud* I, 1321 AB, 1320 C.
[30] *In Cant.* 15; I, 1116 C–1117 B.
[31] Ibid. 4; I, 836 D.
[32] *In illud* I, 1320 A.
[33] *C. Eunom.* I; II, 416 A.

person who] sees the Son sees the Image of the Invisible One and through the Image receives into his understanding the imprint of the Archetype."[34] Thus we enter into the love of the Father that he cherishes eternally as his infinite image: "You have loved them as you have loved me. For if the Father loves the Son and if we are all in the Son, transformed into his body by faith in him, it is a necessity that he who loves his Son should also love the Body of his Son as he loves his Son himself. We are this Body of his Son."[35]

---

[34] *C. Maced.* II, 1325 D–1328 A.

[35] *In illud* 1, 1321 B. Thus we discover *explicite* in Gregory's work the elements of Augustine's *imago trinitatis*. (Cf. Bergardes, Ἡ . . . διδασκαλία Γρηγορίου τοῦ Νύσσης [Thessalonica, 1876], 26.) The human soul is at once a rational substance, intelligible word, and spirit, in which she is perfected (*In illud* I, 1340 B). In this way she possesses "figures, images, and shadowings" of the Trinity (*In illud* I, 1341 B; cf. I, 140 B; II, 17 A). Similarly the soul is νοῦς, λόγος, and ἀγάπη and thereby the image of God: *De hom. op.* 5; I, 137 C (cf. 1333 B). Therefore there is in us "a figurative trinity in unity with respect to image and likeness" (I, 1332 A). Cf. a similar line of thought in the *Great Catechesis* 1–2; II, 13–17. The concept of trinity in unity is figured in the soul. So also is unity in trinity and unity in the processes that are held in common (I, 1344 AB).

CONCLUSION

At the end of this study we should like to disengage from Gregory's religious philosophy a few methodological principles that are implied in all his thought and that alone render it possible and coherent. They are, it seems to me, three in number.

1. The first can be formulated in this way: since the fundamental problem of this philosophy is that of Presence, or, what amounts to exactly the same thing, that of Existence, the methodology of thought that alone can respond to this formal "object" of his inquiry can only be an existential method. In fact, the principle posited by our Introduction, that is to say, the ontological superiority of the ὅτι ἐστίν over the ὅ τί ἐστιν, of "existence" over "idea", is found confirmed by the whole of our study: life is above desire, presence (παρουσία) is above image, and the miracle of continual arrival (ἐπιδημία) is above even presence, inasmuch as it would tend to be established in duration and habit. To this "object" there corresponded in our Introduction the subjective act of faith, understood as the essential comparative of knowing. But this going beyond knowing tends necessarily to be widened in a *life*. It then becomes the realization of thought through action, which is the proof of conceptual truth. There is, indeed, no other means of assimilation to the object that is precisely the transcendence of life relative to thought. By action, therefore, the object is introduced to the interior of the subject, and the reflection of action is existence that is pondered over and—*if* action has truly taken place and is continued—existential thought. There is thus a strict reciprocity: "No faith without works, and no works without faith."[1] In all strictness there is no other criterion of theological truth. "For he who in truth and in a proper way turns his attention to 'theology' [θεολογία] will have demonstrated by this very fact that his life is in perfect harmony with his faith."[2] This conformity, which means essentially an openness of thought toward that which surpasses it, is the immediate introduction into mystical theology. Far from being opposed to one another, dogmatic theology and mystical theology are

---

[1] *In Eccles.* 8; I, 748 B. Cf. *Vit. Moys.* I, 377 BD.
[2] *In Ps.* 14; I, 577 D.

inseparable. Indeed, if theology is conceived of as a dynamic realization, they are identical. This is how all the Fathers understood it, most
particularly Origen and the Cappadocians. Gregory of Nyssa, who in
this instance follows quite closely the second theological discourse of
Gregory Nazianzen,[3] leaves no doubt on this subject:

> Theology is a steep and hardly accessible mountain. The great majority
> of people reach only the foot of it and that scarcely. But if anyone is
> a Moses, it will happen that in climbing the mountain he will become
> capable of hearing the sound of trumpets, a sound which, so the story
> goes, becomes louder and louder as one rises higher. The trumpet that is
> so terrifying to the ear is doubtless none other than the proclamation of
> the divine nature. It seems loud at the first hearing. But it becomes ever
> louder and closer to the ear as the goal becomes less and less distant. . . .
> And if the multitude cannot stand this voice from on high but prefer
> to commit to Moses the personal knowledge of ineffable things, so that
> the people may be taught afterward what he has learned in his education
> on the mountain, this also happens all the time in the Church: it is not
> everyone's business to press on toward the comprehension of mysteries.
> But the people choose from their midst the man who is capable of the
> divine to which his compatriots generously lend their attention, as they
> hold for true all that the person who is initiated into the mysteries of
> God will bring to their hearing.[4]

Gregory can risk this esotericism because his existential principle
serves him as a base and a criterion. If the mystagogue is not truly
purified before beginning his ascent, he will not be able to undertake
it. He will hear nothing. "Since he is pure, he will be able to risk
the mountain [καθαρὸν γενόμενον, οὕτω κατατολμῆσαι τοῦ ὄρους]."[5]
   2. The second principle flows from the definitively metahistori-
cal, not metaphysical, character of the object. The God "above God"
(which is to say, the God who is above the God of the philosophers),
the God "beyond hope" cannot be the object of a system, like Eunomius attempted in his arid, theological rationalism. *Epinoia* remains
midway between the subject and the object. Theology is merely an
"inventive approach". And this is so, because the object is a free Person. Thus there is a strict and definitive correlation between the *word*
of God and what the creature *hears* (in the double sense of perceiving

---

[3] PG 36, 28.
[4] *Vit. Moys.* I, 373–76.
[5] Ibid., 373 D.

by hearing and of comprehending). This infrangible *tantum-quantum* is yet again an expression of the fact that the word of God is at once λόγος and δύναμις. "Who then would be so completely childish as not to understand the mutual and internal relationship between hearing and the word, that there is no auditory energy if nobody speaks, or an active word that would not be directed to somebody's ear?"[6] The object of "theology" is thus strictly limited to what "the trumpet" clearly wants to make heard from on high, from Θεὸς λέγων (the God who speaks).

This relationship takes its absoluteness from the fact that it is founded on the identity of the intellect and the divine will itself, an identity that leaves no place for the realm of "things that are possible". Not only are intention (προαίρεσις) and action (πρᾶξις) identical in God (whereas in the case of the creature an active power [πρακτικὴ δύναμις] is not necessarily in action [τῆς ἐνεργείας ἐκπλήρωσις],[7] but, what is more, there is indeed an identity between will (βούλησις) and power (δύναμις): "There is a coincidence between will and power, and the measure of power is none other than the will itself."[8] The power of God is measured by his will as much as will is measured by power. The reason for this is very simple: "All that can be thought of in God is act and action." "The will is transformed without any intermediary [ἀμέσως] into the proposed end."[9] And the characteristic word returns in this regard: ἀδιαστάτως.[10] This identity of will and power is completed at length in the still more fundamental identity between will and intelligence: τὸ δὲ θέλημα σοφία ἐστίν. With the prevision of what will need to be done, the realizing power of things is identical: συνέδραμεν. "The two make only one [ἓν ἀμφότερα]."[11] Therefore creatures are at once both rational, because they arise from supreme wisdom, and also subsisting acts of free will: "(Existing) essence is the subsistence of the will. [Ἡ δὲ τοῦ θελήματος ὕπαρξις οὐσία ἐστί]"[12]

---

[6] *C. Eunom.* 12; II, 980 A.

[7] Ibid., 988 A–B.

[8] Ibid. 2; II, 488 A. σύνδρομός ἐστι τῇ βουλήσει ἡ δύναμις καὶ μέτρον τῆς δυνάμεως αὐτοῦ τὸ θέλημα γίνεται. This is explained in identical terms in: *In hexaëm.* I, 69 A.

[9] *C. Eunom.* 12; II, 988 B–C: "Everything that is intended in [God] is productive and constitutes an action."

[10] *In hexaëm.* I, 69 A.

[11] Ibid., A–B.

[12] *De an. et res.* III, 124 B.

This is the salutary and indestructible contribution of "Nominalism" in all of philosophy, preventing it from achieving a necessity that is independent of divine freedom. Augustine formulated it in terms of a lapidary adage: "*Cujus voluntas rerum necessitas est* [whose will is the necessity of things]."[13] For Gregory, the same identity is established between omnipotence (τῆς παντοδυνάμου ἐξουσίας), wisdom, will, and act (ὅπερ ἂν σοφῶς τε καὶ τεχνικῶς ἐθέλῃ μὴ ἀνυπόστατον ποιούσης τὸ θέλημα).[14] A philosophy that, however unconsciously, would introduce a dualism into God, as if his will came from a source other than his intellection,[15] would only succeed in projecting into God the shadow "of what is proper to our heavy and sluggish nature . . . that is to say, the shadow of willing something without having it or of possessing something without willing it."[16]

This principle, which strictly limits thought to that which God has indeed wished to reveal to us (in nature or in supernature) and which prohibits it from straying into the realm of "possibilities without subsistence" (ἀνυπόστατα θελήματα), is finally shown to be identical to the first principle: since Existence is the formal object of this thought, it is at the same stroke limited to the existent. The introduction of the realm of possibilities remains licit, henceforth, only if it is understood as a "mythical" way of expressing the real. We had reason to believe that the myth of an asexual generation of humanity was understood by Gregory himself as being just such.

3. Finally, we can disengage from the movement our study has examined a third formal principle, that of progression by intensification. A system of notional thought progresses by way of connecting links and extensions, while an existential system of thought, by way of contrast, progresses through an ever more deeply plumbed repetition of the same point. We no longer need to bring forward proofs that this is the essential movement of Gregory's thought. It is evident that the various levels we have superimposed are not found in his work in the abstract and schematic order we have given them. In the constantly reiterated repetition of the same theme, Gregory descends to various depths: sometimes higher, sometimes lower. And let us not

---

[13] *De Gen. ad litt.* 6, 15, 26.

[14] *De an. et res.* III, 124 B.

[15] *C. Eunom.* 8; II, 776 A. "The will does not arise innately from any peculiar source, nor can it be conceived of apart from that which is wished for."

[16] Ibid., 773 D–776 A.

forget that the psychological experience of the philosophy of desire can, insofar as it is an experience, have a sharper and much more poignant character even than certain truths of the philosophy of love, and that the *whole* truth of this experience of desire, at once painful and peaceful, enters positively into the structure of love. Living and lived philosophy, as represented by the philosophy of Gregory and that of the other Fathers, has, accordingly, the right to maintain a freer attitude toward the formulation of its intimate movement. Still it is the case that a more rigid "construction", such as the one we have attempted, can contribute to rendering the most supple twists and turns of this movement more perceptible, thereby permitting us to enter into a deeper contact with the author.

Just now we were using the term "intensification". We could also say "elevation" (*Aufhebung*) over ever-higher levels of thought and being that share one—same and identical—ontological structure. A being limited by its three spatial dimensions escapes from itself, so to speak, through a fourth dimension: time. Thus, for Gregory, the totality of temporal being, which is enclosed, as we know, by the internal finitude of time, even so escapes from itself by way of a "fifth" dimension, which, indeed, presupposes a radical elevation, on the part of God, into the eternal. The eighth day, which must follow the seven temporal days, will be at once day and beyond day, because it will no longer be limited by nights and because it will not be numbered with the others (οὐκέτι δὲ τὴν τοῦ ἀριθμοῦ διαδοχὴν ἐφ᾽ ἑαυτῆς δεχομένη).[17] Phenomenal time (ὁ χρόνος αἰσθητός) forms a perfectly closed *circle* (ἀνακυκλούμενος . . .).[18] But this circle, which is the limit of the creature (τὸ πέρας τῆς κτίσεως),[19] extends into the horizontal, so to speak, and cannot defend itself against a hand that would come to grasp it vertically and lift it to a higher horizontal level.

This miracle of elevation is described to us by Gregory with a particular insistence, since it concerns the glorification of the humanity of Christ. Here the extreme case occurs: "*Dextera Domini exaltavit me* [the right hand of the Lord has exalted me]." The hand of God has seized a creature in order to divinize it. Here Gregory thinks like Origen. The Incarnation and earthly life are still merely like an exte-

---

[17] *In Ps.* 6; I, 612 A.
[18] Ibid. 5; I, 504 CD.
[19] Ibid. 6; I, 609 B.

rior contact between two natures, with the hand of God lying on the chosen being. It is at the moment of the Resurrection that God's hand seizes its prey and lifts it into an unknown dimension. It is a true *super*-elevation (ὑπερύψωσις)[20] that snatches the being from its own measurable limits: οὐκέτι ἔμεινεν ἐν τοῖς ἰδίοις μέτροις καὶ ἰδιώμασιν. "The right hand of the Lord raised him on high, and from being a slave he became Christ the King. From his humble state he became the Most High. From being man he became God."[21] Gregory (in spite of the all of the influences of Methodius that would seem to neutralize those of Origen) is almost even more radical on this point than the latter: in light [the assumed man] becomes light, in the incorruptible he becomes incorruptible, in the invisible he becomes invisible, in Christ he becomes Christ, in the Lord he becomes Lord. "Just as in corporeal mixtures [ἀνάκρασις] a part of the mixture that is quite inferior in quantity is completely transformed [πάντως μεταποιεῖσθαι]"[22] into the other part, thus the humanity of Christ is completely absorbed (κατεπόθη) into this sea of immortality (πέλαγος ἀφθαρσίας). This humanity loses all its own qualities: "weight, form, color, toughness, softness, quantitative delimitation. Nothing of all that one had been able to perceive in it persists when this mingling with the divine comes to raise up the lowliness of corporeal nature all the way to the level of divine attributes [θεϊκὰ ἰδιώματα]."[23] This is Gregory's constant teaching.[24] We shall not enter into the details of his Christology here.[25] Let us mark, however, as we have marked elsewhere regarding Origen, the repercussions that this theory is bound to have on eucharistic doctrine. The glorious Christ is, in fact, according to Gregory, omnipresent, inasmuch as he has been taken away from place (ἀόριστος καὶ ἀπερίγραπτος, πανταχοῦ ὤν).[26] He has become one with God (ἓν δὲ τὰ δύο διὰ τῆς ἀνακράσεως γέγονε).[27] Thus it will not be

---

[20] *C. Eunom.* 5; II, 697 C.

[21] Ibid.

[22] Ibid.

[23] *C. Apollin.* II, 1244 AB.

[24] *C. Eunom.* 5; I, 706 AC–708 CD; ibid. 6; II, 736 D–737 A; *C. Apollin.* II, 1168 A–1221 C and note.

[25] One should consult Karl Holl, *Amphilochius von Ikonium* (1904), 220–35, and J. Lenz, *Jesus Christus nach der Lehre des hl. Gregor v. Nyssa* (1925).

[26] These attributes are those of God. Apollinaris refuses to grant them to the (celestial) body of Christ. Gregory attributes them to him: *C. Apollin.* II, 1160 A.

[27] *Adv. Apoll.* II, 1165 C.

prudent to exaggerate the "physical" side of Gregory's eucharistic teaching. The spiritualization of the body of Christ is such that there can be a question of "glorious nourishment" only in a totally analogical sense. We are far from someone like Saint John Chrysostom! But we are far, as well, from Saint Augustine, for whom Christ was, in his glorious state, "localized" in heaven—"*non est hic* [he is not here]."[28] Whence we have the obscurities of Augustine's eucharistic texts. With respect to the separation effected by Augustine, Gregory finds it already in his adversary Apollinaris and does not hesitate to oppose it:

> Toward the end of his treatise, [Apollinaris] says: "Although he is in heaven by virtue of his body, all the same [Christ] is with us right to the consummation of the world." The author, by separating the inseparable, does not evidently understand who he is that is "with us". For if, on the one hand, he situates the Lord's body in heaven and then, on the other hand, situates the Lord "with us", through this distinction he openly introduces a certain disintegration and a division. . . . As for us, we affirm that Christ . . . has been raised to heaven and that he who has been raised is with us and that there is no dividing to be done, but that just as he is in us [ἐν ἡμῖν], present to each one in particular and "in the midst" of them, so does he traverse all the regions of the created order and manifests himself uniformly to all parts of the world. If he manifests himself incorporeally in us, who are corporeal, he will certainly not manifest himself corporeally to the beings that are in heaven! . . . Whereas [Apollinaris] claims that Christ, while seated in heaven in fleshly guise, will enter into contact with men in a spiritual way.[29]

---

[28] See the penetrating study of Karl Adam, "Zur Eucharistielehre des hl. Augustinus", *Theol. Quartalschrift* 112 (1931): 490–536.

[29] *C. Apollin.* II, 1268 B–1269 A. That famous letter of Gregory's against pilgrimages to holy places is closely related to this doctrine of the Eucharist. It is true that he does not condemn pilgrimages *in themselves*. He even admits that he has drawn some consolation from them (*Epist.* 3; III, 1016 BC). But on the whole, this devotion has no significance for him: "If the Holy Spirit abounds in Jerusalem, can he not be diffused to where we are? . . . The approach to God does not presuppose any spatial change of location. . . ." Do not say that Christ commanded the apostles to remain in Jerusalem. This was the case only until the sending of the Spirit. The Spirit scattered them throughout the earth. At the present time, no place, be it ever so "holy", has preeminence. *Spiritus ubi vult, spirat* (The Spirit blows where it wills) (*Epist.* 2; III, 1012–13).
There is absolutely no doubt that many a time this Alexandrinism carried our theologian beyond admissible limits. In his letter to Theophilus, above all (II, 1272ff.), Gregory goes so far as to see in kenosis a "means" for God to make himself understood by the "weak". The

But will the whole of human nature, the cosmos in its entirety, follow Christ in this rectilinear, vertiginous ascent into God? When Gregory speaks of men and the common resurrection, he does not use the same bold language. However, having said all that we have said about the influence of sin on the body (σάρξ), we need not press Gregory's affirmations on the identity of the fallen body and the risen body too far.[30] Origen himself had admitted this identity, not only of the corporeal form (εἶδος), but of matter itself.[31] Our future body, according to Gregory, "will no longer be of this heavy and coarse constitution, but woven from a lighter and more ethereal thread".[32] And according to certain passages it must be believed that these future bodies of ours will participate in the privileges of the body of Christ himself, "raised in its humanity toward the true Father, in order to make us rise up in our turn, through him, all of us who spring from the same stock".[33] The principle of divinization is universally posited: "Divinity empties itself [κενοῦται] so as to be graspable by human nature. Human nature, in its turn, is rejuvenated, divinized by its mingling with the Divine."[34] The fire that was hidden and smoldering, as it were, under the ashes of the world (οἱονεὶ συγκαλύψας τὸ τῆς ζωῆς ἐμπύρευμα) blazes forth. With its divine spark it inflames the dead shell (ἀνεζωπύρησε τῇ δυνάμει τῆς ἰδίας θεότητος, τὸ νεκρωθὲν ἀναθάλψας) and "pours out in the infinity of divine power the small libation of our nature".[35]

This combination of two affirmations, that of time raised to the eternal and that of nature carried to the divine, brings us to the problem of eternal beatitude. Here also two series of affirmations must be

---

"strong", such as Moses, Elijah, Paul, and Ezechiel, would not have had need of a bodily parousia of the Logos. They would have been able to rise to the point of direct spiritual contact. Here we find the same spiritualism as in Origen, which, when pressed to the limit, would destroy in its foundations the whole meaning of Christianity. This destruction will be seen to occur in the burning mysticism of an Evagrius Ponticus, a mysticism of narrow and fanatical proportions. In the work of the great Doctors, such destruction is impeded by that profound catholicity that fortunately often keeps them from following the logic of their thought right to the limit.

[30] *De an. et res.* III, 76 C; ibid. III, 140 C–141 A.
[31] PG II, 93–100.
[32] *De an. et res.* III, 108 A.
[33] *In Pascha* 1; III, 628 A.
[34] *C. Eunom.* 5; II, 705 D–708 A.
[35] Ibid., 708 B.

synthesized. The first, with the abolition of time, suppresses faith and hope.[36] It promises, without the uncertainties that remain perhaps in Origen, the impossibility of a new fall.[37] It seems[38] as well to promise a knowledge of God that is qualitatively[39] (not structurally!) different from that poor glimpse we possess here below. The other series of affirmations expressly perpetuates the "course" and the "desire". We no longer have to linger on this synthesis, which should emerge from our whole study in its entirety. Nevertheless, it had to be mentioned here as a last example of super-elevation (ὑπερύψωσις).

This third methodological principle, as well, is itself nothing but a particular aspect of existential thought. It is in-depth progress in the knowledge whose object remains ever the same, namely, Presence.

---

[36] *De an. et res.* III, 93 B–96 C; cf. *In Ps.* 8; I, 482 AB.

[37] Gregory, however, stresses that this fixity in grace is itself essentially a grace: *C. Eunom.*; II, 800 A; cf. 632 B.

[38] Notice, in fact, the ἴσως, "perhaps". *In Cant.* 11, I, 1009 D.

[39] Ibid., 1009 D–1012 A: ἑτέρως πάντως (in an entirely different way). . . .

FINAL NOTE

This book had already gone to press when several articles on Gregory of Nyssa appeared. We shall afford ourselves one last note to offer an appreciation of these.

The most important of these articles is that of Alois Lieske, S.J., in *Scholastik*, 1939, "Zur Theologie der Christusmystik Gregors von Nyssa". Lieske recovers the same three fundamental motifs from Gregory's work as we do: radical finitude, image, loving contemplation in a "thick cloud". He understands the human totality on which the totality of the Mystical Body is superimposed in a manner very similar to our own. Nevertheless, even though he concedes a certain "realistic" and "Platonic" side to human unity, he lays a strong stress on the ideal side and underlines the differences between this unity and the unity of the Divine Persons. He sees very clearly that this Platonic unity is not, however, a purely abstract idea but is also the "pleroma" of all individuals. In spite of this, his conception comes closer than ours to that suggested by Hitt and Father Malevez.

A little before this, S. Gonzalez had published a study on the same problem in *Gregorianum* (20 [1939]: 189–206): "El realismo platonico de S. Gregorio de Nisa". He, too, had tried a solution that follows a middle course by relying on the "realistic" side of human unity and insisting on the likeness between human unity and divine unity established by Gregory. Hence the *Quod non sint tres dii* is at the center of his study. We find ourselves fully in accord with him in rejecting all extreme solutions, be they "Platonic" or Aristotelian or Thomistic. We believe, however, that there should be more insistence, even more than that of A. Lieske, on the "Stoic" side of Gregory's thought, with the intent of emphasizing in this way the concrete unity of individual existents. This unity is neither Platonic nor Aristotelian, and Gregory is probably not indebted for the idea to a precise historical influence on the part of the Stoics. It seems, for the most part, to be his own invention, facilitated at most by certain influences from Philo.

In the *Rivista di Filosofia Neo-Scolastica* (30 [1938]: 437–74), Michele Pellegrino devotes a long article to the influence of Plato on Gregory: "Il Platonismo di San Gregorio Nisseno nel dialogo 'Intorno all'anima e alla resurrezione' ". As the title of the article indicates, the author concerns himself solely with the treatise on the soul. He deals above all with the nature of the soul according to Gregory, her origin, her relationship with the body, her likeness to God, and her immortality. In the end, he rejects the hypothesis of an interpolation in the texts that concern the apocatastasis (471). Finally, he declares that he is against the tendency to make Gregory out to be an eclectic thinker (473). However, the "evidente preferenza verso Platone", as Pellegrini says, is correct only for the particular treatise he has studied.

E. von Ivánka's study, entitled "Die Autorschaft der Homilien Εἰς τὸ ποιήσωμεν ἄνθρωπον, . . . " (Byzantinische Zeitschrift 36 [1936]: 46–57), which had escaped our notice when we were drafting this book, seeks to claim these famous homilies for Gregory. Although certain arguments do not appear to be without value, it seems to us, nevertheless, that the principal reason that permits us to doubt their authenticity remains intact in spite of arguments to the contrary: the absence, in Gregory's work, of the fundamental distinction between εἰκών and ὁμοίωσις. The few equivalents that this eminently learned man enumerates with a view to making up for this deficiency do not suffice, it seems to us, for the elimination of the traditional reasons for doubt.

BIBLIOGRAPHY

See also the Bibliographical Note (1988) on pages 189–94. Cited below are the principal works that have appeared on the teaching of Gregory of Nyssa. This bibliography, however, makes no pretense at being absolutely complete.

Ἄκυλας, Α. Μ. Ἡ περὶ ἀθανασίας τῆς ψυχῆς δόξα τοῦ Πλάτωνος ἐν συγκρίσει πρὸς τὴν Γρηγορίου τοῦ Νύσσης. Diss., Athens, 1888.

Aufhauser, J. B. *Die Heilslehre des hl. Gregor von Nyssa*. Munich, 1910 (215 p.).

Balthasar, H. U. von. *Der Versiegelte Quell. Gregor von Nyssa. Auslegung des Hohen Liedes*. In Kürzung übertragen und eingeleitet. Salzburg, 1939.

Bauer, J. *Die Trostreden des Gregorius von Nyssa in ihrem Verhältnis zur antiken Rhetorik*. Diss., Marburg, 1892.

Baur. "Untersuchungen über die Vergöttlichungslehre." *Tübg. Quart.*, 1916–1920.

Bayer, J. *Gregors von Nyssa Gottesbegriff*. Diss., Giessen, 1935.

Bergardes, J. Ἡ περὶ τοῦ σύμπαντος καὶ τῆς ψυχῆς τοῦ ἀνθρώπου διδασκαλία Γρηγορίου τοῦ Νύσσης. Thessalonica, 1876 (93 p.).

Böhringer, F. *Die Kirche Christi und ihre Zeugen*. 2d ed. Vol. 8, *Gregor von Nyssa*. Stuttgart, 1876.

Cherniss, H. F. *The Platonism of Gregory of Nyssa*. University of California Publications in Classical Philology, vol. 11. Berkeley, 1930.

Diekamp, F. *Die Gotteslehre des hl. Gregor von Nyssa*. Part 1. Münster, 1896 (260 p.).

———. *Literargeschichtliches zu der Eunomianischen Kontroverse*. Byzant. Zeitschrift 18. Leipzig, 1909.

———. "Die Wahl Gregors von Nyssa zum Metropoliten von Sebaste im Jahre 380." *Theol. Quart.* 90 (1908): 384–401.

Draeseke, J. "Zu Gregorius von Nyssa." *Zeitschr. f. Kirchengesch.* 28 (1907): 387–400.

———. "Gregorios von Nyssa in den Ausführungen des Johannes Scotus Erigena." *Theol. Studien und Kritiken* 82 (1909): 530–76.

Gomez de Castro, O.F.M., Dr. Michael. *Die Trinitätslehre des hl. Gregor von Nyssa.* Freiburger theologische Studien, no. 50. Freiburg: Herder, 1938.

Gonzalez, S. "El realismo platónico de S. Gregorio de Nisa." *Gregorianum* 20 (1939): 189–206.

Gronau, C. *Poseidonius und die jüdisch-christliche Genesisexegese.* Leipzig-Berlin, 1914.

———. *De Basilio, Gregorio Nazianzeno Nyssenoque Platonis imitatoribus.* Diss., Göttingen, 1908.

Hayd, H., and Fisch, J. *Gregor von Nyssa.* Translation and introduction. 2 vols. Bibliothek der Kirchenväter (Kösel). Munich, 1874, 1880.

Herrmann, G. *Gregorii Nysseni sententiæ de salute adipiscenda.* Halæ, 1875 (49 p.).

Heyns, St. P. *Disputatio historico-theologica de Gregorio Nysseno.* Leiden, 1835 (183 p.).

Hilt, F. *Des hl. Gregor von Nyssa Lehre vom Menschen systematisch dargestellt.* Cologne, 1890 (350 p.).

Holl, K. "Die Theologie des Gregor von Nyssa." In *Amphilochius von Ikonium,* 196–235, Tübingen, 1904.

Horn, G. "L'Amour divin. Note sur le mot 'eros' dans Saint Grégoire de Nysse." *R.A.M.* 6 (1925): 378–89.

———. "Le Miroir et la nuée." *R.A.M.* 8 (1927): 113–31.

Isaye. "L'Unité de l'opération divine dans les écrits trinitaires de Grégoire de Nysse." *Recherches de science religieuse* (1937): 422–39.

Ivánka, E. von. "Die Quelle von Ciceros De natura Deorum II 45–60. (Poseidonios bei Gregor von Nyssa)." *Archivum Philologicum* 59 (1935): 10–21.

———. "Vom Platonismus zur Theorie der Mystik. Zur Erkenntnislehre Gregors von Nyssa." *Scholastik* 11 (1936): 163–95.

———. "Ein Wort Gregors von Nyssa über den Patriarchen Abraham." *Studia Catholica* (1935): 45–47.

———. "Die Autorschaft der Homilien ΕΙΣ ΤΟ ΠΟΙΗΣΟΜΕΝ ΑΝΘΡΩΠΟΝ ΚΑΤ ΕΙΚΟΝΑ ΗΜΕΤΕΡΑΝ ΚΑΙ ΟΜΟΙΩΣΙΝ (Poseidonios bei den kappadokischen Kirchenvätern). *Byz. Zft.* 36 (1936): 47–57.

Kleinheidt, L. *Doctrina de Angelis S. Gregorii Nysseni.* Freiburg, 1860.

Koch, H. "Das mystische Schauen beim hl. Gregor von Nyssa." *Theol. Quartalschrift* 80 (1898): 357–420.

Koperski, V. *Doctrina Sancti Gregorii Nysseni de processione filii Dei.* Rome, 1936.

Krampf, A. *Der Urzustand des Menschen nach des Lehre des hl. Gregor von Nyssa.* Würzburg, 1889 (107 p.).

Lenz, J. *Jesus Christus nach der Lehre des hl. Gregor von Nyssa.* Trier, 1925 (123 p.).

Lewy, H. *Sobria ebrietas*, 132–37. Giessen, 1929.

Malevez, L. "L'Église dans le Christ." *Recherches de science religieuse*, 1935, 257–91 and 418–40.

Maréchal, J. *Études sur la psychologie des mystiques II*, 101–15. Paris, 1937.

Méridier, L. *L'Influence de la seconde sophistique sur l'œuvre de Grégoire de Nysse.* Thesis, Rennes, 1906.

———. *La Grande catéchèse de Grégoire de Nysse.* Greek text, French translation, and commentary. Collection Hemmer-Lejay. Paris, 1908.

Mersch, E. *Le Corps mystique du Christ.* 2d ed., 450–64, 1936.

Meyer, Hans. *Geschichte der Lehre von den Keimkräften von der Stoa bis zum Ausgang der Patristik.* Bonn, 1914.

Meyer, W. *Die Gotteslehre des Gregor von Nyssa.* Leipzig, 1894.

Michaud, E. "Saint Grégoire de Nysse et l'apocatastase." *Revue inter-nat. de théol.* 10 (1902): 37–52.

Moeller, E. G. *Gregorii Nysseni doctrinam de hominis natura et illustravit et cum Origeniana comparavit.* Halæ: E.G.M., 1854 (126 p.)

Pellegrino, M. "Il Platonismo di San Gregorio Nisseno nel dialogo 'Intorno all'anima e alla resurrezione'." *Riv. di Filos. Neoscol.* 30 (1938): 437–74.

Preger, F. *Die Grundlagen der Ethik bei Gregor von Nyssa.* Würzburg, 1897 (56 p.).

Puech, H. C. "La Ténèbre mystique chez le pseudo-Denys." *Études Carmélitaines* 23, no. 2 (1938): 33–53 (in particular, 49–52).

Reiche, A. *Die künstlerischen Elemente in der Welt und Lebensanschauung des Gregor von Nyssa.* Diss., Jena, 1897.

Rupp, J. *Gregors des Bischofs von Nyssa Leben und Meinungen.* Leipzig, 1834 (262 p.).

Slomkowski, A. *L'État primitif de l'homme dans la tradition de l'Église avant saint Augustin.* 1928.

Srawley, J. H. "Saint Gregory of Nyssa on the Sinlessness of Christ." *Journal of Theological Studies* 7 (1906): 434–41.

Stephanou, E. "La Coexistence initiale du corps et de l'âme d'après Saint Grégoire de Nysse et Saint Maxime l'Homologète." *Echos d'Orient* 35 (1932): 304–15.

Stigler, J. U. *Die Psychologie des hl. Gregor von Nyssa systematisch darge-stellt.* Regensburg, 1857 (136 p.)

Stiglmayr, J. "Makarius der Grosse und Gregor von Nyssa." *Theologie und Glaube* 2 (1910).

———. "Die Schrift des hl. Gregor von Nyssa 'Über die Jungfräu-lichkeit'." *Zft. f. Asz. u. Mystik* (1927): 334–59.

———. *Allgemeine Einleitung zur deutschen Ausgabe der Schriften Gregors von Nyssa.* Bibliothek der Kirchenväter, vol. 56. Munich: Kösel und Pustet, 1927.

Unterstein, K. *Die natürliche Gotteserkenntnis nach der Lehre der kappadozischen Kirchenväter Basilius, Gregor von Nazianz und Gregor von Nyssa.* Straubing, 1902–1903.

Villecourt, L. "La Grande lettre grecque de Macaire." *Rev. de l'Orient chrétien* 22 (1920–1921).

Vincenzi, A. *Sancti Gregorii Nysseni et Origenis de æternitate pœnarum in vita futura omnimoda cum dogmate catholico concordia.* 2 vol. Rome, 1865.

Vollert, W. "Hat Gregor von Nyssa die paulinische Eschatologie verändert?" *Theol. Blätter,* 1935, 106–12.

———. *Die Lehre Gregors von Nyssa vom Guten und Bösen und von des schliesslichen Überwindung des Bösen.* Leipzig, 1897 (58 p.).

Weiß, H. *Die grossen Kappadozier Basilius, Gregor von Nazianz und Gregor von Nyssa als Exegeten.* Braunsberg, 1872.

Weiß, K. *Die Erziehungslehre der drei Kappadozier.* Strassb. theol. Studien 5. Freiburg, 1903.

For the literature on purely philological and biographical questions, see O. Bardenhewer, *Geschichte der altkirchlichen Literatur* 3:188–220.

BIBLIOGRAPHICAL NOTE

Compiled by Brian Daley, S.J.

For works published on Gregory of Nyssa before 1985, see:

Margerete Altenburger and Friedhelm Mann, *Bibliographie zu Gregor von Nyssa. Editionen, Übersetzungen, Literatur* (Leiden, 1988).

More recent publications include the following:

I. Editions of the Greek Text:

The series *Gregorii Nysseni Opera*, founded by Werner Jaeger in 1921, supersedes the edition in Migne, *Patrologia Græca* 44–46, for those works that have appeared in it. The only volume to have appeared in this series since 1985 is:

Gregorii Nysseni Opera III/2: ed. J. K. Downing, J. McDonough, and H. Hörner, *Opera Dogmatica Minora* (Leiden, 1988).

A reliable, sometimes critically edited Greek text of many of Gregory's works, with notes and French translation, is to be found in the series *Sources chrétiennes*. These include:

Life of Moses (J. Daniélou; SC 1b);

On the Creation of the Human Person (SC 6);

On Virginity (J. Aubinaeu; SC 119);

Life of Saint Macrina (P. Maraval; SC 178);

Letters (P. Maraval; SC 363).

A new critical edition of Gregory's treatise *On the Dead*, with an Italian translation, introduction, and notes, has been published by G. Lozza (Società Editrice Internazionale; Turin, 1991).

II. Translations:

Recent translations of works of Gregory into modern languages include:

a) *English:*

> *Life of Moses,* tr. A. J. Malherbe and E. Ferguson; The Classics of Western Spirituality (New York: Paulist Press, 1978).
>
> *Letters and Biographical Writings* of Basil of Caesaraea, Gregory of Nazianzus, and Gregory of Nyssa, tr. G. Barrois (Crestwood, N.Y.: St. Vladimir's Press, 1986).
>
> *Homilies on the Song of Songs,* tr. C. McCambley (Brookline, Mass.: Hellenic College Press, 1987).

b) *French:*

> *Great Catechetical Oration,* tr. J.-R. Armogathe and A. Maignan (Paris: Pères dans la foi, 1978).
>
> *Homilies on the Beatitudes,* tr. J.-Y. Guillaumin and G. Parent (Paris: Pères dans la foi, 1979).
>
> *On the Creation of the Human Person,* tr. J.-Y. Guillaumin (Paris: Pères dans la foi, 1982).

c) *Italian:*

> *Homilies on the Lord's Prayer,* tr. G. Caldarelli (Rome, 1983).
>
> *Life of Moses,* with Greek text; tr. M. Simonetti (Rome, 1984).
>
> *Homilies on the Song of Songs,* tr. C. Moreschini (Rome, 1988).
>
> *Life of Saint Macrina,* tr. E. Giannarelli (Milan, 1988).

d) *German:*

> *On the Three Days of Christ in the Tomb,* tr. H. Dröbner (Leyden, 1982).
>
> *Against Eunomius I, 1–146,* tr. J.-A. Röder (Frankfurt/New York, 1993).

III. Reference Works:

C. Fabricius and D. Ridings, *Concordance to the Greek Works of Gregory of Nyssa*, microform; Acta Univ. Goth. (Göteborg, 1989).

Index to biblical references:

H. Dröbner, *Bibelindex zu den Werken Gregors von Nyssa* (Paderborn, 1988).

IV. Congresses and Collections:

a) *Collections containing important articles on Gregory of Nyssa:*

J. Fontaine and C. Kannengiesser (eds.), *Epektasis. Mélanges patristiques offerts au Cardinal Jean Daniélou* (Paris, 1972).

H. Dröbner and C. Klock (eds.) *Studien zu Gregor von Nyssa und der christlichen Spätantike* (Leiden, 1990).

H. Eisenberger (ed.), *Hermeneumata. Festschrift für Hadwig Hörner zum 60. Geburtstag* (Heidelberg, 1990).

b) *Congress volumes:*

L. Mateo-Seco and J.-L. Bastero (eds.), *El "Contra Eunomium I" en la producción literaria di Gregorio de Nisa*, Sixth International Colloquium on Gregory of Nyssa (Pamplona, 1988).

S. G. Hall (ed.), *Gregory of Nyssa: Homilies on Ecclesiastes: an English Version with Supporting Studies*, Seventh International Colloquium on Gregory of Nyssa (St. Andrews, 1990).

V. Monographs and Articles:

C. Apostolopoulos, *Phædo Christianus: Studien zur Verbindung and Abwägung des Verhältnisses zwischen dem platonischen 'Phaidon' und dem Dialog Gregors von Nyssa "Über die Seele und die Auferstehung"* (Frankfurt/New York, 1986).

D. L. Blank, "The Etymology of Salvation in Gregory of Nyssa's *De Virginitate*", *Journal of Theological Studies* 37 (1986): 77–90.

M. Breydy, "Vestiges méconnus bei Pères Cappadociens en syriaque. Lettre de Grégoire de Nysse au moine Philippe", *Parole de l'Orient* 12 (1984–1985): 239–51.

J. A. Brooks, *The New Testament Text of Gregory of Nyssa* (Atlanta, 1991).

A. Capboscq, *El bien siempre mayor y sobreabondante: In Cant 174, 16: aproximación al nexo entre belleza, bondad y verdad en el pensamiento teologico de Gregorio de Nisa, In Cant. Or. V–IX* (Santiago, Chile, 1992).

G. Castelluccio, *L'Antropologia di Gregorio Nisseno* (Bari, 1992).

F. Düngl, "Gregor von Nyssas *Homilien zum Canticum* auf dem Hintergrund seiner *Vita Moysis*", *Vigiliæ Christianæ* 44 (1990) 371–81.

V. E. F. Harrison, "Male and Female in Cappadocian Theology", *Journal of Theological Studies* 41 (1990): 441–71.

M. D. Hart, "Reconciliation of Body and Soul. Gregory of Nyssa's Deeper Theology of Marriage", *Theological Studies* 51 (1990): 450–78.

R. E. Heine, "Gregory of Nyssa's Apology for Allegory", *Vigiliæ Christianæ* 38 (1984): 360–70.

C. Klock, *Untersuchungen zum Stil und Rhythmus bei Gregor von Nyssa: ein Beitrag zum Rhetorikverständnis der Griechischen Väter* (Frankfurt/New York, 1987).

G. L. Kustas, "Philosophy and Rhetoric in Gregory of Nyssa", Κληρονομία 18 (1986 [1990]): 101–46.

P. Maraval, "Un Lecteur ancien de la *Vie de Macrine* de Grégoire de Nysse", *Analecta Bollandiana* 104 (1986): 187–90.

———, "La Lettre 3 de Grégoire de Nysse dans le débat christologique", *Revue des sciences religieuses* 61 (1987): 74–89.

———, "Grégoire de Nysse pasteur. La *Lettre canonique à Letoros*", *Revue d'histoire et de philosophie des religions* 71 (1991): 101–14.

H. Meissner, *Rhetorik und Theologie: Der Dialog Gregors von Nyssa De anima et resurrectione* (Frankfurt/New York, 1991).

E. D. Moutsoulas, " 'Essence' et 'energies' de Dieu selon S. Grégoire de Nysse", Ἐπιστημονικὴ Ἐπετηρὶς τῆς θεολογικῆς Σχολῆς 26 (1984 [1986]): 275–86.

H. J. Oesterle, "Probleme der Anthropologie bei Gregor von Nyssa. Zur Interpretation seiner Schrift *De Hominis Opificio*", *Hermes* 113 (1985): 101–14.

S. G. Papadopoulos, "Γρηγόριος Νύσσης (335–40 –394)," Ἐπιστημονικὴ Ἐπετηρὶς τῆς θεολογικῆς Σχολῆς 26 (1984 [1986]): 195–234.

E. Pietrella, "L'Antiorigenismo di Gregorio di Nissa (*De hom. opif.* 28, ed. Forbes, pp. 276–282)", *Augustinianum* 26 (1986): 143–76.

J.-R. Pouchet, "Une Lettre spirituelle de Grégoire de Nysse Identifiée: l'*Epistula* 124 du corpus basilien", *Vigiliæ Christianæ* 42 (1988): 28–46.

J.-M. Sauget, "L'Étrange périple d'une sentence de Grégoire de Nysse retrouvée dans des 'Paterika' arabes", *Le Muséon* 100 (1987): 307–13.

K. Skouteris, " 'Malum privatio est.' Ὁ ἅγιος Γρηγόριος Νύσσης καὶ ὁ ψευδοΔιονύσιος διὰ τὴν ὕπαρξιν τοῦ κακοῦ (περαιτέρω σχόλια)", Ἐπιστημονικὴ Ἐπετηρὶς τῆς θεολογικῆς Σχολῆς 26 (1984 [1986]) 309–20.

T. Špidlik, "La mistica del martirio secondo Gregorio di Nissa", in A. Quacquarelli and I. Rogger (ed.), *I martiri della Val di Non e la reazione pagana alla fine del IV secolo* (Bologna, 1985), 69–84.

R. Staats, "Basilius as lebende Mönchsregel in Gregors von Nyssa De Virginitate", *Vigiliæ Christianæ* 39 (1985): 228–55.

W. Ullmann, "Der logische und der theologische Sinn des Unendlichkeitsbegriffes in der Gotteslehre Gregors von Nyssa", *Bijdragen* 48 (1987): 150–71.

R. Winling, "La Résurrection du Christ dans l'*Antirrheticus adversus Apollinarem* de Grégoire de Nysse", *Revue des études augustiniennes* 35 (1989): 12–43.

————, "La Résurrection du Christ dans les traités *Contre Eunome* de Grégoire de Nysse," *Revue des sciences religieuses* 64 (1990): 251–69.

R. Darling Young, "On Gregory of Nyssa's Use of Theology and Science in Constructing Theological Anthropology", *Pro Ecclesia* 2 (1993): 345–63.